A LONG ROAD TO

JUSTICE

*A Collection of Short Stories, Essays, and Pieces-
Historical Fiction and Historical Non-Fiction*

Bob Mack

A Long Road to Justice

A Collection of Short Stories, Essays, and Pieces

Historical Fiction and Historical Non-Fiction

Print ISBN: 978-1-66781-425-4 eBook ISBN: 978-1-66781-426-1

DEDICATION

To my wife, Cathy, the Voice for Autumn

To our son, Danny

In memory of my parents

In memory of my favorite teacher, Ms. Freddie Jefferson

Regarding efforts to censor, suppress, whitewash, or bury
the teaching of our long history of racial injustice-

"Those who cannot remember the past are condemned to repeat it."

- George Santayana

TABLE OF CONTENTS

PREFACE

I first learned something about racial injustice, intolerance, and hypocrisy when I was about seven or eight years old in the early 1960s. Early one evening in my hometown of Lake Worth, Florida, Dad walked into the Whispering Palms convenience store while Mom and I waited outside in the car. Right next door to the grocery store was an old laundry mat. Written on the front entrance to the laundry mat were two words- "White Only." I asked Mom what the words meant. She explained them to me. My reaction was something like-That's unfair! That's dumb! Mom wholeheartedly agreed. She told me that the President was trying to do something about it. The next day I was back in school reciting the daily pledge of allegiance to the flag culminating with the words, "With liberty and justice for all."

To this day, I believe that most children would have reacted to the meaning of that "White Only" sign as I did. Most children have an innate sense of what's fair and just and what's not. They don't like bullying. And therein lies the hope of the world. I believe that racism and intolerance are perpetuated from one generation to the next, due to the shattering of that basic sense of fairness which lives within the hearts of children, by their exposure to the bigotry of adults.

History has proven that the road to justice is a long and winding path and an uneven ride. Every effort to expand justice has been met by efforts to block it or to shrink it. For example, throughout history, men and women have paid the price in blood, sweat, and tears, and at times with their very lives, in the struggle for the right to vote. Those efforts culminated in 1965 with the passage of the Voting Rights Act. Despite those heroic and herculean efforts, in 2013, the United States Supreme Court in *Shelby v. Holder,* gutted the 1965 Voting Rights Act by extracting the teeth from the law. Doing so opened the floodgates to the passage of state voter suppression laws throughout the country targeting minorities.

What follows is a collection of fifty short stories, essays, and pieces, mostly in the form of either historical fiction or historical non- fiction. Eight of the pieces concern my own family history. They are mostly stories about justice and injustice; kindness and cruelty; tolerance and intolerance; honor and dishonor; empathy and apathy; altruism and selfishness; cowardice and courage; and devotion to the Constitution and betrayal of the Constitution. Forty- four of the pieces are narrative stories or essays told in verse and rhyme. Six of the longer pieces are written in straight prose. The pieces are intended as a push back against injustice, racism, and intolerance in all of their ugly forms. May that three-headed monster be one day relegated to the dustbin of history, and forever expunged from the human heart.

Bob Mack

MIRACLE ON THE NINTH FLOOR
(Historical Non-Fiction)

Joe's life was on a downhill slide-
He lost his job and he lost his pride;
And then he lost his love, his bride.
He found himself at the end of his rope-
Drifting away on a slippery slope-
Unable to cope for he'd lost all hope.

Pushed close to the edge-
He wound up on a razor's edge-
On the ninth floor of a building's ledge.

For two hours he threatened to leap to his death
      from the Miracle Mile Building on Wilshire
      Blvd., deep in L.A.
In a state of depression, despair, and dismay-
He concluded there simply was no other way.
He dreaded the pain of another day.

Police officers, a police psychologist, and a chaplain
      offered assistance-
And probed for a line of least resistance-
But Joe held fast to his stiff resistance.

When all seemed lost a Superman arrived-
Intent on ensuring that Joe survived.
He looked out from the nearest window and spoke to Joe.
He offered him words to soften the blows-
To lighten the moment he threw in some prose-
To help him to cope with the depth of his woes.

When Joe asked him how he'd appeared out of nowhere so
      quickly, he responded with the following words:
"I'm so fast that last night I turned off the light switch in my
      hotel room and got into bed, before the room was even
      dark!"
"Float like a butterfly, sting like a bee-
The hands can't hit what the eyes can't see!"

For a moment, Joe doubted that his eyes could see-
For the words he was hearing were those of Ali!
Joe thought to himself, how can this be?
Why is he here for a loser like me?

Muhammad Ali, the Champ, and none other-
Reached out to Joe and called him his brother.
Joe responded, You're Muhammad Ali, The Greatest of all
       Time, the ultimate winner.
I'm a nobody, a loser and sinner.

Trying to keep hope alive-
Within Joe's heart that he might survive-
The Champ threw a lifeline to a drowning man-
By listening hard to understand;
Then said to Joe, You're not a loser and a nobody-
You're a child of God, you are somebody.

At times, he continued, we all get knocked down in the ring-
When it happens, it deeply hurts and it deeply stings.
The important thing is to never give up-
Refuse to quit and keep getting up.

Inching closer to the edge-
Joe insisted he was a drowning man and had no purpose-
That he was stuck in the mud below the surface.
Ali responded, We all have a purpose, let's find yours-
And you will find there's something more-
A better life than you've known before-
If you never give up, you'll surely endure.

With those words, Joe unlocked the door to the fire escape
       and Ali approached him.
At last Joe's fate was looking less grim.
Joe embraced Ali and began to cry-
For the Champ had refused to turn a blind eye.
Joe walked with the Champ from the danger up high.

Upon reaching the ground, Ali drove Joe to a hospital,
     to help him work through his lows and his piques-
So life was not so terribly bleak.

Ali bought him some clothes.
Joe was grateful, heaven knows.
For even better than a cash advance-
Joe was given a second chance.

In the moment of truth on that fateful day-
The stars lined up in an unlikely way.
At a time that Joe had become unglued-
On the brink of bidding the world adieu-
Ali appeared from out of the blue!

In the right place, and just in time-
A force for good and a role benign-
With Joe's existence, on the line.

It seemed a Miracle, like parting the sea-
For Joe had found a reason to be.
Despite the absence of guarantees-
Joe believed he was given the key.
To shed his demons and set himself free-
With a little help from his friend, Ali.

THE FORGOTTEN OLD MAN

(Historical Fiction)

The forgotten old man used to stand on the corner-
The one who died without a single mourner.
He'd bake in the sun for the longest time-
Sweating in place while holding his sign:
"Please brother, can you spare a dime?"
Living his life on the poverty line.

Drivers stopped at the nearest light-
And gazed at the old man, so gaunt and so slight.
Most ignored his terrible plight.
Others, they looked the other way-
Messaging him to stay away-
Then drove off on their merry way.

Law enforcement razzed him and harassed him
      and called him a deadbeat-
And they bullied and they browbeat-
To drive him off the city street.

He died alone as he'd lived alone.
There was no one to contact, no one to phone.
He was laid to rest in an indigent grave.
No words were spoken for the life that was broken-
Only the gravedigger's offhand remark:
That there was no soul there to be saved-
Only an old man who took more than he gave.

The truth was buried with him, inside of his grave.
The truth of what he once had been, so strong and so brave.
The countless lives he had helped to save-
And the terrible price that he had paid.

For the ghosts of the dead from the Vietnam War-
Flashed through his head like open soars-
The remnants of his second tour.

Returning to an ungrateful nation-
He self-medicated with drugs and with rum-
Society wrote him off as no more than a "bum."

What enabled him to rebuild his life?
His precious child and his beautiful wife.
Two times saved and two times blessed-
He strove to give them his level best.

He worked his job, paid his taxes, and supported his family with
        the sweat of his brow.
He viewed these responsibilities as a Sacred Vow.
He rejoiced in family outings with his wife and his little girl-
People noted that they seemed to be his whole world.

And it was said of him that he knew how to keep hope alive-
Never settling just to survive.
No matter how hard the times he continued to strive-
So that one day his family might prosper and thrive.

All of the hope, the love, and the pride-
Disappeared on a family Sunday drive.
For a split second he laughed and took his eyes off
        the road to look at his child-
It was the last time that he ever smiled.

A sudden flash- and two lives taken in a fatal crash!
Gone forever was the life he had built-
Replaced by remorse and survivor's guilt.

He self- medicated with drugs and with rum-
Society wrote him off as no more than a "bum."
A second coming of post-traumatic ghosts
        was far more than he could overcome.

Years after he was laid to rest-
His name was discovered- his truth was uncovered-
By a Veteran's Group on a Veteran's Day-
Checking the indigent graves that day.

Money was raised and his casket exhumed.
He was laid beside those that he loved in his life-
His precious child and his beautiful wife.

The forgotten old man at long last-
Could rest in peace from a tortured past.
A three-gun salute- the rifle blasts –
And taps was played for the price he had paid-
Remembered, respected, and honored at last.

TRUDY LOWE AND JOHNNY LEE
(Historical Fiction)

They grew up in the segregated South, dirt poor.
When he glanced upon her, he felt like the richest
      person alive, to be sure.

He was afraid to tell her, to let her know-
He was madly in love with Trudy Lowe.
Johnny Lee gazed upon her often, for she was the girl next door.
She seemed, however, miles away, maybe more.
Often, when she happened to glance his way-
He'd freeze in fear and turn away.

Due to the color of their skin-
They were the objects of threats, of racist sin.
They were treated like second class citizens, they attended
      second class schools, and opportunities were few.
But when the U.S. entered WWII-
Johnny knew what he had to do.
For he was a patriotic American, through and through.

After enlisting in the Army, with a month to go before setting out-
He resolved at last to confront his doubts-
And found the courage to ask her out.

To his shock and overwhelming joy, she said, "Yes."
He felt that he'd been truly blessed.
They took long walks together while holding hands. They attended
      Church and picture shows-
And she kissed him goodbye when he had to go.

And tenderly, she placed a specially inscribed locket with chain
      around his neck, to be worn close to his heart-
Something with which he'd never part.

He whispered in her ear-
And told her not to fret or fear.
He promised her he would survive-
And return to her from war alive.

As the horrors of war dragged on in years, they corresponded.
He lived for her letters.
They replenished his soul, made everything better.
The same was true for her, until his letters stopped coming-
For the moment of truth in the war was coming.

Johnny was a member of the 320th Barrage Balloon Battalion,
the first African-American unit to hit the beaches on D-Day.
They were among the first infantry troops facing fire that fateful day.

Strapped to Johnny and the other members of his segregated unit,
were steel cables supporting hydrogen filled balloons
attached to soda can sized bombs.
They embraced their role without any qualms.
The balloons were designed to blow up dive-bombing German
fighter pilots attempting to strafe U.S. soldiers landing
on Omaha Beach-
To keep the soldiers safe from their reach.

As a Battalion Balloon Flyer-
About to face the hell and the fire-
He took a moment to say a prayer-
To help him save the men out there.
And he prayed to God that he might be spared-
To return alive to his Trudy Lowe-
The promise he'd made her long ago.

As shots were fired upon his buddy, Johnny instinctively
threw his body in front of him and tackled him,
saving his life!
The buddy who'd spoke of his kids and his wife.

Johnny was shot in the leg!
And a bullet rang out and grazed his head!
Another inch and he would have been dead.
Somehow, he managed to forge ahead-
And he scaled the beach wall, dead ahead.

He joined a U.S. anti-aircraft gun team, and he
          received first aid-
Which brought him back when he'd begun to fade.
He assisted the team in liberating Saint Lo, Paris, and all of France-
As Patton's Army steadily advanced.

Upon his discharge from the service, Johnny was awarded a
          distinguished service cross and a purple heart.
All he could think of was to follow his heart-
And return to his love so deep in his heart-
To ask for her hand, "till death do us part."

During the war, Johnny's family had joined the Great Migration-
To avoid the clutches of racist damnation.
They'd moved to the Big Apple. It was goodbye to Alabama-
They'd had their fill of its threats and its drama.

Upon Johnny's arrival in New York, his family
          gave him a hero's welcome and a beautiful greeting-
A precious reunion but one only fleeting.
He told his parents of all that he planned-
Of his deep love for Trudy, how he yearned for her hand.
How he'd saved for a ring to place on her hand-
And he prayed she'd say "Yes," to proposed wedding plans.

He called Trudy and told her he was driving to see her
          the very next day!
They expressed their love in a beautiful way.
He told her, "I have something to ask you, something to say-
It'll have to wait for the following day."
They said good night and excitedly prayed-
For the hours between them to tick away.

His parents warned him not to drive to Alabama, to stay away-
They feared he'd fall prey to the KKK.
But Johnny believed it was a New Day-
He'd fought for freedom and the American Way-
So why would harm be coming his way?
He'd proudly wear his military uniform with medals in
        full regalia, like a suit of armor to protect him from harm-
No reason for fear, no need for alarm.

One day, two days, then a week went by-
His parents called Trudy but he hadn't arrived.
Trudy broke down and began to cry.
He'd kept his promise to return from war,
        he had survived-
But now she sensed he wasn't alive.

Six months passed and nothing was heard-
Of Johnny's fate, not a single word.
Then one day, the nude decomposed body of a black male
        was located in a wooded area just over the
        Alabama border, hanging from a tree.
There was no evidence revealing who it could be-
Decomposition disallowed an ID.

As the body was about to be taken away-
To a potter's grave that terrible day-
A police dog alerted to a shiny object barely sticking
        out of the soil, not far away.

It turned out to be, a broken pink locket in the shape
        of a heart-
Broken in pieces like a broken heart.
As if it was saying, "till death do us part."

When the locket was repaired and pieced together,
        the following words were clearly inscribed-
Identifying the victim who hadn't survived:

Trudy Lowe loves Johnny Lee-
This locket brings you home to me.

1968 - THE DEATH OF A DREAM?

(Historical Non-Fiction Essay)

It was a time of hope- destroyed by hate-
That ill-fated year of '68.
MLK, the drum major for justice, the doer and dreamer-
Was changing the world as he fought to redeem her.

In 1963, in a Letter from a Birmingham Jail-
He asserted the movement would surely prevail.
He explained to his critics, "Why we can't wait"-
To stand up for justice and resist all the hate.

His moral leadership and courage led to the demise of Jim Crow segregation
        laws, poll taxes, and literacy tests through enactment of the 1965
        Voting Rights Act and enactment of the Civil Rights Act of 1964.
This landmark legislation provided protections for the rights of
        minorities as never before.

In 1967, he spoke out against American involvement in the Vietnam War-
And our economy sacrificed for that terrible war;
And our boys left dead or dying at death's door.

Having led the fight against laws of inequality-
He turned his attention toward economic equality.
In April 1968, he backed the Memphis sanitation workers' strike
        for safer working conditions and a living wage.
Two months earlier, two sanitation workers, Echol Cole and Robert Walker,
        were crushed to death by the compactor of a garbage truck which
        malfunctioned. The City's pattern of disregard for safe working
        conditions amounted to a moral outrage.

As strikers marched while holding up signs saying, "I am a man"-
King backed and supported their moral stand.
But a man with a rifle shot him dead and altered the future-
The damage to justice yet to be sutured.

In the years following his death, his nonviolent resistance to unjust laws-
Was tainted by violence which set back the cause.
He fought for a dream, not a dream deferred-
But a bullet rang out and silenced his words.

What if he'd not stepped out onto the balcony of the
      Lorraine Motel-
And the world had avoided that moment of hell?
And his voice had gone on like a liberty bell?

Would we now be closer to justice and further from hell?
Some insist that it's hard to tell.
But it matters not for on that day-
The man with the rifle had his say.

Seeking solace from that terrible day-
Looking for someone to lead the way-
Many turned to RFK.
He ran for President, a national campaign-
To stop the war, the death and the pain.

Grief-stricken since the death of President Kennedy,
      his beloved brother-
He empathized and felt the pain of others.
He believed that the suffering of minorities, working
      class whites, and the hungry and poor-
Must be directly addressed and never ignored.

He called for law and order and justice for all-
While healing divisions and tearing down walls.
He championed young and old, Christians and Jews,
      whites and blacks-
Moving forward and never back.

He believed that all people could come together and learn to unite-
To rise above their common plight;
For a better life, well worth the fight.

He once said that "each time a man stands up for an ideal,
      or acts to improve the lot of others, or strikes out against injustice-
      he sends forth a tiny ripple of hope."
When he won the California primary, we seemed to be rising
      from a slippery slope.

He seemed poised to win the nomination and become our next leader-
His momentum was strong, so many believers.
But a man with a gun shot him dead and altered the future-
The damage to justice yet to be sutured.

Upon his death, those ripples of hope were all but replaced,
      by ripples of violence and hopeless despair:
Over 21,000 Americans died "Over There"-
In Vietnam, in the Nixon years.

Those ripples of hope were also replaced by ripples
      of doubt and government mistrust.
Vietnam and Watergate led to distrust.

RFK spoke of those things people had in common,
      and inspired them to unite.
Nixon stoked division- youth against "hard-hats,"
      blacks against whites.

Kennedy's voice, to unite the people and end the war-
Was silenced that night forevermore.
His body was placed on a funeral train-
The final journey of his Last Campaign.

Up to two million people lined the tracks-
Young and old, blue- collar workers, policemen and firemen,
      whites and blacks.
They wished to bear witness and pay their respects-
They glanced at his train, took time to reflect.
Many stood tall and simply saluted-
For he'd made them feel they were all included.

He fought for justice, not justice deferred-
But a bullet rang out and silenced his words.
What if he'd not entered the pantry, the scene where he died-
And dodged a bullet with luck on his side?
And the world had avoided that moment of hell-
And his voice had gone on like a liberty bell.

Would we now be closer to justice and further from hell?
Some insist that it's hard to tell.
But it matters not for on that day-
The man with the handgun had his say.

Does 1968 speak to us? What does it say?
That violence and chance have the final say-
Those gunshots shaping the present day?

Is that all we take from '68?
The loss of hope and the triumph of hate?
The long-ago death of a long-ago dream-
Is there something more that we can glean?

King and Kennedy reached for the stars while
    fighting for change.
Perhaps the people can reach for the same.
If they choose to do so and follow their lead-
Perhaps they'll choose to help those in need.

The Declaration of Independence and the Constitution,
    King asserted, constituted "a promissory note to
    which every American was to fall heir"-
A promise of justice for all to share.

He asserted that in regard to people of color, America had
    "…defaulted upon that promissory note"-
Justice denied through suppression of votes.

King proclaimed that "the arc of the moral universe is long but
    it bends toward justice."
So it's never too late to take up the cause-
Of fighting for justice and fixing our flaws.

If we approach it this way and fight the delay-
Then maybe one day we'll be able to say-
That infamous year has at last been redeemed-
No longer viewed as the death of a dream.

ELIANA'S DREAM
(Historical Fiction)

Fifteen-year-old Eliana Goldberg was a lonely girl and an only child with a shy and retiring nature. As a Jewish girl attending middle school in the early 1960's in a predominantly Christian community, she was ostracized by her teenage peers. Her painfully shy nature, diminutive size, and skinny build made her an easy target for bullies. She often bore the brunt of cruel anti-Semitic harassment by classmates. On one occasion, a yellow star of David was painted on her desk. Another time, a cut out photo of a rat was pasted onto the front of her locker. On yet another occasion, a sketch of Eliana with an elongated nose was left on top of her desk.

Eliana did her best to stay clear of her tormentors. While she was diminutive of size, she was speedy of foot, and she had the ability to change directions quickly. On many occasions, she simply fled and outran those with ill-intentions.

She pushed the bounds of her own shy ways in an effort to reach out toward others; But due to peer pressure, or perhaps due to latent anti-Semitic prejudice of their own, other students failed to intercede on her behalf. Eliana was unable to develop any real friends in whom she could confide or count on to have her back.

Eliana's dad had died of cancer when she was but a little girl of five. While her mom, Ellen Goldberg, was loving and supportive, she was forced to work two jobs to make ends meet. Very often, she did not get home until 8:00 at night. As a result, the isolation Eliana experienced at school extended into a lonely latchkey kid type of existence at home. Despite her loneliness, Eliana deeply loved and respected her mom, and she bore no resentment toward her; And because she sensed how hard her mom worked to support the two of them, she did not want her mom to worry about her. She chose not to burden her with her own troubles at school.

She coped with her isolation and loneliness by immersing herself in a world of books. She had a quick, bright, and curious mind, and she devoured books in the areas of history and biography. She also kept up with the news and world events. The book that affected her more deeply than any other, the book that spoke to her on so many levels, was "The Diary of Anne Frank." She developed a deep feeling of kinship with Anne and her family and friends. She read about the danger, fear, and isolation that they endured day after day for 25 months hiding from the Nazis within the suffocating atmosphere of The Secret Annex. She found herself hanging on Anne's every word, including the following words: "I get frightened myself when I think of close friends who are now at the mercy of the cruelest monsters ever to stalk the earth; And all because they're Jews." In light of the torment she endured in school, Eliana identified with Anne's words. She felt as if Anne was speaking to her personally and directly. She also identified with Anne's teenage angst, her feelings of isolation and loneliness. She was inspired by Anne's courage, hope, and love of nature. As she read the Afterward to the Diary, Eliana was heartbroken to learn that all the members of The Secret Annex were betrayed and eventually murdered by the SS in Nazi Concentration Camps, save for Anne's Father, Otto Frank, the lone survivor.

For all her admiration for Anne, Eliana felt that she lacked Anne's strength of personality and courage. Whereas Anne had been an outgoing extrovert in school, and often the center of attention, Eliana viewed herself as introverted, quiet, and shy. Temperamentally, Eliana found herself identifying more with Anne's older sister, Margot, who was murdered by the Nazis at the age of 19. Anne described Margot in her diary as an excellent student, hard-working, kind and considerate to a fault, reserved, and quiet. Eliana yearned to know more about Margot, and how she coped with anti-Semitism, danger, and fear. Perhaps, she thought, understanding Margot better would help her in her own life, in coping with the threats and harassment at school. She wished that Anne had written a lot more about her sister than she did.

As the bullying and threats continued incessantly at school, Eliana's fear, panic, and depression grew dangerously close to a breaking point. She tried to think of new ways to make friends, and to create for herself a zone of safety. She developed an interest in tennis upon reading the autobiography of Hall of Fame tennis player, Helen Jacobs. She learned that Ms. Jacobs, who was Jewish, had not been stopped by anti-Semitism from rising to the top of the tennis world, or from becoming a commander in the U.S. Naval Intelligence Agency during WWII. Eliana learned that Ms. Jacobs had authored a number of books, including a book entitled, "Gallery of Champions, a Collection of Biographies of Female Tennis Pros." Eliana thought that she too would like someday to become a writer, just as Anne Frank had aspired to become a journalist and a writer. Reading about Ms. Jacobs also led Eliana to begin thinking about trying out for the middle school tennis team.

Despite her trepidation due to the threats and racist tropes she'd endured, and despite her retiring nature, she mustered up the courage to show up for the first day of practice. She wound up having a good time at practice. An outgoing girl named Hope asked her to be her practice partner. They spent the entire period hitting together. Given her quickness which had been honed running away from bullies, Eliana found that her footwork was coming easy to her. Hope told her that she had natural talent for the game. She asked Eliana to be her practice partner the next day. Eliana readily agreed. Hope gave her a quick hug, and then hurried off, telling her that she needed to get home to babysit her little brother.

For the first time since the school year began, Eliana's heart was light, and she was filled with happiness and hope. She walked over to the general area where the kids had left their tennis bags and racquet covers. As she gathered up her tennis bag, she noticed that her racquet cover was missing. She looked everywhere but couldn't find it. She thought maybe another girl had picked it up by mistake. As she walked over toward her bicycle to ride home, she was pleased to spot at a distance that her racquet cover was wrapped around the handle bar. As she took hold of it, she saw pasted onto the front of the cover, a Nazi Swastika! Eliana dropped the cover, dropped her tennis bag, dropped to her knees, and screamed! After a few moments, she looked up upon hearing a group of students laughing, cursing, and making fun of her from a nearby school sidewalk; And then, she was wounded by the "unkindest cut of all." Among those laughing at her, she gazed upon the figure of Hope.

In the days that followed, Eliana sank deeper into depression and despair. Not long thereafter, her mom, while at work, received a call from the school advising her that Eliana had not shown up for school for almost a week. Upon arriving home on a Thursday evening, Ms. Goldberg found Eliana in bed, groggy and half asleep. She confronted her daughter about missing school. "What's going on, Eliana? Why are you skipping school? Talk to me." While Eliana intended no disrespect to her mom, in that moment she was unable to break through the shell of her interior isolation so as to utter a single word. Try as she might, Ms. Goldberg could not get her daughter to open up to her. Finally, Eliana told her mom that she wished to go to sleep. Her mom made her promise to return to school in the morning, and to sit down with her after school and tell her what was going on. Upon Eliana agreeing to do so, her mom hugged and kissed her and left the room.

Contrary to what Eliana had told her mom, she spent a sleepless night. Earlier in the week while skipping school, she had spent endless hours alone in her room. She had also taken long walks, wondering around aimlessly in "quiet desperation" and hopeless depression. Her mind was saturated with the bullying, the threats, the fear, the racist tropes, and Hope's betrayal. In her despair, she came to the conclusion that she could no longer go on living in this life. Because she had no friends with whom to share social activities, she had accumulated most of her monthly allowances since the beginning of the school year. Earlier that Thursday, she had made her way to a sordid part of town where drug trafficking was the order of the day. While there, she purchased a deadly cocktail of illegal drugs.

In recent weeks, Eliana had discovered a trail which extended deep into some nearby woods, and led to a partially hidden hollow. She had begun visiting this beautiful and peaceful hollow as a place of refuge and escape from her misery at school. She considered it her Secret Hiding Place. It was there that she intended in the morning to take the lethal cocktail to escape her pain. She had grown at peace with her decision; But after her mom left her room that Thursday evening, Eliana's mind began racing with indecision. Her hesitation was attributable to her deep love for her mom. She didn't wish to hurt her, and she deeply regretted the pain and heartbreak she would cause. All through the night, Eliana wrestled with her decision without getting a wink of sleep. Near sun-up, exhausted and sick at heart, she sat down and wrote her mom the following note: "Dear Mom, I have tried so hard, so very hard, to cope and go on living in this world; But the constant barrage of threats, bullying, anti-Semitic hatred, fear, and social isolation I have endured at school, is more than I can continue to bear. I cannot go on. You have been as kind, loving, and caring a mom as a daughter could ever hope to have. I love you with all my heart. Please forgive me. Your loving daughter, Eliana"

That morning, Eliana dressed for school, gathered up her school books along with her bagged-up cocktail of drugs, and placed them in her bicycle basket as if she was preparing to ride to school. Her mom reminded her about the talk they were to have that evening. At that moment, Eliana hugged her and began to cry. "What's wrong, dear?" her mom asked. Eliana gathered herself the best she could as she wiped away her tears, and replied, "Nothing, Mom. I love you." She then got onto her bike and began riding off. As she did so, she looked back over her shoulder and waved goodbye.

As Eliana reached her final road and pedaled down the trail leading to her Secret Hiding Place, a feeling of peace and calm came over her. No longer would she be faced on a daily basis with threats. No longer would she be bullied, targeted, and terrorized by mindless hate. By the time she reached the hidden hollow that bordered the woods, the sky was deep blue, and the sun shone brightly upon the dew drops in the bright green grass. Even as she sat down upon a towel and laid out the deadly cocktail of drugs, she marveled at the peace and beauty of the woods and hollow. She allowed herself a few minutes to take in the splendor and tranquility of her surroundings. She heard a rustle in the wooded area. About 50 yards away, she spotted a mother deer and her fawn walking gingerly from the woods into the hollow. Eliana looked on as the deer and her fawn chewed upon weeds and the succulent grass. At the nearby lake, a mother duck led her ducklings across the water. Graceful songbirds flew against the background of the deep blue sky. The peaceful scene had a hypnotic affect upon Eliana, and her lack of sleep from the night before began to overcome her. Unable to keep her eyes open, she laid down upon her side and sank into deep, rapid eye movement sleep, the kind of sleep associated with the stuff of dreams.

"Eliana, wake up. It's me, Margot. You've wanted to know more about me. So let's talk."

"I can't seem to move or to open my eyes, but I hear your voice. How can this be? You and your sister perished long ago in Bergen Belsen."

"You trust your own ears, don't you, Eliana? Do you not trust me?"

"In school I have learned not to trust. I have been tormented by bullies and my trust has been betrayed. But if you are telling me that it is truly you, then I will believe you."

"We have much in common, Eliana. As you know from reading Anne's diary, our family too was betrayed. Our hiding place, The Secret Annex, was turned from our place of salvation into the site of our betrayal; But it isn't too late for you, Eliana. There is still time for you to turn this hiding place of yours into your place of salvation."

"It's too late for me, Margot. There is nothing to be done."

"It is so beautiful here, Eliana. Even while we were hidden away in the Secret Annex, my sister fell in love with the beauty of nature. As she looked out through a window in the attic upon the branches of the chestnut tree behind the Annex, and as she gazed upon the seagulls flying against the background of the bright blue sky, she drew strength and hope which helped her to carry on. You too, Eliana, can draw strength from the beauty of the woods and the hollow, the deer and her fawn, the duck and her ducklings, and the graceful songbirds, as reason enough to carry on."

"Margot, your sister described you in her diary as reserved, quiet, and perhaps somewhat shy. I'm a lot like that. My nature rendered me unable to cope at school. I was too weak. I lacked the strength and the courage to go on. Tell me, Margot, how did you cope before you went into hiding, and during the two years after you went into hiding, with the dangers and threats posed by, in Anne's words, 'the cruelest monsters ever to stalk the earth?' How did you cope with the fear of bombs dropping on The Secret Annex? How did you carry on?"

"First of all, Eliana, you are confusing your own quiet, sensitive, and caring nature for weakness. It is not. Each of us must be true to our own nature. My mother sometimes got on my outspoken sister's nerves, by telling her that she should behave more like me. Mother was wrong about that. Anne didn't try to behave like me; And I didn't try to behave like her. There is nothing wrong with trying to stretch yourself to overcome your shyness, for that would make life easier for you. Sometimes it takes years to overcome shyness; But having a weakness that needs strengthening, does not make you a weak person. Your kind and caring nature defines you as a person of strong character."

"As for me, Eliana, it was difficult to cope with the danger of being discovered by the Nazis, and with the danger of bombs dropping on our hiding place. But I was surrounded by family and friends. We drew strength from each other. We had terrible rows within The Secret Annex. We got on each other's nerves. But at the end of the day, we leaned on each other. We were all going through the same hardships. There was strength in numbers. In contrast, you've had no one to assist you, Eliana. You were one person being ganged up on and bullied by many others. You weren't weak. You did the only thing you could do, which was to try to stay clear of the danger. The point is, Eliana, that there are different sources of support. If you cannot find it from your peers at school, you must look elsewhere. The first time you confided in your mom was when you left her your note, when she was no longer in a position to help you."

"I know, Margot. I love Mom very much, and she has worked so hard to support us. I didn't want to worry her with my problems."

"She's your mom, Eliana. Worrying about you, helping you with your problems, and guiding you, is part of the way she expresses her love for you. She would want you to confide in her. When Anne and I were facing the horrors of Auschwitz, our mother watched over us and protected us the best she could, every step of the way. Her unconditional love and support were critical to our survival at Auschwitz. As you know, we didn't have her with us at Belsen. The Nazis sent Anne and me on to Belsen to face starvation and typhus without her."

"I guess I should have told Mom at some point. I tried to make friends at school, Margot. I really did. I even went out for the tennis team and discovered that I enjoyed playing tennis. I thought I'd made a friend, but she betrayed me."

"Eliana, before we went into hiding, I too enjoyed playing tennis. I made many friends at a tennis club in Amsterdam. Maybe you gave up too easily. Maybe if you kept going to practice and the others saw your talent, your quickness around the court, some of the girls would have grown to respect you. That might have led to friends who would have had your back."

"You're only fifteen, Eliana, and you should have had the luxury of being a happy go lucky kid, and of maturing and growing up at your own pace; But the haters have forced your hand. You have no choice but to put away childish things and to grow up fast; Just as Anne and I were forced to do while in hiding, and later on in the concentration camps; With your mom's support, you can fight back in your own way, with quiet courage and conviction. You can expose the abuse you've endured, while demanding that the school principal take action to end that abuse and to hold the abusers accountable. If your school principal won't take action, you can alert the media. You can speak out against anti-Semitism and racism with your voice, or perhaps with your pen, like Anne. If necessary, you can transfer out of that school. It's not the only school in the world."

"The main thing, Eliana, is that you must recognize your self-worth and the intrinsic value of your life; And by standing up for yourself, you would also be honoring the memory of all six million of us Jews who were slaughtered and annihilated from the face of the earth, 'by the cruelest monsters who ever stalked the earth.' You would be honoring our memory by affirming that Never Again will our people be humiliated and victimized by racists, while people in positions of power to stop it, do nothing. You would honor our memory by affirming that vicious bullying will never drive any one of us into a suicidal holocaust."

"That all sounds hard, Margot, really hard; And I've been so depressed. I don't know if I can cope with life and go on."

"Often, Eliana, doing the right thing is hard, really hard; But that's the challenge and the price of not giving up; And that's why it's important to enlist the help and support of others; And a furry friend can provide comfort and support while lightening one's heart. Before we went into hiding, Anne and I had a cat named Moortje. After we went into hiding, we became attached to Peter's cat, Moushi. Each cat was a great source of comfort to us. You might think of getting a cat of your own. Cats are natural born counselors and therapists for humans."

"I do like cats, Margot. They're affectionate when it suits them; Aloof when it suits them. And they do seem to delight in observing the world from a hidden position while grinning about it with an air of superiority, like the Cheshire Cat."

"Eliana, notwithstanding her diary, Anne never had the opportunity to realize her dream of becoming a journalist or a writer. I never had the opportunity to pursue my dream of becoming a maternity nurse in Palestine after the War. Everything was stolen from us; But you have a chance to reach for your dreams, a chance for a future, and a chance to shape it. If you'll only refuse to quit on yourself. If you'll firmly resolve to speak up for yourself. If you'll gather the drugs and throw them away, while choosing to live for another day."

A complete silence hung in the air as Margot's words, all of them, filled Eliana's mind and heart. After a time, her eyes opened and the long silence was filled by the sounds of nature within the hidden hollow. Eliana had no idea how long she'd been asleep, except for the fact that it was now quite hot outside and she found herself in a pool of sweat. The deer and her fawn were no longer present. The duck, however, was now waddling back toward the lake with her brood of tiny ducklings following close behind. For a moment, the story of Mrs. Quackenbush, written by Anne Frank in response to her teacher calling her Ms. Quack Quack for talking too much in class, filled Eliana's thoughts. She said to herself, "Better to talk too much like Anne, than to fail to speak up for yourself or to quit on yourself, like me." And with those words, Eliana picked up the deadly cocktail of drugs from her towel, followed behind the ducklings, and tossed the drugs far out into the lake!

She climbed onto her bicycle and pedaled directly home. As she approached her house, she observed a policeman standing right outside her front door. The officer had just returned from conducting a neighborhood search for Eliana. "Who are you?" the officer asked. "I'm Eliana Goldberg." The officer immediately yelled out, "Ms. Goldberg, come outside, Eliana's home!" Ms. Goldberg threw open the front door and threw her arms around her daughter like she'd never let go! During their embrace, no words were shared between the two of them, only tears.

After a time, they engaged in a brief conversation while still outside.

"I'm sorry, Mom, I'm so sorry. Please forgive me."

"Are you ok, dearest? Are you injured in any way?"

"I'm ok, Mom. I'm fine. I'm so sorry that I scared you to death."

"I read your note. I regret that I was so blind to your plight. I would like to help you, Eliana. I would like for us to go see your principal together."

"Yes, Mom. That's exactly what I had in mind."

"Also, Eliana, given the ongoing bullying and threats you've encountered at school, I'm going to arrange for you to receive counselling services from the school psychologist. No arguments, dear. Promise me you'll go."

"Yes, Mom, I promise. There is something else that I truly believe would be of help to me."

"What is that, Eliana?"

"I would like to adopt a cat."

"A cat?"

"Yes, Mom, a cat. Let's go inside. I have so much to tell you."

Eliana turned toward the officer and apologized for all the time and expense that she had caused.

"That's ok, young lady. I'm just glad you're ok. It appears that you and your mom have much to talk about. I'll leave you to it."

Ms. Goldberg stated, "Thank you so much for all of your support, officer."

Once inside, Eliana told her mom all about the cruelty she'd endured since the school year began. She told her all about Margot Frank visiting her in her dream at her lowest point, and filling her with determination to go on living, to fight back against bullying and anti-Semitism, and to take control of her life. Eliana and her mom agreed to speak together with her principal and with her teachers first thing Monday morning. They would demand that each of Eliana's tormentors be held accountable. Before the school board, they would give voice to the need for a humanities course addressing the consequences of bullying, racism, and intolerance. They decided that if they weren't taken seriously, they'd alert the media. Perhaps most importantly, Eliana and her mom agreed that from there on in, they would keep the lines of communication open between the two of them on a daily basis, and be there for each other through thick and thin.

That evening, after Eliana had fallen into a deep sleep, Margot visited her once again.

"Well, Eliana, it's great to see that you've returned home to your mom."

"Yes, Margot, and I tossed the deadly cocktail of drugs into the lake. Mom and I are going to speak to the principal on Monday morning. I'm going to receive counselling services from the school psychologist. I'm going to demand that my tormentors be held accountable. Before the school board, Mom and I are going to voice the need for a humanities course addressing the consequences of bullying, racism, and intolerance. If nothing's done, we'll alert the media."

"That's it, kiddo. Now you're fighting back and standing up for yourself. My spirited sister, Anne, would be proud of you; As I am proud of you. Now you need to get some rest. Starting tomorrow morning, a whole new life, a better life than you've ever known, awaits you."

"Will I ever hear from you anymore, Margot? Will you visit me again? You've been a lifesaver. You have helped me so much, and I will miss you terribly."

"Thanks to my sister, our family and friends who hid together from the Nazis within The Secret Annex, will go on living forever through her diary. So whenever you wish to visit, all you have to do is reach for your bookcase and pull from the shelf your copy of The Diary of Anne Frank."

"I wish that Anne had written more about you in her diary, Margot, so that I could feel closer to you while seeking words of wisdom in the troubled times."

"All you have to do, Eliana, whenever it moves you to do so, is to read between the lines, and I'll be there for you."

With her mom's support, the support of the school psychologist, and with a little help from her cat, Mooksie, who she and her mom picked up from the shelter the day after she returned home, Eliana overcame the forces of anti-Semitism, hatred, and intolerance in her life, as well as her own demons. In the years that followed, she went on to realize her dream of becoming a successful journalist and writer. She used her writing skills to speak out against bullying in school, and to battle anti-Semitism and racism in all of their ugly forms.

She became an accomplished and avid tennis player throughout her life. Her opponents referred to her as diminutive in stature but large of heart, and light on her feet. Later in life, she married and had a daughter of her own named Sophie, who she and her husband adored.

Shortly before Sophie went off to begin her freshman year of college, Eliana shared with her the story of how Margot Frank visited her in her dream, and infused her with the strength to overcome during the lowest point in her life. As Eliana explained to Sophie, "She seemed so real, and her impact upon my life was so profound. It seemed like she was more than a visitor in my dream. It was as if I'd somehow communed with her spirit."

During Sophie's senior year at college, she phoned her mom and informed her that she'd decided to write her senior thesis on the Frank family and The Holocaust. She told her that some new photographs had recently been released in regard to the Frank family. Sophie said that she'd email copies of the photos to her the next day. Upon receiving the photos the next evening, Eliana scrolled through them until she came across a photo of Margot surrounded by a group of friends. Margot and the other girls were pictured side by side at an Amsterdam Club with their wooden tennis racquets and white tennis outfits on display. As Eliana continued to stare at the photo, Sophie called her on the phone and said, "Mom, you were right! Anne never mentioned in her diary that Margot played tennis, but you were right! I recall that before I went off to school to begin my freshman year, you told me that Margot had revealed to you in your dream that she enjoyed playing tennis. The photo of Margot and her tennis playing friends bears that out. Maybe it truly was something more than a dream."

After saying goodnight to Sophie, Eliana put down her phone, reached for her bookcase, and pulled off the shelf her copy of The Diary of Anne Frank. It was the same old copy of the diary that she had revisited again and again throughout her life, in the happy times and in the troubled times. She opened the diary to begin reading, glanced over at the tennis photograph of Margot on her computer screen, and expressed these words aloud: "Thank you, Margot, for saving my life. I've always known you were more than a dream, for I've never stopped reading between the lines."

LOVING CHOPIN
(Historical Fiction)

Paul Stone was a distinguished violinist and teacher at the Hoch School of Music in
      Frankfurt, Germany, before the War.
When his daughter, Anna, was five years old in 1932, her God-given talent for piano
      revealed itself on Paul's piano at home, to be sure.

Paul asked his close friend, Aaron Greenburg, an accomplished pianist and fellow teacher
      at the Hoch School of Music, if he'd work with Anna at the school-
To develop her talent and provide her the tools.

Aaron, whose family had emigrated to Germany from Poland years earlier,
      readily agreed.
As he introduced her to Bach, Beethoven, Mendelssohn, Mozart, and Chopin, she
      progressed with amazing speed.

In April 1933, soon after Hitler and the Nazi Party ascended to power, Jewish members
      of the teaching staff at Hoch, including Aaron, were unceremoniously fired.
It mattered not- they'd been greatly admired.

Aaron was forced to scrape out a living working at his dad's haberdashery store;
And Paul paid him as generously as he could to continue working with Anna in
      her home, a labor of love which Aaron adored.

Even as Anna progressed as a pianist in leaps and bounds, her physical
      health declined.
She suffered from asthma which left her at times-
Completely bedridden, or mostly confined.

No matter the challenge or how steep the climb-
Aaron stood by her in the difficult times.
When her symptoms subsided, she was anxious to grind-
And swiftly catch-up, for all the lost time.

Anna and Aaron shared many a laugh-
Like the times she hit the wrong note with great conviction, magnifying
    the gaffe!
In addition, Anna refused to allow her darling Sasha the Cat to
    be locked away.
So every so often without any warning, Sasha turned into the Red Baron,
    landing on top of the keyboard as Anna played!
Instead of getting angry with Anna for refusing to lock her away-
Aaron utilized Sasha's keyboard landings to lighten the moment in a special way.

Anna affectionately referred to Aaron as "Maestro."
On those occasions when Anna felt she'd completed a piece while in the flow-
She'd turn to him, beam, and say, "What do you think of that, Maestro!"

Often, Aaron's wife, Nina, accompanied him to Anna's home. During the lengthy
    piano lessons, Nina and Anna's mom, Emma, became fast friends.
They looked forward to their chats and the time that they'd spend.

They discussed the anti-Semitic Nuremburg Laws of 1935 which stripped Nina, Aaron,
    their families, and all Jewish people of their citizenship and their civil rights.
Nina spoke of the growing fear felt by Aaron and herself for their family's safety, and
    for the safety of their Jewish friends, as hatred and darkness eclipsed the light.

The years passed, and Anna continued to blossom.
Her proficiency on the Beethoven, Mendelssohn, and Mozart was nothing short of awesome!
But then, in 1938, Anna was stricken with a severe asthmatic flare-up which landed
    her in the hospital.
Her condition was serious and she wasn't improving, not even a little.

Aaron and Nina visited Anna and her parents in the hospital every day-
Determined to back them in every way.
They also made sure that Sasha was cared for and got enough play.

Anna was weak and she seemed so sad-
On many levels she felt so bad.
She told Maestro she had so much to give-
But she deeply feared that she wouldn't live-
To develop her talent and realize her dreams-
It was all in the balance, or so it all seemed.

Aaron and Nina, who had no children of their own, had grown to love Anna. They
    viewed her as their God child with her parents' blessing.
They leaned over her hospital bed and assured her that she'd be healing and soon
    progressing.

The next day when Aaron and Nina showed up at the hospital, Aaron had a black eye,
    and his face and arms were badly bruised. Their home had been ransacked, and
    the windows of the haberdashery smashed and broken.
The expression of anti-Semitic hatred had metastasized beyond words that were spoken.
Hitler's SA had engaged in the "Night of Broken Glass."
For Aaron and Nina, the writing was on the wall, their greatest fears had come to pass.

Anna exclaimed, "Oh Maestro, you're hurt!"
"Don't worry, Anna, I'll be ok. You just get well. Don't cry, dear Anna, your eyes will
    swell."
"Nina and I need to speak with you and your parents." He walked
    over and shut the hospital room door.
As they all stood around Anna's hospital bed, Maestro spoke in a solemn tone that he
    hadn't used before.

He explained that he and Nina had no choice but to immediately leave Germany for
    France. It was now too dangerous in Germany for Jews to remain.
The Nazis would kill them or place them in chains.

"Your mom and dad, he stated, have offered to hide us in your home; But we've been
    seen coming over too often. That's the first place the Nazis would look.
We'd be quickly discovered and our goose would be cooked."

Overwhelmed by her weak physical condition as well as the news of their leaving,
    Anna once again began to cry.
Maestro pulled up a chair, sat down next to Anna's bedside, reached for her hand, and
    said, "I have a story to tell you Anna, please let me try."

"Frederick Chopin, the great Polish composer, like yourself, suffered serious
        lung issues from early on.
His illness never stopped him from composing the most consistently beautiful and
        melodic classical piano music ever written. He was a phenom."

"It never stopped him from composing the exquisite Nocturnes. It never stopped him
        from composing the Mazurkas, the Polonaises, the Waltzes, the two Sonatas,
        the four Ballades, the four Scherzos, the four Impromptus, the 24 Preludes, the
        24 Etudes, his two piano Concertos, and more-
All of them masterpieces, more creative, beautiful, and powerful piano music than
        anything written since or before."

"Chopin 'made a single instrument speak a language of God,' wrote his lady friend and
        famous writer, George Sand.
You, Anna, have magic in your heart and in your hands.
If you are willing to fight your illness with all of your heart and all of your will
        and make your stand-
You will one day become a concert pianist as you have dreamed, performing
        throughout the world in many lands."

"The Etudes are probably among Chopin's most difficult pieces to play. While they are
        beautiful and powerful, they are also studies. Each of them challenges the
        piano student to master a particular technical difficulty. Master the Etudes,
        dear Anna, and you will realize your dream.
You will rise to the top as they say of cream."

"I wish to ask something of you, Anna. My favorite of Chopin's compositions is his
        Revolutionary Etude. Chopin was very patriotic. His Revolutionary
        Etude constituted a powerful in your face expression of defiance in response to
        the Russian attack upon Warsaw during the 1830-31 Polish uprising- a revolution
        that was crushed.
Chopin fought back in the only way that he could. He utilized his artistic genius to
        weaponize his piano as a powerful paint brush."

"When Chopin died, the world suffered a great loss.
He was buried in France, but his heart was transported by his sister, Ludwika, at his
        instruction to where it belonged, his beloved Poland, at the Church of
        the Holy Cross."

"One day, Anna, after Hitler's Nazi menace has been eradicated from the world,
        I would like for you to travel to my beloved Poland and perform the
        Revolutionary Etude, before a live audience as an expression of defiance-
A message to tyrants everywhere of non-appeasement and non-compliance."
"Will you do that for me, Anna"? Maestro implored.
"Yes, Maestro, you can rest assured."

As Maestro and Nina prepared to leave, hugs were exchanged by all. Maestro quietly
        handed to Paul a gift for Anna, to be opened after Maestro and Nina were
        on their way.
It turned out to be a gift which Anna treasured for the rest of her days.

The inside cover contained a note written by Maestro which he had shown to Nina.
        The note read as follows: "Dear Anna, this book contains all 24 of
        Chopin's Etudes. I utilized it to learn to play the Etudes when I was a young
        boy growing up in Poland. Aside from my wedding ring, it is my most treasured
        possession. Now it is yours.
I hope that it provides pleasure for you which endures.
Like Chopin, you will one day make the piano 'speak a language of God.' Unlike
        Chopin, to say it with brevity-
Yours will be a life of health and longevity."

Four days after Aaron and Nina left for France, Anna's health improved enough
        for her to return home. Soon thereafter, she tackled the Chopin Etudes
        with commitment and drive.
After a time, she felt she was bringing the music alive.

Two months went by. Then one evening, Anna's parents held a family meeting-
At the dinner table while they were eating.
Paul revealed that he'd received a call from a wealthy man named Mark Cook,
        a close friend of Maestro who lived in America. At Maestro's request,
        Cook was offering to bring the entire family to America, to enable Anna
        to study piano at the Julliard School.
Anna couldn't believe her ears, it sounded so cool!

Cook had informed Paul that Maestro was confident that upon hearing Anna play-
Julliard would enroll her in the school right away.
In addition, Julliard was in need of an additional musician-
And they were prepared to offer Paul a teaching position!

Cook had also passed along to Paul, Maestro's message that there was excellent medical
practice in America, which would provide opportunities for Anna to
receive effective treatment for her asthmatic condition-
By availing herself of first-rate physicians.

Paul and Emma wanted only the best for their daughter so there was
nothing to debate.
They were all excited about the move and they couldn't wait!
But Anna said to her parents, "Mama, Papa, please. I want so much to go, but only if
Sasha comes along as well. I must have my cat!"
"Of course, she's coming along, her parents replied. Our family would be incomplete
without Sasha the Cat!
So she's coming along, and that's that!"

The family was grateful beyond words to Maestro and to Mark Cook. Paul called Cook
and thanked him for his generosity, and told him they were coming. The
family also contacted Maestro and Nina, expressing their thanks as well as
their love.
The opportunity awaiting them in America felt like a wonderful blessing from above.

Paul and Emma rented out their home, packed up their things-
And the family set off to experience the American Dream.
Anna held Sasha in her arms while thinking of America and Julliard, and beamed.

Just as Maestro predicted, Anna was immediately accepted at Julliard when they
heard her play! She threw herself even more into mastering the Etudes. Her
fingers flew across the keyboard as she spread her wings in full flight.
Everything about The Julliard School felt perfect, just right.

Almost a year and a half went by as the family adjusted to life in the States.
The whole family, including Sasha who insisted upon being spoiled, agreed that life in
America was going great.

Overseas, however, things were far different. Through radio reports and newspaper
    accounts, Anna and her parents followed closely with alarm and great sorrow,
    the horrible news from Europe. Beginning in April 1940, the Nazi blitzkrieg
    rolled over Norway, Denmark, Luxembourg, Belgium, and the Netherlands;
    And then, in June 1940, France fell as well.
For Anna and her family, it was a moment of hell.
They prayed that God would watch over Maestro, Nina, their families, and keep
    them well.

Anna supported Maestro and Nina in the only way that she could. She immersed herself
    in her studies at Julliard with complete dedication.
She soaked up instruction like a sponge, achieving a first rated education.
Initially, she had focused upon Chopin mostly to honor Maestro; But very soon, she
    fell in love with Chopin's music on her own.
Each new Chopin piece she mastered, felt like a milestone.

Even as she committed herself to mastering the Etudes, Anna learned that the Nazis had
    banned the performance of Chopin in Poland, which they had occupied
    since September 1939.
The Nazis were worried about the patriotic fervor that Chopin's music stirred in the
    hearts of the Polish people, and in their minds.
That knowledge stirred within Anna's heart the motivation to practice even
    harder, to grind.

Anna continued to suffer periodic asthmatic flare-ups which landed her in
    the hospital and off her feet.
Nevertheless, she refused to become demoralized or give in to defeat.
After not very long she'd rise to her feet.

After years of bloodshed, Nazi Germany surrendered on May 7, 1945.
After looking into the abyss, American and Western European democracy survived.
Soon thereafter, the Holocaust, including the horror of the extermination camps, was
    revealed for all the world to see.
It was almost impossible to fathom or comprehend the full measure of its depravity.
The Nazis had murdered and connived-
Six million Jews had not survived.

Anna and her parents had not heard a word from Maestro or Nina since Germany's
       1940 occupation of France.
By February 1947, close to two years after WWII ended, there was
       still no word. Had Maestro and Nina survived? There seemed little chance.

In May 1947, soon after her 20th birthday, with the support and recommendation of her
       teachers at Julliard, Anna took a major step toward realizing her dreams. She
       was chosen to perform a piano recital at Carnegie Hall!
Anna and her parents were completely enthralled!

Before too long the moment arrived.
She'd come so far and she had survived.
With her adrenalin bursting at the seams-
She began her recital with sure things.

Her fingers flew through the Mendelssohn and the Mozart
       with the greatest of ease-
As if a first-time recital at Carnegie Hall was little more than a breeze!

Before her final selection, Anna stood up, turned toward the audience,
       and addressed them directly while talking slow-
There was something she wanted the people to know.

"Ladies and Gentlemen, my final piece of the evening is dedicated to a very
       dear friend who provided me the spirit, the drive, and the means to
       reach for my dream of playing before you today. In a very real sense,
       I owe him my life-
For his help and his kindness, and that of his wife."

"His name is Aaron Greenburg, a gifted musician and teacher, born
       in Poland, who adored his compatriot, Frederick Chopin, as do I.
Listening to the beauty and creativity of Chopin's music is the purest
       means of understanding why."

"My family and I believe that Aaron Greenburg who I called Maestro,
       his wife, Nina, and the rest of their families, were murdered by hate-
Condemned by Nazi anti-Semitism to a horrible fate."

"Hitler bragged that his Reich would last a thousand years.

It lasted a dozen years.

It is Chopin's music which will last a thousand years.

Which is another way of saying that in the long course of history, despite
       everything, love and beauty will ultimately triumph over hate.

Unfortunately, for so many innocent people slaughtered along the way, it
       is far too late."

"So now, to honor my friend and teacher, I wish to play for you his favorite piece,
       The Revolutionary Etude, as a final in your face send off to Nazism,
       Fascism, and despotism everywhere, that they might be forever
       expunged from the earth.

And in their wake, a time for rebirth."

While it had been the hardest piece for Anna to master, when the time came to step up
       and perform-

She played it with passion, conviction, grace and ease, at the very top of her form.

Upon completion of those four abrupt, staccato, and thunderous chords that finalized the
       Revolutionary Etude, there was a momentary pause.

Then, suddenly, Carnegie Hall broke into thunderous applause!

Afterward, Anna was greeted backstage with hugs and kisses from her parents, and from
       the team of teachers from Julliard. For Anna, it was a precious and triumphant
       moment to be sure;

But then came the knocking on her dressing room door.

The Theater Director passed a note to Anna, telling her it was from a female
       member of the audience who had asked to be heard-

An audience member who asked over and over to see Anna, refusing to be deterred.

"Tonight, you truly 'made the piano speak a language of God,'" the note read.

The words shocked Anna into stopping dead.

She immediately asked the Theater Director to escort the note writer to her
       dressing room. Anna awaited the woman as her heart raced.

She remained physically frozen, locked in place.

Very soon the woman knocked, then entered the dressing room. She
        appeared physically infirm and very frail.
She also looked sickly and deathly pale.

She appeared only vaguely familiar at first.
But when the woman smiled, Anna felt that her heart would burst!
For she recognized that it was Nina, and none other-
The woman she loved as her precious Godmother!

Anna reached out and held her tight.
Her parents joined in to reunite.
The teachers beheld this joyous sight.

Between tears shed by all, Nina explained that she had clung to the hope
        that Maestro, as well as their family members, had endured the death camps
        and come out alive;
But after a time, she was forced to accept that she alone had survived.

Nina continued with more to say.
"It was a blessing, Anna, to be here today-
For the incredible thrill of hearing you play!
I was also keeping a promise I made to Maestro while in hiding in France-
That if I survived the war without him, I would hear you in concert at my
        very first chance."

"That's how absolutely certain he was, Anna, that you would overcome your
        illness to become a concert pianist as you had dreamed.
Maestro loved you, Anna. He believed in your talent, and he held you in
        the highest esteem."

"He said to me, 'While you are together with Anna and her family and friends after
        her recital, please share a brief moment with them and say Kaddish for me.
Then let go and let me be.
Join them for a celebration of Anna and her courage, and all that she will have achieved-
For she never gave up and she always believed.' "

At that moment, they all gathered close together as Nina said
        The Jewish Prayer.
In their hearts and in their minds, Maestro was there.

Nina, Anna, her parents, and the Julliard teachers, went out for
      dinner and celebration-
To celebrate Anna, the concert pianist sensation!

During the course of dinner, Nina proposed the following toast to Anna.
      "If Maestro had lived to hear you play tonight, he would no doubt have recalled
      Robert Schumann's words upon introducing the 21-year-old Chopin and his
      music to the world; And he no doubt would have quoted those words upon
      toasting you, as I shall do in his place tonight."
With those words, Nina stood up, raised her glass of champagne, and said,
      "Hats off Ladies and Gentlemen, a genius!"

Anna, unlike Chopin, would go on to live a long and healthy life, just
      as Maestro predicted.
Due to advances in medicine, she was neither sickly nor continuously afflicted.
She was able to manage her asthma and keep it at bay-
So it wasn't controlling and ruining her days.

Anna married and eventually had children of her own whom she adored, a little boy and
      a little girl.
The children reminded her of the Chopin Preludes, beautiful and perfect like little pearls.
She and her husband raised them to be tolerant and accepting of all people regardless of
      race, religion, or class.
They taught them lessons they hoped would last.

At Anna's insistence and with the blessing of her husband, Nina lived with them as
      a treasured member of their family; And to the children, she remained a loving
      Great-Godmother for the remainder of her days.
Her influence upon the children was invaluable in so many ways.

Anna kept her promise to Maestro and travelled to Poland to perform
      The Revolutionary Etude. She did so with faithfulness and devotion.
She captured the Etude's raw emotion.

She always contributed a portion of her concert earnings to the Frederick Chopin
      Society in Warsaw, Poland-
And to the promotion of human rights in Poland-
For so long lost and so long stolen.

In the years that followed, Anna raised money through her recitals and concerts for The
    American Lung Association. She raised additional money for the purpose
    of fighting and eradicating childhood disease-
Determined to bring it to its very knees.

She also established a Foundation of her own located in the center of New
    York City, known as the Aaron "Maestro" Greenburg Center for Ethnic and
    Religious Tolerance. The Foundation was dedicated to the promotion of
    tolerance throughout the world, and to the elimination of anti-Semitism and
    other forms of religious, ethnic, and racial discrimination-
To fashion and mold more enlightened nations.

Throughout her long and illustrious career as a concert pianist, Anna contributed
    generous portions of her own earnings to the Foundation's cause.
It meant more to Anna than the loudest applause-
To help shape a world that embraced humanity-
A world which rejected the hate and insanity.

A CAUTIONARY TALE
(Historical Fiction)

Immigration attorney Johnny Sanders' Memorial Service was filled with
     scores of his Hispanic clients.
They viewed him as their champion, a committed legal giant.

Johnny had devoted his entire adult life to assisting indigent
     immigrants fleeing violence in their own
     countries, by seeking asylum in the United States.
For many of them, he had rescued their lives from a deadly fate.

A number of them spoke at his service of his dedication,
     his compassion, and how deeply he cared-
How thanks to his efforts their lives had been spared.

His only surviving relative, his sister Rose-
Described him as a devoted, loving brother, heaven knows.
She also revealed that despite his loving care for her, as well
     as the satisfaction he took from assisting his clients,
     he'd been a sad and tortured soul who'd lived a lonely life.
He'd broken up with the woman he loved, who would have
     become his loving wife.
Shunning personal happiness, had been his way of life.

As a result of Johnny's lifetime of distinguished service, his Memorial
     Service was attended by a writer, David Snow.
There was much information he wanted to know.

After the service, he gently but persistently prodded Rose to share
     with him the answer to several questions:
     Why had Johnny devoted his entire adult life exclusively to
     assisting those seeking asylum? Why had he denied himself
     opportunities for happiness in his personal life?
What were the reasons for his inner strife?

Despite a huge measure of initial reticence and reluctance, Rose agreed
     to meet with David Snow in her home for an interview in two weeks' time,
     to share with him the story of her brother-
In the hope that it might serve as a wake-up call to others.

David met with her at her home as arranged and listened intently,
  hanging on Rose's every word. She was at times emotional,
  at other times controlled.
This is the story that began to unfold:

As a teenager growing up in Texas near the border, Johnny had joined a gang
  that harbored deep racial resentment against immigrants who they would
  target, threaten, taunt, and berate-
Acting out on their senseless hate.
Anyone who looked "foreign," they'd bully, belittle, and demean-
Calling them dirty, diseased, and unclean.

When Johnny was seventeen and Rose was ten, seventeen-year-old
  Sergio Hernandez and his family moved onto their neighborhood block.
Thanks to Johnny and his gang, Sergio had to watch his back, round the clock.

Sergio was zoned to the same high school as Johnny, Friendship High.
It was difficult to avoid crossing paths with Johnny and his bullying gang,
  though he constantly tried.
All too often, the other students turned a blind eye.
The bullying went on for weeks and months on end.
Sergio couldn't count on a single friend.

One day in speech class, Johnny listened to Sergio as he stood before the class
  and told about his family; About how his parents had led he and his
  little sister, Gabriela, on a dangerous and desperate thousand- mile
  trek from Honduras to Texas. They were fleeing not only poverty, but
  the life-threatening violence of Honduran gangs.
They'd fled after seeing a neighbor who couldn't pay tribute to the gangs,
  strung up and hanged.

Johnny listened stone-faced, completely unmoved by Sergio's words.
His attention was grabbed by the last thing he heard.
Sergio stated that his family had been granted asylum, and that his
  Dad, Manuel Hernandez, worked as an orderly at Goodwill Hospital,
  having been issued a lawful green card.
Johnny suspected that Sergio's story about asylum and the green card
  was nothing but a fabrication, a canard.
He suspected that Sergio's dad possessed nothing more than a faked,
  counterfeit card.

At the very end of that school day-
Johnny and two of his fellow gang members, Jason and Justice,
        cornered Sergio in the usual way.
Outside a building with no one around-
They punched him out and continued to pound.
They grabbed Sergio by the collar, and shoved him up
        against a wall.
There was no one to help him- no one to call.

As Jason and Justice held Sergio by the collar, Johnny told Sergio that he was
        going to call ICE on the office phone and make an accusation.
He was going to tell ICE where they could round up a family of illegal
        immigrants for jailing and deportation.

He was going to tell ICE that Sergio's dad, Manuel Hernandez, worked as an
        orderly at Goodwill Hospital. He was going to give them
        Sergio's family's home address-
Ratting them out, he expected, with enormous success!
He elevated Sergio's panic and stress!

While Jason and Justice held Sergio up against the wall-
Johnny left to make the call.
Upon his return, Johnny laughed at Sergio and gloated,
        "I called ICE and the deed is done, it was no problem at all!"

Johnny, Jason, and Justice had upcoming football practice with forty minutes to kill-
They held Sergio in place, taunting him against his will.
Sergio was scared and feeling ill.
After forty minutes went by, they callously laughed and shoved him away-
As if he was nothing but discarded prey.
From the moment they released him, Sergio was on a mission, and he'd find a way!

Like Paul Revere, he furiously pedaled on his bike toward Goodwill
        Hospital to warn his dad, the ICE agents were coming!
He ignored exhaustion, the pain from his beating, and the burning in his legs.
        There would be no succumbing!

The hospital was located midway between Friendship High and Sergio and Johnny's neighborhood block.

About 100 yards before reaching the hospital, Sergio experienced a terrible shock!

A car flew by and struck a young girl on her bicycle who was riding home from her nearby elementary school.

The driver took off like a scared and panicky, heartless fool.

Sergio instantly jumped off his bike and ran over to the little girl.

Pouring out of her left thigh was a stream of blood!

Sergio realized he must nip the bleeding in the bud!

He stripped off his shirt, and applied it as a tourniquet to control the bleeding.

While holding the tourniquet in place, he lifted her into his arms and raced on foot to the hospital entrance, recognizing that time was fleeting.

As he ran, he comforted her, telling her she would be ok.

While his inner voice continued to pray.

As he approached the glass doors at the front entrance to the hospital-

Sergio observed two cars marked ICE, and two uniformed ICE agents inside.

He ran inside without breaking a stride.

He raced up to the receptionist who was talking to the ICE agents, while yelling that it was a medical emergency!

He begged for medical help for the young girl with the greatest of urgency.

Not long thereafter, Johnny, who was at football practice, was notified by an office staff member that he needed to go immediately to Goodwill Hospital due to a family emergency.

The staff member told him that it was a matter of utmost urgency.

Upon arrival, Johnny was directed to the fifth-floor surgical unit where he met up with his mom and dad.

He learned that his little sister, Rose, was in surgery, and her injury was bad.

Her femoral artery had been seriously damaged when she was struck by a car on her way home from school.

Johnny hugged his parents, then collapsed and cried over news so cruel.

For the next two hours, Johnny and his parents waited and prayed-
Asking God to render His Aid.
And then, in an instant, the surgeon emerged and gave them a smile.
She wouldn't be walking for quite a while;
But she'd keep her leg and eventually heal-
And she'd also recover all of her feel!

The Dr. told them that her rescuer had saved her leg and probably her life,
	by wrapping around her bleeding femoral artery, the shirt off his back.
He'd utilized his shirt as a tourniquet in the nick of time. He had the knack.

After receiving the joyful news, Johnny and his parents asked exactly how
	Rose had gotten to the medical center.
The downstairs receptionist explained the story of how she entered.
She explained how Rose's rescuer, a teen who appeared to have been beaten up,
	burst through the sliding glass doors carrying Rose in his arms with his
	shirt wrapped around her leg to control her bleeding.
He desperately cried out for the help she was needing.
He exclaimed that she'd been the victim of a hit and run strike!
While leaving school, while riding her bike.

The family asked for the whereabouts of the rescuer who they wished to thank.
The receptionist explained that that would be impossible, for the rescuer
	and his dad had figuratively "walked the plank."
For immediately after the rescuer turned Rose over to the medical staff,
	he and his dad, Manuel Hernandez, a hospital orderly, were taken into
	custody and whisked away by federal agents.
The agents weren't interested in the life saving assistance the teen had provided
	Rose. They had no patience.

The receptionist explained that the teen was so determined and desperate
	to save Rose, that he ran inside to get her help, undeterred by the uniformed
	ICE agents standing right inside the front door-
Or by their marked cars parked right outside the door.
She added that she'd never in her life seen such an act of selflessness- never before.

With a pained expression, Johnny asked, "What was the teen's name?"
	"Sergio Hernandez," the receptionist replied.
Johnny held his head in his hands, and broke down and cried.

He asked, "Is there any chance we can see Sergio and his dad? Please, oh please,
       is there any possible way?"
"I'm sorry, it's impossible," the receptionist replied. "For the Feds have taken Sergio
       and his dad into custody to deport them, to send them away."

"The receptionist was correct," Rose said to David Snow. "Johnny never saw
       Sergio again, and he never had the opportunity to apologize for his behavior-
Or to thank him for having saved my life, for being my savior."

Rose told David that it was only recently upon his deathbed, that Johnny
       revealed to her that the teen who saved her life, Sergio Hernandez, was
       someone he had tormented, beaten, and ratted out to ICE.
Sergio and his family had paid a terrible price.

Johnny had never revealed these facts to another soul.
He'd hidden them away from all human knowledge, like the secrets of a black hole.
He had cloaked in secrecy his guilt and his shame.
He had no one else but himself to blame.

As he neared his death, Johnny had one final secret to share with Rose-
The most dreadful cause of his lifelong woes.
Finding it difficult to speak with a burning throat-
Johnny gestured for a pencil and paper to write her a note.

He also pointed to a footlocker at the end of his bed, which he gestured for
       her to open. As she did so, he proceeded to write.
She opened the footlocker, felt around, and eventually spotted a 63-year-old
       Honduran newspaper clipping, deeply buried and hidden from sight.
Rose, who was fluent in Spanish, held the dusty and faded clipping up to the light.

The clipping was an obituary which read as follows:
       "Seventeen-year-old Sergio Hernandez was shot and killed by
       gang members only two days after his deportation back to Honduras
       from the United States.
He was a kind soul and a loving son and brother, murdered by hate."

As knowledge of the fate of her rescuer, her guardian angel from long ago,
      sank in, tears welled up and she began to cry.
Accompanied by a painful sigh.
Johnny physically and emotionally struggled to voice the words, "I'm so sorry Rose.
I should have told you years ago, heaven knows."
Two days later he passed away.
At last his demons had faded away.

As Rose related this revelation to David Snow, her tears welled up once again-
Just as they had in the moment back then.
"If it is too painful, I will leave the fate of Sergio out of my piece, dear Rose."
"Thank you, David, but it needs to be included in your piece for Johnny's sake,
      I suppose."

As she expressed those words, Rose reached into her pocketbook and
      handed David the note written by Johnny as she looked
      through his footlocker, two days before he passed away.
These are the words he wrote that day:

"There was nothing that I could ever do to right the wrong.
My shame's been buried for far too long.
Let it serve as a cautionary tale to others-
To treat each other as sisters and brothers."

STICKIN' IT TO JIM CROW
(Historical Fiction)

Jada Patterson grew up in the 1920's in Birmingham, Alabama, the heart and soul of
    the segregated South. It was short on heart and scant of soul.
Birmingham specialized in racial discrimination, terror, poll taxes, and literacy tests, to
    keep minorities away from the polls.

Jada's parents were educators, and because they were black, they taught at a
    segregated public elementary school.
They disdained racism and discrimination sanctioned by Jim Crow laws,
    as disgraceful and cruel.
They could not abide the enormity of America's hypocrisy-
Condoning the treatment of minorities as second- class citizens in a democracy.

They viewed the country's founding principle of equality, "that all men are
    created equal"-
Interpreted by the U.S. Supreme Court in 1896 as sanctioning "separate but equal"-
As a ruse, a convenient means to further abuse.
They were determined to protect their daughters, Jada and Kia, from the horrors
    of racism, by teaching them to rise above it-
To stare it down and mentally shove it.

Birmingham wasn't satisfied with segregation of blacks through Jim Crow.
In the midst of segregation, it erected statues of confederate generals as an in-your-face
    reminder to black people that they were second class citizens- to harden the
    blow and to let them know-
They'd remain forever, low man on the totem pole.

While their teacher salaries were low, Jada's parents managed to make ends meet even
    through the Great Depression years.
In the face of economic decline and the KKK, they refused to give in to panic or fear.
When around Jada or Kia, they exuded confidence, full of good cheer.
By any definition they were financially poor.
Yet they viewed themselves as rich, for they had each other and the kids they adored.

They instilled within their children a love of reading and learning, and a firm
    belief that all things were possible-
That with hard work and determination, nothing was impossible.

Jada and Kia, while six years apart, had much in common. They were
       each very bright, and they took great pride in their schoolwork
       in which they excelled.
Their teachers said of each of them that their effort level was unparalleled.

They were each fleet of foot and ran like the wind. Kia was the fastest runner
       in her sixth- grade class.
By the end of her races, her rivals were passed!
As for Jada, she was undefeated in high school track.
She rose to the top and never looked back.
As a senior, setting nationwide records in the 100- and 200-meter-dashes,
       was her special knack.

Jada and Kia adored the family's one- year- old Golden
       Retriever, Rusty.
They introduced him to their friends as "their trusty companion, Rusty."
At those times when they were feeling sad and needed a lift-
Rusty cheered them up- he had the gift.

Despite living in the south under an oppressive system of apartheid-
The entire Patterson family went about their lives, with heads held high
       and a sense of pride.

Upon Jada's graduation from high school and Kia's graduation from elementary school,
       the whole family went out for a celebration dinner. Jada spoke of her dreams
       and future aims.
She aspired to become a nurse; And she dreamed of running in The Olympic Games!

Over the next five years, Jada worked toward a B.S. degree from Tuskegee
       University. All the while, she continued to train toward her
       Olympic dream. She graduated as a certified registered nurse with a
       B.S. degree in 1943.
At that moment, with her country at war facing Nazi tyranny-
And despite being forced to live under Jim Crow tyranny-
Her overwhelming thought was, "My country needs me."

She enlisted in the U.S. Army Nurse Corps.

She was sent to the British colony of Burma in 1944.

There she served British and American forces who were fighting invading forces
from Japan. The injured men were grateful for her competence and touched
by her compassion, and welcomed her as an angel of mercy.

For them, the color of her skin was irrelevant, not a matter of controversy.

Jada served in a semi-mobile medical installation in the area of a combat zone.

As casualties mounted, so did the moans.

She cared for them all like her very own.

At times she worked while bombs were falling-

Helping the wounded, true to her calling.

During her stressful tour of duty treating soldiers close to the front-

Jada was sustained and comforted by letters from the home front.

She was delighted to learn that Kia was following in her footsteps, dominating the
competition in high school track.

Jada told Kia how proud she was of her when she wrote her back.

Jada also loved hearing stories about Rusty-

Which revealed how smart, kind, and funny he was, and how trusty!

While Kia and her parents were extremely proud of Jada's service-

They were continuously concerned for her safety, worried and nervous.

They were thrilled to greet her in late 1944 at the Birmingham Airport upon her
discharge from the Service.

Pinned to her uniform was her Medal for Distinguished Service.

Hugs and kisses were exchanged, and they all went out for a homecoming
dinner celebration.

They felt a wonderful sense of joy and exhilaration.

Jada spoke of her future plans with a great sense of determination.

She intended to find employment as a nurse in a Birmingham hospital. She
expressed optimism that her service to country would surely break down
walls of segregation.

Her parents reminded her that Jim Crow was still alive and well in Birmingham,
and would raise its ugly head despite her distinguished military service, her
wartime nursing experience, and her education.

In response, Jada smiled and said, "We'll see."
She then turned and embraced her sister with a sense of glee.
She said, "Kia, I'd like you to do something for me.
I'd like you to help me train for my Olympic dream by hitting the track, you and me!"
Kia lit up like a Christmas tree!

Jada turned toward her parents and said, "For a time, I'd like to work in
        your classrooms as a volunteer, helping out with your girls and boys."
They responded, "By all means," and hugged her with a sense of joy.
The evening was topped off when they arrived home and Jada received from Rusty,
        The Big Greeting!
It was a delightful reunion, for Rusty assured a high energy meeting!

Jada spent the next few weeks working with the boys and girls.
After her wartime service in Burma, she especially loved working with children,
        viewing them as precious pearls.
She also began training with Kia by her side.
While getting back into shape, she learned what a gifted sprinter Kia had
        become, matching her stride for stride.
Jada smiled at her sister with joy and pride.

After three weeks had gone by, Jada decided that it was time to get back to work.
She missed working with other nurses and doctors committed to helping patients
        through mutual teamwork.

She set out early in the morning intent on landing a position-
Working beside committed health care workers and physicians.
Thus began her life-changing hour-
Which threatened to cause her life to sour.

She marched into a Birmingham hospital wearing her Army
        Nurse Corps uniform-
So the hospital would be aware of her service, fully informed.

Despite her service to country in the Army Nurse Corps, and despite her
        meritorious service medal, she was turned down flat by the hospital
        administrator. He told her she was standing in a "white only" hospital
        and needed to go.
After arguing for a time, Jada retorted, "Take your bigotry and discrimination and
        shove it! To hell with Jim Crow!"

As Jada stormed out of the room and headed for the hospital exit, she was greeted
with cursing and racial slurs directed against her by two twenty- something
white men sitting in the waiting room. She looked directly at them without
saying a word, and exited through the doors-
Recognizing that they deserved to be completely ignored.

Jada got into her car and drove off. About eight minutes down the road, she turned
off the main drag onto a quiet road which circled into a small business area.
As she approached an area of the road which ran parallel to a deep ditch, a
large pick-up truck drove up beside her at a high rate of speed. As she looked
over, she viewed the faces of the two men from the hospital who had spouted
their hate!
Instinctively, she hit the gas pedal to accelerate!

The pick-up truck sped up and intentionally rammed the driver's side of her car,
forcing her off the road and into the ditch! As Jada's car plunged
into the ditch, it rolled onto its side.
The last thing she recalled was her head banging against the dashboard and searing
pain through her right thigh.

A shopper outside one of the nearby businesses viewed the hit and run with shock.
She immediately ran to a pay phone and called the cops.
The distance from the ditch to the Birmingham "white only" hospital was less than
ten minutes away.
But upon being removed from her car within the ditch, Jada was driven the opposite way.

She wound up in a hospital located outside Birmingham, forty-miles from the ditch.
She didn't wind up there based upon a glitch.
The ambulance driver had deliberately chosen not to drive to the "white only" hospital
located less than ten minutes away.
Despite her serious injuries, he drove her to the hospital far away.

Jada had suffered serious damage to the femoral artery in her right leg, resulting in
the loss of a great amount of blood. She had also incurred bruises and bumps
to her head and torso, as well as a concussion. Upon her arrival at the hospital,
Dr. Don James performed emergency surgery upon her torn femoral artery.
Immediately following surgery, Dr. James briefed Jada's family who had been notified and arrived.
He explained that as a result of damage to Jada's femoral artery, the tissue in her right
thigh had been oxygen rich blood deprived.

His biggest worry, he explained, was that Jada could develop gangrene in her right leg, in
      which case he'd have to amputate.
The next day or two would determine the outcome. For the time being, all they could do
      was pray and wait.

Regarding the crash, Dr. James told the family that according to reports, Jada's
      vehicle had rolled over into a ditch as a result of being broad-sided by a
      hit and run driver.
The Dr. emphasized that Jada was fortunate to have been a survivor.
The family, stunned and shocked by the news, hugged each other and cried.
They remained together for the night at Jada's bedside.

The next morning, they were still with Jada when she awakened. They each held her
      hand and smiled. She was on heavy meds, dozed on and off, and said little.
As for the fate of her leg, Dr. James was noncommittal.

Another day went by. The family was then directed into a conference room to meet
      with Dr. James. They were all seated nervously awaiting the doctor when he
      entered the room.
He greeted them with a smile, not gloom!

"She'll keep her leg and she'll walk again," he said.
The family embraced and tears were shed.
After thanking the doctor for saving her leg, Kia asked, "My sister is a gifted
      sprinter with Olympic dreams. Will she race?"
With sadness upon his face, Dr. James cut to the chase.
"The damage to the tissue in her leg is too severe. She'll walk and jog, and
      maybe she'll run; But she won't run at a world class pace."

Dr. James continued, "Let's talk to Jada together tomorrow, when I expect her
      to be clear-headed."
It was a moment of truth that the family dreaded.

The next day, they all met with Jada as planned. For the first time, she
      was able to tell them what happened. She told them about the two guys
      from the Birmingham hospital waiting room who spouted racial slurs,
      before stalking and intentionally ramming her car.
She asserted that after ramming her car into a ditch, "They took off like the
      cowards they are."

Dr. James explained to Jada how serious the damage to her leg tissue had been,
    and how her leg had been at risk. Then he once again cut to the chase:
"Jada, you'll keep your leg, you'll walk and you'll jog, and maybe you'll run-
    but you won't run at a world class pace."
As the news sank in, Jada was feeling both saddened and shocked-
Filled with the sense her world had been rocked.

Her family tried to comfort her, but she felt deeply depressed.
Dr. James administered medication to reduce her pain and to help her to rest.
Upon her falling asleep, her family shut the light.
They thanked Dr. James and returned home for the night.

The next day, Jada asked for Dr. James to ask him a question:
    "If I had been taken to the white only Birmingham hospital located only a few
    minutes from the ditch, instead of being driven to this hospital forty
    miles from the ditch, would my leg have been in a position to fully
    heal? Would the difference in time have mattered?
Please, Dr. James, I have a right to know, for I've been wronged and battered."

Dr. James hesitated. Jada insisted, "Please doctor, tell me the truth. Just tell me.
If I'm to cope with this, I need the complete truth. That's key."

"The main problem, Dr. James explained, is that the tissue in your right thigh
    was badly compromised and damaged due to inadequate blood supply
    for too long. If emergency surgery had been immediately performed
    at the Birmingham Hospital located only a few minutes from the ditch, then yes,
    Jada, your leg might have been in a position to fully heal.
You were rendered a raw deal."

Later on in the day, Jada's family told her they had something to discuss with her.
    Her dad said, "Jada, you've needlessly suffered this terrible blow.
We've had it with racial violence, second class citizenship, and Jim Crow.
We believe it's time to cut ties with Alabama, time to go."

"A great renaissance has taken place in Harlem among the black community in literature,
    the arts, and music. We'd like to move there when you are sufficiently healed.
    Harlem offers all of us a chance for a new life filled with open doors, new
    opportunities, and a chance to grow.
It will help you recover from this difficult blow."

Jada looked over at Kia and said, "You'd be leaving your friends as well as your
        high school during your junior year."
Kia replied, "I'll make new friends. Please Jada, I no longer wish to be here-
Living in a climate of hatred and fear.
Let's move to Harlem for a new life there."
Jada's mom chimed in, "Just think about it, dear.
We won't leave unless it's a decision we all share."

The next day, Jada presented her family with a short poem she'd written
        which contained her answer. It read as follows:
        "Jim Crow Alabama, you've altered my fate-
        Damaged my body with senseless hate.
        So long and goodbye don't bother to phone-
        Till Jim Crow has died, you're no longer my home."

A few days later, Jada was greeted upon her homecoming from the hospital
        by Rusty, who lightened her heart while making her laugh-
Seeming to cut all her sadness in half.

A month later, the entire family packed up their belongings and set out upon the
        long journey to Harlem. They joined what became known as the
        Great Migration. During long stretches on the car ride north,
        Jada sat quietly, petting Rusty while lost in thought.
Her future seemed like a gordian knot.

Upon arrival in Harlem, the family immediately rented an apartment. In light
        of their years of experience, Jada's parents soon landed jobs teaching
        in a public elementary school.
Kia enrolled in public high school.
While thinking about her own future, Jada once again spent time working in her
        parents' classrooms. She loved working with the girls and boys.
It brightened her outlook and brought her joy.

In addition, Jada said to her sister, "If you'll allow me, I would like to coach you as a
        sprinter to help you win a scholarship, to be the best you can be."
Once again, Kia lit up like a Christmas tree!

As Jada focused upon training her sister and working with her parents'
  students, it slowly dawned upon her what she wished to do-
The future life she wished to pursue.
She accepted that her Olympic dream was dead-
Replaced by new dreams for the years ahead.

She was bent on striving to pursue a mission-
Applying herself to become a physician.
To work with children as a pediatrician.

She read that Florence Nightingale, the Founder of Modern Nursing, had
  pioneered the idea of animal assisted therapy to relieve stress and anxiety
  in patients. Jada recognized how Rusty had helped her to emotionally heal.
His healing affects had been quite real.

She decided that she would one day utilize canine and feline assisted therapy in
  her own practice, to assist children who were disabled, sick, or injured.
  That was her dream and that was her hope-
A means of helping children to cope.

In addition to becoming a pediatrician, Jada was filled with another dream-
Of a time when freedom was at last redeemed.
She'd work for the day she'd be able to say-
To the Birmingham Clinic that turned her away-
"Take your 'white only' signs and tear them to shreds!
For the country has changed and Jim Crow's dead!"

Would she realize her dreams by forging her way?
One thing is clear at the end of the day.
With her uncommon courage, out on display-
Nothing was going to stand in her way!

SOMETHING TO SMILE ABOUT
(Historical Fiction)

Julio Chavez's childhood was bereft of smiles.
Born with a cleft palate and a cleft lip, he lived a life of
      tribulations and trials.
While among his classmates, he was often ridiculed and reviled.

Due to his combination of clefts, he experienced eating difficulties
      and suffered from malnutrition-
Which was detrimental to his learning, reasoning, and cognition.

He also experienced speech and language development difficulties,
      and hearing issues; And his teachers had difficulty understanding
      him when he spoke. As a result, he fell further and further
      behind in school.
All the while, he was often served up as a schoolyard pinata,
      a target of ridicule, the brunt of bullying, insensitive and cruel.

Over time, this abuse instilled within Julio a kind of social anxiety and insecurity.
He lived a life of ostracism and obscurity.
By the beginning of the fourth grade, Julio's parents had heard enough.
They marched in and pulled him out of school, in a huff.
In an effort to shield their son from discrimination-
They wound up schooling him at home in isolation.

Even as Julio lived a sad and lonely life, a Foundation in central
      Texas known as Austin Smiles, was improving the lives of
      children everywhere.
Many plastic surgeons working on behalf of the Foundation,
      specialized in pediatric care.
They performed life-changing plastic surgery upon children born with
      cleft lips and cleft palates- answering their prayers.

Some of the pediatric plastic surgeons felt morally motivated and compelled
      to follow the example of the humanitarian organization, Doctors
      Without Borders-
To rescue children no matter where they lived, from a lifetime of suffering
      from cleft disorder.

One such doctor who was committed to helping children who didn't have access to
     treatment and care in the U.S., was Dr. Sandy Clausman, or Dr. Santa Claus,
     as he was affectionately called by the children whose lives he repaired.
Dr. Clausman's motto was that all children must be spared from a lifetime
     of isolation, and of being scared.
Like Santa Claus, he wished to bring joy into the lives of all the children for
     whom he cared.

Dr. Clausman took time off from work in Texas in an effort to assist
     children in other countries suffering from cleft lips and cleft palates. Doing so
     became a mission of devotion.
He believed that doctors should have access to all children in need, unencumbered by
     borders, barriers, political climate, or oceans.
On one such visit, he travelled to El Salvador to perform plastic surgery upon children
     with clefts, for free.
The surgical procedure unlocked the door to a new life. It was key.

One of the children he set free-
Whose life was changed to the nth degree-
Was Julio, whose home was in El Salvador.
Julio would be condemned to a shut-in life of misery, no more!

Julio's surgery gave him a smile by reconfiguring his face.
His difficulties and demons began melting away with hardly a trace.
He began eating better, resulting in improved nutrition-
Which in turn improved his ability to learn, his cognition.

Upon returning to school, he was no longer compromised, ostracized, or
     unfairly handicapped.
As a result, while he was behind, he rapidly closed the gap.
Now that his teachers could understand him-
They recognized that his ability to learn was sharp, not dim.

As for those who had behaved as bullies-
He bore them no anger. He forgave them fully.
For Julio, there was no room for the dark.
He embraced every moment as a beautiful sunlit walk in the park.

Having experienced so much pain, he felt nothing
     but empathy toward others.
He embraced his peers as sisters and brothers.

Years passed, and Julio grew up while continuing to excel in school-
While living by the highest standards, including the Golden Rule.
He sought to identify children within his community who were afflicted by clefts.
     He reached out to them all-
To ensure they felt worthy- to help them walk tall.
Whenever he learned that a doctor with Austin Smiles was visiting El Salvador to
     perform surgery over the years-
Julio made sure that all children with clefts were referred to the doctor's care.

Julio went on to graduate college, followed by nursing school.
He landed work as a nurse at a local hospital, where he gained a
     reputation for empathy, a steady hand, and for keeping cool.

One afternoon in early September, Julio learned that Dr. Hopman, an
     Austin Smiles doctor, was coming to his hospital to perform
     surgery upon a child with a cleft palate. Julio sought out
     Dr. Hopman after the surgery, and asked for a helping hand.
He asked for contact information for Dr. Clausman, so he could write
     him as planned.
Julio wished to thank the man who'd blessed him, when he was but a child-
Who'd changed his life of misery, to one in which he smiled.

Dr. Hopman informed Julio that he'd recently learned that Dr. Clausman
     had taken an extended leave of absence, because his college age
     son, Donny, was hospitalized and seriously ill.
After providing the specifics, Dr. Hopman stated, "Donny needs a Miracle, the
     intervention of God's will."
Julio asked Dr. Hopman to provide him the name and address of Donny's
     hospital, if he could.
Dr. Hopman, without hesitation, told Julio that he surely would.

Several months passed and back in Texas, Dr. Clausman and his wife,
     Susan, were at their son, Donny's, hospital bedside round the clock,
     praying for a Christmas blessing-
As time grew short and the need was pressing.

Only days before Christmas, the doctors informed the Clausmans that
        they needed to carefully reanalyze some recently received medical records and
        medical samples, while running some more
        blood tests. In addition, they needed to change Donny's dressing.
They asked the Clausmans to return home for some sleep, as they
        exuded signs of stressing.
Initially, the Clausmans resisted.
But eventually they agreed when the doctors insisted.

Early the next morning, around 8:30 a.m., Dr. Clausman received the
        following phone message from the hospital: "You and your wife
        must come right away. The news is good, but don't delay!"

Upon arrival, Dr. Clausman and Susan met with Donny's surgeon,
        Dr. Doan, at the nurses' station-
Hoping for news of Donny's salvation.
Dr. Clausman immediately asked, "Have you found a match for Donny at last?"

Dr. Doan responded, "Yes sir, I believe we have. It looks promising.
        Our tests have shown that the donor's blood and tissue types,
        appear to be compatible with the blood and tissue types of your son.
        Your son's antibodies have not attacked the donor's cells.
As long as that remains the case, your son's operation can go forward,
        and all should go well."

Elated, Dr. Clausman and Susan asked Dr. Doan to provide them contact
        information for the deceased donor's family. They wished to thank
        them in some meaningful way.
Dr. Doan responded that he couldn't provide such contact information- that
        there was no way.

At that moment, as Dr. Clausman and Susan looked a bit confused,
    Dr. Doan led them into Donny's hospital room. Donny and a
    visitor were having a chat.
The Clausmans looked over where the visitor sat.

After a few moments, the visitor looked back at them, stood up from his chair, and
    spoke these words:
"My name is Julio Chavez. I'm here on a U.S. Visa from El Salvador.
I've seen you Dr. Clausman, once before.
Many years ago, when I was a child living a life of isolation, you reconfigured
    my face and gave me a smile. That procedure amounted
    to a second chance at life for me, a gift which opened many doors-
To happiness and fortune, I'd never known before."

"Good news for Donny is long overdue.
Please be assured that I've thought this through.
This is something I'm determined to do-
For Donny, your wife, and also for you."

"Through the donation of my kidney, I wish to
    provide a second chance at life for your son.
Some things in life are meant to be done.
I am certain that this is one."

What followed were smiles, and tears, and laughter. Finally, Dr. Doan stated,
    "Ok folks, time to get ready. Let's do it. Let's get this done."

In short, the surgery was successful! Donny recovered slowly but surely in stages.
His parents viewed Julio's gift of life to their son, as a Christmas Blessing
    for the ages.
One lifesaving Miracle had led to another-
And Donny and Julio bonded as brothers.

CHARLOTTESVILLE
(Historical Non-Fiction Essay)

In Charlottesville, Neo-Nazis and white supremacists lit
 tiki-torches and marched through the night-
With minds full of malice and hearts full of spite.

"Jews will not replace us," they demagogued and ranted-
"Soil and blood," they shouted and chanted.
Nazi salutes, swastikas, and goose-stepping were on full display-
Tolerance and humanity were soundly betrayed.

One of the racists deliberately accelerated and rammed his car into a
 crowd that was protesting against the Nazi rally.
A young female activist was struck and killed in a tragic finale.

On national television, the former President declared there "were very fine people,
 on both sides." He thus asserted a moral equivalency between the
 white supremacists and Nazis and those who called them out-
An assertion that constituted a betrayal of decency, beyond a reasonable doubt.

Betrayed was the memory of six million Jews murdered in the Holocaust,
 wiped out of existence.
And the memory of those who gave their lives in the Resistance.

Betrayed was the memory of Jackie Robinson-his guts, his courage, and his
 ability as he put everything on the line-
To break through and flatten Major League Baseball's color line.

Betrayed was the memory of Emmett Till and thousands of others who
 were tortured and lynched.
And the courage of Rosa Parks who refused to give up her seat on a
 Montgomery bus, unwilling to flinch.

Betrayed were the sit-in and the wade-in activists and the freedom riders; And the
 memory of Medgar Evers and of Chaney, Goodman, and Schwerner
 who were murdered registering blacks to vote-
While the Ku Klux Klan choked decency by the throat.

Betrayed as well were the demonstrators of Birmingham who stood up to
     fire hoses, billy clubs, and police dogs; And the demonstrators of
     Selma, including John Lewis, who were attacked and battered at the
     Edmund Pettis Bridge marching for the right to vote; And Ruby Bridges
     and the Little Rock Nine who put their lives on the line-
Desegregating schools, crossing the color line.

Betrayed were the memories, contributions, and sacrifices of all those who
     have stood up to Jim Crow-
Who shed their blood and absorbed the blows.

Race-baiting by means of moral equivalencies, Anti-Semitic dog whistles,
     and racist tropes-
Are leading the world down a slippery slope-
Which strengthens hate and weakens hope.

Better to march toward freedom and seek the light-
Than to chant with torches in the dead of night.

SCAPEGOATING THE "BOGEYMAN"
(Historical Non-Fiction Essay)

In Mein Kampf and in his speeches, Hitler referred to Jews as vermin,
    parasites, and rats.
He scapegoated Jews for a "stab in the back":
Germany's surrender in WWI-
A war he seethed that could have been won.

He scapegoated "Jewish bankers" in America for Germany's
    economic collapse.
Making them the brunt of bogus anti-Semitic attacks.

These vicious lies paved the way to a Holocaust-
At a heartbreaking and unspeakable cost.
Six million Jews were murdered and gassed-
The world will remain forever aghast-
At the eternal horror of that ugly past.

Yet anti-Semitism remains alive and well.
To avoid repeating that time of hell-
Sound the alarm and ring the bell:
For Vigilance IS forever needed-
So racial slurs don't go unheeded.

In the name of "manifest destiny," the U.S. Government stole land
    from Native Americans while dehumanizing them as savages. Under
    pressure from President Andrew Jackson, Congress enacted into law
    The Indian Removal Act of 1830. Under the legislation, approximately
    60,000 Cherokee, Creek, Chickasaw, Choctaw, and Seminoles were forcibly
    removed from their fertile lands in the Southeastern United States. They
    were relocated to relatively barren and infertile land in the Oklahoma Territory.
    Thousands perished on forced death marches which took place over a period of twenty years.
They succumbed to starvation, exposure, and disease, amidst the unforgiving conditions,
    along The Trail of Tears.

For four centuries, black people in America have been racially slurred as "nigger,"
    "boy," and "pickaninny"-
All "in the land of the free."
Racism has resulted in Jim Crow segregation laws, voter suppression laws, the Ku Klux
    Klan, lynchings, and housing discrimination. It has resulted in discriminatory "red
    lining" practices by banks making it harder for black people to obtain loans needed
    for the purchase or renovation of homes, or in order to start-up a business. It has
    resulted in the past destruction of black homes and businesses which eradicated
    an important source of future intergenerational wealth within the black community.
    For years it resulted in segregated public schools.
If this is to be the "land of the free," than why do we sanction behavior so cruel?

The former President referred to Hispanics seeking asylum as drug addicts, rapists,
    and criminals-
Slurs that were blatant, nothing subliminal.
He referred to them less as undocumented immigrants and more as "illegal
    aliens," dehumanizing them more-
Branding them falsely as caravans and hordes:

Invading our country, raping its women, and stealing its jobs-
Like an out-of-control remorseless mob.
Like swarming locusts devouring crops-
A wicked crisis for the nation to stop-
By a cost-exorbitant impenetrable wall-
Which the President promised he'd surely install-
To keep them away for the good of all.

History has proven over and over that branding, dehumanizing, and lying about
    minorities in this manner, opens the door to discrimination-
Endless cruelty and extermination.

Following Japan's attack upon Pearl Harbor on December 7, 1941, approximately
200,000 Americans of Japanese ancestry living on the west coast, were
rounded up by the government in a climate of stoked hysteria and racism.
They were forced from their homes and relocated to concentration camps
built within the United States of America. They were imprisoned within
those concentration camps by barbed wire and armed guards. Many lost
their homes, their businesses, and their cars, or were forced to sell them at
woefully deflated prices.

Many Japanese Americans spent up to three years locked up within the crowded camps.
They endured the hot summers and the cold winters while sleeping in uninsulated
barracks which often lacked running water. In many cases they were humiliated,
forced to share communal men's and women's latrines which lacked partitions or
stalls. Hot water was often limited. Perhaps worst of all, they lived under a cloud
of suspicion with their patriotism called into question. In 1944, the U.S. Supreme
Court in *Korematsu v. United States*, placed its seal of approval upon this
unconstitutional and moral outrage. It upheld the constitutionality of the evacuation
and imprisonment of Japanese Americans within their own land-
Treating them like second- class citizens at the mercy of a high command.

Ironically, even as the patriotism of Japanese Americans was called into question, many
of their sons volunteered to fight for America in WWII. The 442nd
Regiment, composed almost entirely of Japanese American soldiers, became
the most decorated infantry regiment in U. S. military history. In all,
approximately 33,000 Japanese Americans served in the military during
WWII. Around 800 were killed in action. One would like to think that
this shameful period of injustice, of imprisoning Japanese Americans and
questioning their patriotism at the very moment their sons were overseas fighting
with unmatched valor to preserve freedom and democracy, has over the years led
to positive change. History, however, has proven that the more things change, the
more they stay the same-
Racism has stayed alive and well, and readily inflamed.

Case in point: In June 1982, Vincent Chin, a 27- year-old American of Chinese
    descent, was brutally bludgeoned to death in Metro Detroit. Vincent was
    an industrial draftsman employed with an automotive supplier. He
    worked weekends in a restaurant as a waiter in order to supplement his income.
    On the evening he was savagely beaten with a baseball bat, he and his friends
    were celebrating his upcoming wedding at his bachelor party. During the
    time frame of his murder, due to the high cost of oil, many Americans
    began purchasing smaller, more fuel- efficient cars manufactured in Japan.
    The auto-makers in Detroit began laying off workers. This resulted in a climate
    of racial hostility and resentment, and the scapegoating and targeting of
    Americans of Asian ancestry. The two men involved in Vincent's murder, one
    of whom had been laid off by Chrysler, were alleged to have spouted racial slurs
    as they assaulted him. Both men were charged with second degree murder.
    They each plea bargained their charges down to manslaughter. They were
    each sentenced to three years- probation and a $3000 fine. Neither of them
    served time in prison for their vicious hate crimes. As for Vincent Chin's
    fiancée and friends, they honored his life at his funeral, instead of at his wedding-
The consequence of senseless hate, metastasizing and spreading.

On August 3, 2019, a gunman walked into Walmart located in El Paso with a
    semi-automatic firearm. He opened fire, killing 23 people and wounding 23 more.
    The gunman had apparently driven over 600 miles from his home on a twisted
    mission to target and massacre Hispanic people. The police concluded that
    the gunman had posted an anti-immigrant white nationalist "manifesto" on-
    line, shortly before committing the massacre. The former President never expressed
    one iota of remorse for spouting racist tropes which inflamed a climate of
    anti-immigrant white supremacist hate.
Instead, he doubled down on his racist tropes and his anti-immigrant hate.

In 2020, in the midst of the COVID pandemic, the former President repeatedly
referred to the deadly disease as "Kung-Flu." This politically expedient racist
trope, stirred and stoked an upsurge of threats and violence directed against
those of Asian descent. The racial harassment and violence continued into 2021.
On March 16, 2021, a mass shooting took place at three spas or massage parlors
in Atlanta, Ga. Eight people were murdered, six of whom were Asian women.
Once again, the Scapegoater- In- Chief, while no longer President at the time of
the shooting, never expressed one iota of remorse for having utilized the
bully pulpit to spout racist tropes which inflamed a climate of threats, violence,
and bullying, targeting people of Asian ancestry. Why would he? The racial
slur was the thing that he meant-
The choice of his words revealed his intent.

Why must people scapegoat a "bogeyman," running down "others"-
Of a different religion or a different color?
Why don't they view each other as brothers?
Why are minorities so often degraded?
Is all human life not equally sacred?

Maybe one day before it's too late-
We'll decide that it's time to eliminate hate.
And maybe the future will lead to a day-
When a Skywalker soaring from far far away-
Will feast her eyes and lovingly say:

Do you see that part of the Milky Way?
The "big blue marble's" over that way.
Our cherished Home, the beautiful Earth-
United by people of equal worth.

JOURNEY TO A STOLEN DREAM
(Historical Fiction)

More than life itself, Olivia Ramos loved Nina and Carlos,
      her little girl and her little boy.
They were her life, her pride and joy.
Trapped in a world that was seemingly cursed-
She always put her children first.

Her family was destitute, desperately poor-
She tried to give them something more.
Despite the hardship of their plight-
She wanted them to read and write.
She worked with them most every night.

Each day in Honduras, life became more unbearable-
Conditions seemed beyond repairable.
Vicious gangs demanded "tribute"-
There was no choice but to contribute.

It was pay the tax or pay the piper-
Go along or dodge the sniper.
Since she lacked the money to pay the "tax"-
She lived in terror, she couldn't relax.

Danger lurked inside her home as well-
Her husband beat her until she swelled.
The straw that broke the camel's back-
The thing that made her up and pack-
Her children's cries from the violent whacks-
Her children's cuts from her husband's smacks.

Thus began a deadly journey-
The kind that leads to morgues and gurneys.
To protect her kids so they'd survive-
She had to risk their very lives-
By taking flight to the Lone Star State-
On a thousand-mile trek to salvage their fate.
She was willing to risk most any strife-
To give her children a better life.

For Olivia was filled with the American Dream-
For a better life, or so it seemed.
She planned to apply as refugees-
In the land of generosity-
In the land of opportunity-
Where her children would be safe and free.

They set out in the deadly heat-
Walking on their tired feet-
On gravel roads while breathing dust-
Just in time to catch the bus.
Which headed north toward Mexico-
Where dangers lurked, they'd come to know.

Bus line shelters along the way-
Where buses stopped at the end of the day.
Where she and her kids would opt to stay-
For a respite from exhausting days.

They dozed on dirty concrete floors-
They'd wake up with their bodies sore.
Another torment of the night-
The ravages of insect bites.

Food and water in short supply-
There was no money and nothing to buy.
Her hungry kids would start to cry.
When others shared a little food-
She accepted it with gratitude.

On two occasions her bus was robbed.
She held her breath and quietly sobbed.
She was filled with dread they'd end up dead.
She feared her kids being stolen away.
She held her breath and silently prayed.

She dreaded most the bus-line checkpoints-
Where immigrants were seized at gunpoint-
By Mexican authorities checking IDs-
Threatening their chance of remaining free.

When the moment arrived to disembark-
They started walking through the dark.
She joined a group of others fleeing-
To help ensure her kids' well-being.
For safety lie in greater numbers-
Safe from attack and abuse by others.

The level of their fear increased-
As they headed for the dreaded "Beast,"
    "The Train of Death"-
Where limbs were lost like items of theft.
As immigrants crowded atop the train-
Exposed to the elements the heat and the rain-
A slip and fall meant death and pain.

Boarding the train with children in hand-
Olivia spotted a place to stand.
She kept them close and tightly in hand-
As they rode across the Mexican land-
Toward the U.S. border as they had planned.

On the second night aboard The Beast-
A storm broke open from the east.
Nina and Carlos were chilled to the bone-
By morning time, Carlos was prone-
And Nina soon began to groan.
The exhausting journey had taken its toll-
Their foreheads felt like burning coals.

The Beast pulled in and made a stop-
Her kids were carried from the top-
By exhausted souls aboard the train-
Who held them up with might and main.
They carried the kids to a quiet retreat-
Where they rested their bones while off their feet.

A change of clothes and food and water-
Were received by Olivia and son and daughter.
It was critical help from caring providers-
Received by desperate Death Train Riders.

After two days of rest and care-
Strengthened by their mother's prayers-
The children's fever finally broke.
She made them laugh by telling jokes-
A spirit-raising master stroke!

It was soon time to reboard The Beast-
To finish their journey come famine or feast.
They were badly sunburned, with little to drink and little to eat-
They arrived at the border an unlikely feat.
For death itself they'd managed to cheat.

They disembarked at the Texas border, late at night-
And crossed the border before the light.
Seeking asylum, they surrendered to the border patrol-
Believing they'd reached their desired goal.

But U.S. policy was heartless and mean-
Like being engulfed in the Perils of Pauline.
Olivia was charged with illegal entry-
She was treated quite harshly, not a bit gently.

Her children were seized and taken away-
Placed in cages and locked away.
Olivia was put into Kafa-esque detention-
With nothing to break or relieve the tension.

She begged for information concerning the welfare and
        whereabouts of her children; But no one would say.
Her worry intensified with each passing day.

Her initial claim for asylum was determined to be sincere.
Her fear of conditions in Honduras, was held to be a "credible fear."
She next awaited a full Due Process asylum hearing before a judge.
But the length of the wait she had sorely misjudged.

Days turned into weeks and months. It felt like forever.
Her endless questions about the welfare of her kids,
      proved a futile endeavor.
Desperate to find them, she requested release and awaited a
      hearing. As the other detention inmates expected-
Her request for release was flatly rejected.

Olivia feared she'd never see her children again.
She had no clue as to how reunification would take place, or when.
The government's policy of separating children from their parents so
      as to discourage immigrants from seeking asylum, had provided
      no mechanism for ensuring that reunification took place. No records
      were kept to prevent children from being placed-
Without so much as leaving a trace.
The country she held in the highest esteem-
Had snatched her children and stolen her dreams.

Nina and Carlos felt frightened and lost-
Separation from Mom had exacted a cost.
Yearning to see her they imagined a way-
To see her at bedtime at the end of the day.

They savored the moments and begged her to stay-
But when morning time broke, she'd slip away-
Like vanishing moonbeams at the dawn of day.
For her visits were only the stuff of dreams, there was
      no other way.
And the mother and child reunion seemed years of pain
      and heartache away.

THE DREAMER AND DOER
(Historical Fiction)

She was brought to America on a wing and a prayer.
Her parents yearned to elevate her above a life of poverty Over There.
They admired America as the land of opportunity for a decent life, a living wage,
    and sufficient money.
They revered America for its heart and generosity of spirit, a promised land
    of milk and honey.

From the time Maria Diaz was a little girl until fully grown-
She turned obstacles into steppingstones.
She struggled mightily when she started school-
For kids could be thoughtless, and sometimes cruel.
At times, she was the subject of ridicule.
Many did not accept her at first-
For being different, for her Mexican heritage, she was cursed.

As she studied hard and mastered English-
Prejudices faded, they were partially extinguished.
And because she was smart as a whip and extremely giving-
Kids flocked to her for help without misgivings.
She turned down no one for she was forgiving.

It was said of her that when she flashed her friendly, open,
    and big-hearted smile-
It would have melted the stone-cold heart of the most aggressive
    Croc on the River Nile!

Her parents had brought her to America at the tender age of two.
When she started school, she pledged allegiance to the red, white, and blue.
It was the only flag that she ever knew.
She saw herself as an American, through and through.

As she progressed through school, she reached beyond her comfort zone.
She continued to grow, coming into her own.
She developed strong convictions and a mind of her own.

In community college, she studied American History and developed a deep
    reverence for the heart and soul of America, its principles and institutions-
As established by its Founding Fathers in the Declaration and Constitution.

She studied the Constitution, including the Bill of Rights, with a passion-
Which some viewed as over the top and out of fashion.
Her studies filled her with a sense of commitment and compassion-
For all those who had been targeted for discrimination or hate.
She dreamed of a life in politics or law, to fight for others, to change their fate.

From the time Maria was a little child until fully grown-
Her parents worked their fingers to the bone.
To make ends meet, they worked as housekeepers, janitors, meat packers,
    and fruit-pickers with the sweat of their brow-
Providing a good home and opportunities for their beloved
    Maria was their Sacred Vow.

They faced many dangers along the way-
Of being exploited and falling prey-
At the hands of unscrupulous employers who would barely pay-
Who threatened to inform INS of where they stayed-
Who provided unsafe working conditions which wouldn't
    pass muster in the light of day.
At times, they hid in the shadows, in hiding places undisclosed-
To avoid being detected and ultimately exposed.

Despite these hardships, nothing diminished their love or
    Maria's love for America, and their belief in the American Dream-
And they continued to hold America in the highest esteem.

Unfortunately, their love for America was unrequited and unreturned-
By a President who dehumanized immigrants at every turn-
As convenient scapegoats for the "base" to spurn.

The President spouted an anti-immigrant fable known as "The Snake."
An Aesop's Fable, an ethical guide for the education of children it was not,
    make no mistake.
In essence, the fable compared immigrants to poisonous snakes.
The story told of a woman who nursed back to health a frozen snake-
Which turned out to be a fatal mistake.
For the snake returned the favor by poisoning her with a bite
    from which she'd never awake.

The message which the President wished for people to take away:
The Big Lie that immigrants seeking asylum and a better life for themselves
    and their children, will harm America and should be kept away.

The message fanned the flames of anti-immigrant resentment and hatred
    long submersed-
Like molten lava ready to break the surface with an explosive burst!
The message characterized America not as a melting pot to be blended together-
But rather, as a homogenous pot contaminated by immigrants to be tarred and feathered.

The Scapegoater-In-Chief took steps to rescind measures intended to protect Maria and
    the other "Dreamers" from deportation-
Acts of betrayal and moral abdication.
Are the "Dreamers" to be racially profiled, rounded up as usual suspects, and deported-
And their dreams and contributions to our country needlessly thwarted?

In this poisonous anti-immigrant climate, what is to become of Maria who was
    brought here through no fault of her own?
Is she to be unceremoniously rejected and disowned-
By the only home that she's ever known?

And what of her dreams of becoming an advocate and champion on behalf
    of those Americans who have been targeted for discrimination and hate?
What's to become of those dreams and what is her fate?

Maria's life, as well as the lives of 690,000 other "Dreamers," have been
        thrown into flux, limbo, and doubt-
While some leaders conspire to remove them, hoping to throw them out.

In the meantime, Maria and the other "Dreamers" carry on: going to school,
        working their jobs, aspiring to military service, paying their taxes,
        serving as teachers, dreaming and doing-
While those with crocodile smiles and stone-cold hearts, actively plan
        and plot their undoing.

THE INFAMOUS STATUE OF REJECTION
(Historical Fiction)

In the name of "protection," we have changed our direction-
Built a Statue of Rejection, which implores:
Keep away, your tired your poor your huddled Muslims yearning
      to breathe free.
Keep them far far away from me.
Keep away the wretched refuse of your teaming shore-
Whether fleeing famine or war.

Send not those south of the border-
They bring only disorder.
No matter your plight, come not day or night.
Stay away, out of sight, for good!

All who hoped to enter here-
Abandon hope and disappear, for good!
For those of you, here already-
We'll round you up, fast and steady.

Yo, Statue of Liberty, your time has passed-
I'll direct the future at long last.
Send not these, the homeless tempest-tossed to me-
I'll dim my lamp, and barricade the door!

SEEKING OUT MY IRISH ROOTS
(Personal History)

For many years since Dad's passing in 2010, I've been absorbed
      by the question: Who was the ancestor on Dad's side of
      our family tree-
The direct blood line ancestor from Dad to me-
Who escaped the deadly Irish Potato Famine and arrived in New York
      City filled with the American Dream?
Who could it be?

The only family member Dad spent time speaking about was
      my Grandpa John, his beloved dad.
Dad called him as good a man and as good a dad, as good
      a role model as he could have had.
Exactly the way I felt about Dad.

Years earlier during a trip to the National Archives, I discovered
      that Grandpa John's dad, Edward McGinness, was born in
      New York City in 1861.
Upon reflection, it appears that Edward's dad, my great great grandfather,
      must have escaped the Irish Potato Famine of 1845-55,
      to come to America. He was the one.

But who was he? What was his name? Who could it be?
To unlock the truth, I needed the key.
Slowly an insight dawned upon me.

Near the end of his life-
After the loss of Mom, his beloved wife-
Dad flew to N.Y. from Florida and visited Cavalry Cemetery,
      the resting place of Grandpa John and the other members
      of our family tree.
As he paid his respects, he photographed the names on the family
      marker, photos he later passed on to me.

Above Edward McGinness' name on the family marker
     were three names: James McGinness Died 4/13/1895;
     Elicha McGinness Died 12/23/1897; and John McGinness
     Died 6/18/1899.
I call them "The 3 Amigos!" One of them was Edward's dad, the Irish
     ancestor of my direct blood line.
But which of them was it? I needed a sign.
I knew that Grandpa John was born in 1900.
Did that tell me something I pondered and wondered?

I poured over the photographs of the marker seeking an answer
     for hours on end. I lost track of time.
For reasons I couldn't explain, my eyes focused upon the name,
     John McGinness, who died in eighteen hundred and ninety-nine.

In a state of exhaustion, I laid my head down upon the desk next to
     the photos and closed my eyes. Suddenly, the room began
     spinning faster and faster!
As if time was bending, out of control and courting disaster!

As my heart raced like it was about to burst, the spinning abruptly
     stopped! I opened my eyes and found myself standing in the middle
     of a beautiful bright green meadow, facing a small wooden home on top
     of a hill. I approached a farmer passing by and asked him where I was.
     He ignored me completely, as if he hadn't heard a word I said.
     It soon dawned upon me that I was trapped in a kind of out of
     body theater of the absurd-
While I could see and hear, I could be neither seen nor heard.

I was drawn to the small wooden home on top of the hill. Upon reaching
     the front door, I turned the knob and walked inside.
A young man was standing over his father's bedside.

"Promise me, John, that you will escape this deadly potato famine with your brothers,
     James and Elicha. The McGinness name must survive. This is my dying wish.
     You must lead your brothers from this blighted land to the land of milk and honey,
     to the promise of America and a new chance at life."
"Yes Dad, you have my word, I promise- no matter the hardships, no matter the strife."

Upon his father's passing, John gathered up the little savings he had in the whole world.
He used the money to bribe a ship's security guard into allowing him and his
brothers to board the ship which was already full.
Fortunately, his money talked, it exerted pull.

While friends ashore waved The Three Amigos a hearty farewell-
The twelve- week voyage to America turned into a living hell.
The term "coffin ship" was aptly used. Living conditions aboard the ship were horrific.
Twelve hundred poor and destitute immigrants were crammed like sardines into
steerage. There was an insufficiency of food and water and an abundance of rats!

Due to a lack of basic hygiene, outbreaks of cholera, typhus, and dysentery spread like
wildfire throughout the ship. Three out of 10 Irish immigrants died along the
way. The disease- ridden bodies of the dead were tossed into the sea. Legend has
it that when "coffin ships" from Ireland embarked-
They were trailed through the water by hungry sharks.
Sharks expecting an easy feast-
Upon bodies discarded to the Belly of the Beast.

The Three Amigos managed to survive the horrendous conditions and stormy weather-
By looking out for each other and sticking together.
Whatever little food and water they each acquired, they shared. They attended to each
other upon becoming ill. In addition, their youth served them well.
It helped them survive their living hell.

Midway through the voyage a fire broke out!
Amid the panic the screams and the shouts-
The brothers raced to put it out!
They exited steerage and pried open the door to a burning cabin. They saved
a couple by pulling them out!
The captain called them heroes. He elevated them from steerage, authorizing
them to move about.

When they arrived at last in N.Y. Harbor in 1855, they were not welcomed
by the Statue of Liberty "lifting her lamp beside the Golden Door."
For America received Lady Liberty as a gift from France in 1885, and not before.

Yet John and his brothers already believed in The American Dream and
        The Golden Door-
A dream that new opportunity was in store-
For a better life than they'd known before.

They were not processed through Ellis Island, which didn't open until 1892.
Rather, they were processed through Castle Garden; And given America's open door
        policy at the time, they were processed through.

They wound up living in an overcrowded, rundown tenement, in one of the
        poorest slums of the city streets.
For several months they remained jobless with almost nothing to eat-
Exhausted and drained by the oppressive heat.

Each time they applied for work it was the same old story:
        "No Irish Need Apply."
They'd say hello and were told good bye.
Despite the rejection they continued to try.

In the midst of these desperately hard times, John came up with a
        strategy to pursue.
He contacted the captain of their coffin ship on his next voyage through.
The captain provided John and his brothers with written character references to help
        them get hired fighting fires.
When John and his brothers showed up at the City Fire Dpt., they were
        miraculously hired!

Years passed as the brothers worked toward a better life. They served
        the city, fighting hundreds of fires in the rundown tenements
        with their faulty wiring.
The work was dangerous and enormously tiring-
But helping others was also inspiring.

In 1863, riots broke out in N.Y. City in opposition to the military draft which President
        Lincoln had signed into law.
Many of the rioters were Irish immigrants barely squeaking by on low- income wages.
        Their emotions were raw.

Many rioters resented being forced to fight for the liberation of slaves who
      they feared would "steal" their jobs.
They were furious with Lincoln and the federal government, feeling as though they
      were being robbed.

The Rule of Law and The Golden Rule were sacrificed upon the twin altars
      of racist resentment and economic fear;
Any pretense of civilized behavior deteriorated like a thinly layered veneer.

Blacks were lynched, a black church and orphanage were set on fire, and
      homes were set ablaze-
By a violent mob in a fit of craze!
John and his brothers fought the fires amid the strife-
Resolved to protect both property and life.

Appalled by the senseless deadly riot-
John spoke up for peace and quiet.
He spoke before an angry mob, facing down its rage and ire-
To stop the violence and quench the fire.

"People, listen to me! he pleaded. On my dad's death bed, he implored me
      to escape The Famine by leading my brothers to America. I'm sure
      many of you have similar stories. Dad wanted my brothers and me to
      have a chance to make a decent living and to build a better life. I expect that
      many of you have similar hopes and dreams for happiness and opportunity.
I know these are difficult times for all of us; But even in the face of poverty, war,
      and life's daily struggles, I beg you to reject hatred and racism, and to come
      together with a sense of unity."

The moment after John McGinness spoke those words, my vision went dark
      and the world went silent! I felt the world spinning faster and faster-
As if time was bending and courting disaster!

As my heart raced like it was about to burst, the spinning abruptly stopped! I found myself
      back home in a state of sweat, slouched over my desk next to the photos of the
      family marker. As I slowly regained my bearings, my eyes were once again drawn
      to the name of John McGinness, who died in 1899.
Was he truly an ancestral hero who had risen to the occasion, come rain or come shine?

Did he truly honor his dad's dying wish that he escape The Famine by leading his
    brothers to America on a daring trip?
Did the Three Amigos save the couple trapped in the cabin aboard the ship?
Did the brothers survive horrendous conditions and stormy weather-
By staying close and sticking together?
Did they serve together battling fires during the New York City Draft Riot?
Did John McGinness call for calm and peace and quiet?

Did he truly speak to that riotous mob and appeal to their better angels-
    urging them to reject hatred and racism while embracing hope and unity?
As well as a sense of a caring community?

Was my journey to the distant past real? Were my visions true?
Can I ever be sure? How I wish I knew.
Some things, I suppose, we can never know for sure-
They're shaped by our hearts into family lore.

So which of The Three Amigos was Edward's dad, my direct blood line
    ancestor? It makes sense to me that Edward named his son, John,
    born in 1900, after his own dad, John McGinness, who died one
    year earlier in 1899. Do I know this with certainty, can I ever be sure?
I'm a little more certain than I've been before.
I'll consider it more than family lore.

Edward's decision to name his son, John, after his own dad, John McGinness,
    who died the year before-
Reveals something else, something more.
I believe he would have done so only if John McGinness was a good dad
    and an honorable man.
And hero or not I've come to see-
That's what means the most to me.

INTOLERANCE TAKES A PERMANENT HOLIDAY
(Historical Fiction)

Justin owned a cake and coffee shop and became known
    as the neighborhood baker.
He developed a reputation which preceded him as
    the wedding-cake maker.

He named his shop The Baker's Dozen. The derivation of the
    name had to do with Medieval bakers avoiding injustice,
    avoiding a beating.
They'd throw in an extra loaf of bread upon selling a dozen,
    to avoid being accused of "selling short" and flogged for cheating.

Justin's shop was popular, inviting to all, for he was
    chatty and witty.
The Baker's Dozen became a gathering place and a
    melting pot in the heart of the city.

Because the shop was located within the crowded city,
    Justin paid close attention to crime reported on the news.
As a man who viewed himself as God-fearing and devout,
    unlawful behavior was something he couldn't excuse.

When a gay couple asked him to bake a cake-
Not a birthday cake, but a wedding cake-
He refused to do so on "religious grounds,"
    that was his take.

He told the couple he was a Christian who opposed gay marriage-
And explained that his intent was not to disparage-
Though he understood that the U. S. Supreme Court had upheld
    the constitutionality of gay marriage.

He told the couple that he believed in the Passion, the suffering and
    death of Jesus, whom he referred to as The Good Shepard.
The couple asked if he was familiar with the suffering of
    Matthew Shepard:

The young man who was beaten, tortured, tied to a fence post,
  and left to die in dire straits-
A murdered life and a stolen fate-
Victimized in an anti-gay crime of hate.

Justin admitted he was well-aware of the murder of
  Matthew Shepard, yet he still refused to bake the
  cake on religious grounds.
The couple sensed a scarcity of Amazing Grace: that in light
  of the refusal, Justin was Lost and yet to be Found.
And they argued that the refusal was illegal on constitutional grounds.

As the couple walked out, they threatened to sue.
They had every intention of following through.
They believed it was simply the right thing to do.
For allowing the baker to discriminate against gays by
  refusing to bake a wedding cake on the basis of
  "freedom of religion"-
Needed to go the way of the carrier pigeon.

While the couple filed the lawsuit, they wished to
  proceed with their wedding plans.
So they strolled through the city, searching for another
  baker with able hands.

As they happened upon The Baker's Dozen just after
  closing time, they saw a tall man inside the store pistol-
  whipping Justin with a dark colored gun!
As their minds absorbed it, they were momentarily stunned!

Then, with no further hesitation, they burst through the door, tackled
  the attacker, and grabbed the gun!
Suddenly the robber was the one who was stunned!

They held the robber at gunpoint, called the cops, and attended
  to Justin, controlling his bleeding and rendering aid.
They comforted him, and on his behalf they silently prayed.
The police arrived, arrested the robber, and Justin was saved!

For three days and three nights, Justin recovered in his hospital bed-
While a myriad of thoughts raced through his head.
He thought of the gay couple who'd ensured his survival-
By risking their lives upon their arrival.
The couple for whom he'd refused to bake-
What he'd baked for others, a wedding cake.

A refusal based upon "freedom of religion," to bake the cake
        since the couple was gay.
Yet he'd cared not about the couple's sexual orientation
        when they burst through the door and saved the day!
He felt nothing but gratitude for having been saved-
By the couple who acted in a manner most brave.

Upon his release from the hospital, Justin sought out
        the couple to express his gratitude.
He apologized for what he'd come to view as his own
        "religious freedom" platitudes.

Justin had internalized a different religious precept to
        live by: that it's better to give than to receive or to take.
He thanked the couple for saving his life, and stated, "Please drop by
        The Baker's Dozen in the morning when you awake."
They said that they would. Justin was thankful, make no mistake.

Upon saying goodbye, he smiled and stated, "Since I know you'll be
        coming I will bake the cake!
And it's on the house, your wedding cake!"

Justin was as good as his word; And his religious intolerance
        took a holiday-
Without delay and for the rest of his days.

Yet his transformation begs a question which still remains
        to the present day:
Why must so many people be directly affected in a personal way-
Before rejecting intolerance not for a moment, but forever and a day?

RESCUER ON FOUR PAWS
(Historical Fiction)

Once he'd lived the American Dream. Upon completion of high school, Scott Candle built his own small business from the ground up. It was a building material and supply company located in his home city of Detroit. He didn't grow rich but he wasn't poor. He stood on his own two feet as a man of independent means. As for those he employed, he paid them as generously as he could, and he treated them even better. He provided extra bonuses to celebrate their birthdays, their marriages, and the birth of their children.

His parents, both of whom had been chain smokers, died by the time he reached his forties; And given that he was an only child from a small family, he experienced a number of years of loneliness after they died; But he kept it to himself and displayed nothing but good cheer and optimism in the presence of his employees.

Luck finally came his way when he met and fell head over heels for his beautiful girlfriend, Susan. Before long he proposed, and to his delight, she accepted. Two years later they had a little girl, Annie, who they were both nuts about. They spoiled her at every turn, providing her dancing, gymnastics, and tennis lessons. She loved all of her activities; But most of all, she loved and adored animals. When her parents gave her a little tabby kitten for her sixth birthday, she danced while holding her kitty. When she put it down, it danced at her feet. She immediately named it Dancer.

Over the next three years, Scott reveled in the blessing of his wife and daughter and in the success of his business. But then, like the unwelcome arrival of a torrential storm, hard times hit as the bottom dropped out of the nation's economic foundation. The 1970's "stagflation," recession combined with high inflation prompted to a large extent by the Arab Oil Embargo, resulted in long lines at the pump to purchase highly expensive gas. The high cost of oil was passed along throughout the economy resulting in skyrocketing inflation. As prices soared, consumer spending plunged. When the Federal Reserve initially raised interest rates in an effort to fight inflation, the high cost of borrowing slowed down economic activity even more. Less people could afford to purchase automobiles and homes. As the housing market tanked, many building and supply companies like the one owned by Scott were put out of business.

At first, in an effort to keep his business open without firing any of his employees, Scott was forced to reduce their wages and their hours; But after a time, his business was no longer making ends meet. Interest rates were too high for Scott to take out a loan to keep his business afloat. Heartbroken, he was forced to close his business and let his employees go.

Things slowly but surely grew worse for Scott on the home front as well. Over the next year, he persistently but unsuccessfully sought employment. All the while, the family's savings were steadily and inexorably drained, drip by drip. When Scott could no longer afford to fill up his gas tank at the inflated prices, he began relying upon public transportation to perform his daily job search. Susan's moral support began to wane as she became increasingly frustrated and alarmed by the family's economic decline. As savings dried up, Scott and Susan began taking out their frustrations and growing sense of helplessness upon each other. At times, squabbles intensified into raised voices and bitter arguments over the scarcity of money needed for food, clothing, medication, utility and phone bill payments, mortgage payments, cat food and vaccinations for Dancer, as well as movie and fun center money for Annie.

Though it deeply hurt his pride, Scott grew desperate enough to call upon friends for loans to tide his family over- to allow him to keep food on the table, make the mortgage payments, and pay the utility bills. When he was unable to pay back the loans, his requests for additional loans from friends were no longer welcome; And then, as autumn approached, the family was beset by a one-two punch to the gut. First, the utility company cut off electricity to their home. The very next day, the bank initiated foreclosure upon their home.

A few days later, after another fruitless day of seeking employment, Scott returned home to an empty house! Susan had taken Annie and moved out with all of their things! She left behind for Scott only a note which read as follows: "Scott, my parents came for Annie and me, and we've gone to live with them in Lansing. I won't allow our daughter to face the freezing autumn and winter weather while living in a home without electricity. You are no longer the man I married. You have proven incapable of supporting our family. I am leaving you for good."

Devastated, Scott called Susan's parents over and over, but no one answered. After two days of unanswered calls, his phone service was cut off. He lacked the money to pay the bus fare for the 91- mile trip to Lansing.

Shortly thereafter, his home was foreclosed upon and sold on the open market to enable the bank to secure the unpaid balance on its mortgage loan. Scott was forced to seek housing in a homeless shelter/ rescue mission. The mission allowed homeless people to stay as overnight guests three times a month for free. It opened at 3:30 p.m. daily. After the first three nights, there was a charge of $6.00 a night. Breakfast and dinner were provided, along with shower facilities and a daily change of clothing.

Scott began panhandling at a street corner in order to pay the nightly $6.00 fee, and in order to raise the bus fare needed for a trip to Lansing in an effort to reunite his family. After two months, he raised enough money to cover the bus fare to and from Lansing. Upon arrival at Susan's parents' home, he was informed that Susan and Annie were no longer staying there. They told him that Susan had met another man, and that the two of them along with Annie, had moved out west somewhere. Scott asked where they went. They told him that Susan had refused to tell them where they were moving, because she didn't want Scott to locate them.

Scott grew angry and accused them of lying. He told them that he intended to hire an attorney and a private investigator to find Susan and Annie. He warned them that they'd be charged with interference with child custody for refusing to tell him of Susan and Annie's whereabouts.

For all his bold words, Scott was unable to afford the cost of hiring an attorney or an investigator. Upon his return to Detroit, the only world that he'd known, he got back to panhandling. He did so in order to continue to cover the nightly fee at the homeless shelter. Also, he had to raise money to cover the cost of the daily bus fare needed to continue his job search throughout the city. Despite his relentless job search efforts, he continued to spin his wheels upon a track of futility.

While he eventually recovered from the devastation of his wife leaving him, he remained deeply broken-hearted over the absence of Annie from his life. His determination to reunite with her was the thing that drove him on and kept him going. Over time, as the futility of his efforts to find work continued, depriving him of the financial means to search for Annie, the hole in his heart was filled by mounting depression. As a result, he began self-medicating, turning to drink and eventually to drugs in an effort to drown out his pain and sorrow. The substances were provided to him by a few of his friends among the homeless community. There were periods when he binged for days or weeks on end. There were times when he was so intoxicated, so ill, or so cold, that he was unable to stand outside panhandling to raise the $6.00 a night fee at the shelter. Since most shelters had a policy that the first few nights each month were free, Scott began moving from shelter to shelter during those periods when he was physically unable to panhandle.

There were stretches when he was too high or too sick to make it to a shelter. On those occasions, he often remained outside sharing makeshift living quarters with other homeless folks. He hoped that there was safety in numbers. There were other times when exhaustion overcame fear, and he laid down to sleep in deserted areas of the city. On a few occasions he was roughed up by would-be robbers. His greatest safeguard from harm was the fact that he possessed nothing of any real value upon his person to steal.

On one occasion while Scott was panhandling out in front of a shopping center, a shopper who resented panhandlers called the law. Scott was given a trespass warning by law enforcement. He was told that he would be arrested if he entered back onto the shopping center property. Despite that warning, there were times when he was so hungry or when his memory was so addled by drugs, that he returned to the shopping center only to be arrested for trespass. Sometimes, being arrested for trespass and spending a few days or weeks in county jail was actually preferable to life on the outside. Jail time offered "three hots and a cot," and it provided shelter and a temporary respite from the bone-chilling cold of old man winter. In addition, a period of county jail time provided Scott's system an opportunity to dry out from the drugs. As his thinking cleared, his undying hope that he would one day see Annie would well up within him, and fill that empty and lonely space within his heart.

On several occasions upon release from jail, Scott would avail himself of faith-based drug classes offered by many of the shelters. He was provided the opportunity to attend chapel and to receive a combination of drug counselling and spiritual guidance. For a time, the counseling seemed to do him some good. He even began seeking employment again. Unfortunately, he continued to be confronted with the fact that a high school diploma failed to open doors of opportunity for him. As doors remained tight shut, the hope in his heart inspired by his memories of Annie, once again gave way to hopelessness, despair, and a return to alcohol and drugs. This revolving door of hope and despair, drug usage and drug treatment, homeless shelters and homelessness, became the twin realities of his existence. This was the life he continued to live, as days, weeks, and months grew into years. Eventually, twenty years went by as Scott struggled on a daily basis just to survive.

Finally, Scott woke up one morning in a homeless shelter and concluded that he was but one step above the walking dead, existing but not really living. As he showered and got dressed, a deep resolve came over him. In a strange way, it brought with it a sense of great relief. He decided to skip a "last meal," and to walk straight to a nearby bridge. He intended to jump from that bridge to put an end at last to all of his unending sorrow and misery. As he stepped out of the door into the freezing cold just before sun-up, hellbent upon his mission, he heard what sounded like an almost imperceptible high-pitched pathetic cry. He stopped and listened but heard nothing. As he continued walking, he heard the sound once again, only this time a little more insistent and a bit louder. Suddenly, something hopped out of nowhere and landed at his feet! It turned out to be a gray and white little kitten, a tabby. The kitten nestled against Scott's feet. While it purred and seemed quite affectionate, it also appeared very skinny, frail, and sickly. It kept sneezing on and off. Scott thought to himself, "It won't survive another day without food." He smuggled out some breakfast food and milk from the shelter to give to the kitten. The kitten ate ravenously in between sneezes. It then curled up at Scott's feet and went to sleep. For a moment, Scott thought of continuing on toward his moment of destiny at the bridge; But then he thought to himself, "If I leave this kitten behind, it won't survive another winter's night in the city." He went back inside the shelter, looked through the yellow pages of a phone book, and located the nearest veterinarian's office. He then gathered up enough loose change from his travelling bag to cover the cost of the bus fare to the next bus stop, which was located about a mile from the veterinarian's office. He placed the kitten into his open travelling bag and boarded the next bus. Upon being dropped off, he walked the additional mile to the office while carrying the kitten within the bag.

When he presented the kitten to the vet who went by her first name, "Dr. Sally," he told her the following:

"Dr. Sally, I cannot pay for the kitten's treatment." Fighting back tears, he continued: "Years ago, my wife took our little daughter and left me when I lost my small business due to the 1970's stagflation. Ever since, I've lived in and out of homeless shelters. This morning I was on the brink of ending my life. But then, this kitten appeared out of nowhere. It looked so sickly and helpless. I was afraid that if I took it to a shelter and they saw how sick it was, they'd put it down. Please, Dr. Sally, I'm begging you, please save it."

"What is the kitten's name?" Dr. Sally asked.

"I haven't named it. Is it a girl or a boy?"

"It's a girl."

"Well, I haven't named her. I gave her some food and milk from the shelter. She kept sneezing while looking so sickly. I didn't think she could survive another winter's night on her own."

Dr. Sally looked over the kitten and responded, "Mr. Candle, you were probably right. But if I am going to accept her as a patient, she'll need a name."

Scott thought for a moment and responded, "Call her Dancer."

Dr. Sally examined Dancer, and diagnosed her as suffering from a serious upper respiratory infection accompanied by a high fever. Upon completion of the examination, she spoke to Scott as follows: "Dancer is suffering from a serious respiratory infection. She is quite sick. I have a proposal for you, Mr. Candle. I will board Dancer here at the office while providing for her treatment and care. Since you've run a business, I believe you've got what it takes to assist for a time in my office. You could work in the reception area along with other members of my staff. Your job would be to greet animal owners and to check in their animals for treatment. This would provide you the opportunity to work off the cost of the treatment and care of Dancer. You could work off the cost of her vaccinations as well. I will pay for your bus transportation between the shelter and my office. I will advance you the cost of buying work appropriate clothes. If you do a good job, I will hire you on as a full-time employee earning full-time wages." Dr. Sally held out her hand and said, "What do you say, Mr. Candle, is it a deal?"

Scott hesitated for a few moments. He then smiled, shook her hand, and gave her his word that he would work hard to pay for Dancer's treatment. He said, "Please Dr. Sally, please pull Dancer through."

Scott was better than his word. He worked hard, and he conscientiously showed up for work on time. Each day he checked on Dancer's progress, and he sat with her during his breaks. In addition, he treated all pet owners and their pets with great kindness. He also went the extra yard to fit in with the staff and to assist with all tasks he was called upon to do.

One evening after Scott had been working at the office for a couple of months, Dr. Sally invited him over to have dinner with her family which included her husband and two children. She told Scott that she'd drop him off at the homeless shelter after dinner. On the drive over, she informed him that she'd also invited to dinner a friend of hers, a fellow veterinarian. She said to him, "I met my friend at that week long National Veterinarian Convention in California which I recently attended. I had to make a speech about the therapeutic effects of animals upon humans. I hope you don't mind, Scott, but without using your name or identifying you in any way, I told the story about how a helpless stray kitten named Dancer had lifted a Detroit man up from the lowest point in his life. I described how Dancer had moved the man to care for her and to get her help. I explained how the man did so at a time that he was on the brink of taking his own life due to the loss of contact with his daughter, the loss of his business, and the heavy burden of years of homelessness. One of the young veterinarians in the audience was quite moved by my story. She came up to me and we spoke, and we went to lunch together. We became fast friends during the rest of the convention. She's come to pay me a visit and to discuss the job offer I made her.

Soon thereafter, they arrived at Dr. Sally's home. She introduced Scott to her husband and two little children, who greeted him warmly. They all sat down together in the living room. A few minutes later the doorbell rang. Dr. Sally said, "It must be my veterinarian friend." She got up to answer the door. She led her friend into the living room to meet everybody. While looking directly at Scott, Dr. Sally said, "I'd like all of you to meet a fellow veterinarian and a very special friend of mine. Her name is Dr. Annie Lawson."

Dr. Lawson stared at Scott for a few moments and then cried out, "Daddy, it's me, Annie, your daughter!"

Scott gazed upon her in shock and disbelief, and then exclaimed, "Annie! Sweet Jesus! Annie, is it really you?"

"Yes, Daddy, it's me."

Without saying another word, they embraced in a stream of tears.

In the twinkling of an eye, the dinner changed into a reunion celebration of unbridled joy and laughter. After a time, Dr. Sally and Annie walked into the kitchen to bring out the strawberry shortcake dessert. When they returned, Scott asked, "What took so long? I've been dying to taste the strawberry shortcake!"

Toward the end of dessert, Scott grew very quiet. He looked sad and began to tear up.

Dr. Sally asked, "What's wrong, Scott?"

Scott looked over at Annie and asked, "When are you flying home to California, dear?"

Before Annie could answer, Dr. Sally broke in and stated, "The bad news, Scott, is that Annie has to fly home in the morning. The good news is that as we prepared to bring in the strawberry shortcake, Annie responded to the offer of employment which I made her at the conference. The answer she gave me just minutes ago was, 'Yes,' she is accepting a veterinarian position with my office!"

"That's right, Daddy! In the next few months, I intend to move to Detroit with my husband, Andrew, and your two grandchildren who are four-year-old twins!"

As Scott took all of that in, he broke down in tears. "But Annie, he cried, don't you have to talk this over with your husband? How do you know that he is willing to move to Detroit?"

"Andrew and I have discussed the possibility of such a move ever since Dr. Sally offered me the position while we were at the conference. Andrew said to me, 'Annie, if you have truly discovered the whereabouts of your dad after so many years and you wish to be near him, then we'll move to Detroit as a family. The children have not yet started kindergarten; And I believe that I have the entrepreneurial chops to open up a successful restaurant anywhere. So it's all up to you, Annie.' "

Struggling to hold back his tears, Scott asked, "Please tell me a little about my grandchildren, Annie. What are they like?"

"Wendy loves to do cartwheels and to dance, like me; And she's already turning into a little bookworm."

"And her twin? What is she like?"

"Her twin is a little boy. He appears to be a natural ballplayer. He's already hitting pitched- in wiffle balls a country mile!"

"What's the little slugger's name? Scott asked. Is it Al, after Al Kaline, the Detroit Tigers Hall of Fame slugger?"

"No, Daddy. Our son's name is Scotty."

At that moment, Scott placed his face into his cupped hands and once again wept uncontrollably.

Annie pulled from her wallet a few pictures of Scott's grandchildren to share with him. Scott stared at the pictures while smiling, weeping, and laughing all at the same time! A series of revelatory moments of disbelief and joy in a single evening, filled and lightened the gaping hole in his heavy heart.

Annie stood up and knelt over her dad while placing her hand upon his shoulder. She revealed that when she'd come of age, she'd flown to Detroit from her home in California to search for him. She also stated that when she was able to afford it, she had hired a number of private investigators at various times in an effort to locate him. Scott explained that he'd been living on the street for long stretches at a time; And he told her that during other periods, he was forced to live shelter to shelter, never staying in any one shelter for very long.

The next morning as Annie was about to board her plane to California, she hugged her dad and said, "I'm so sorry, Daddy, that I wasn't able to find you sooner. I promise that upon my return, you'll never be alone again." Scott told her how much he loved her, and how much he was looking forward to meeting her husband and his grandchildren.

When the meeting finally took place at the Detroit airport a few months later, Scott instantly fell in love with his grandchildren. He greeted them with the kind of love and affection that he'd yearned to shower upon Annie all those years she was growing up without him. In the years that followed, he attended all of Wendy's dance recitals; And he never missed any of Scotty's little league baseball games. Often, the whole family went out to the ballpark together to root on their beloved Detroit Tigers!

Annie and Dr. Sally grew as close as sisters, and they constituted an outstanding veterinarian team. Between the two of them, they were experts in both traditional western veterinary medicine as well as eastern remedies such as acupuncture. Dr. Sally continued to elevate Scott's level of responsibilities within the office, and he grew into an invaluable member of the office staff. Scott also developed a warm friendship with Annie's husband, Andrew. Scott utilized his own knowledge of running a small business to assist Andrew in getting his new restaurant off the ground.

As for Dancer, while her survival had been touch and go for over a week, she pulled through! She made a complete recovery thanks to the skill and care of Dr. Sally and her staff, as well as Scott's loving moral support. Later on, to celebrate that blessing, and to celebrate the fact that she was promoting Scott to the status of full-time employee, Dr. Sally provided the entire staff with a beautiful cake to share. It was Scott's favorite, strawberry shortcake! The frosting formed a picture of Dancer, The Comeback Kitten! A small piece of cake fit for a kitten was provided to Dancer. With the staff present, Dr. Sally presented Scott with two figurines with wings. One was a molded figure of a cat, while the other was a molded figure of a man. At the base of each figurine were the words, "Guardian Angel." As Dr. Sally explained, in a very real sense, Dancer and Scott had served as each other's Guardian Angel, rescuing each other's lives.

After thanking Dr. Sally for his promotion, the figurines, the cake, and the gathering, Scott addressed the doctor and her staff as follows:

"Dancer and I have been fortunate enough to have been blessed by a second Guardian Angel in our lives, who rescued both of us when things looked hopelessly grave. That Guardian Angel, Dr. Sally, is you. In addition, your entire staff has embraced Dancer and me with nothing but kindness. You might say that this office has become our Promised Land. I can only say to all of you, thank you from the bottom of my heart for saving us both."

Unlike her namesake, Dancer received a lifetime of love and attention from both Annie and Scott. After Scott saved up enough money for a down payment, he moved into his own home with Dancer. Annie and her whole family visited Scott and Dancer at their home regularly for the remainder of their days. Often, Wendy performed little living room dance recitals, dancing for her grandfather while holding Dancer in her arms. And just as Dancer's namesake had danced at Annie's feet so many years before, whenever Wendy put Dancer down on the floor, she danced around at Wendy's feet to her grandfather's delight.

For the rest of Dancer's life, despite protests from Scott who offered to pay for her checkups and treatment, Dr. Sally refused to prepare an invoice for her care. She insisted upon treating Dancer during her office visits as a distinguished and privileged citizen-cat. She referred to Dancer at various times as Top Cat, Top of the Heap, the stray Pauper who became a Princess, and Scott's Rescuer on Four Paws. As Dr. Sally liked to say, "Treatment for Dancer is all in the family and on the house: Pro Bono care for Numero Uno!"

THE TENNIS MATCH THAT MATTERED MOST

(Historical Non-Fiction Essay)

On its surface it was a carnival and a circus, an exhibition
      match that didn't mean a thing-
The 1973 "Battle of the Sexes" between Bobby Riggs and
      Billie Jean King.

No major title was at stake- not Wimbledon, the U. S. Open,
      the Australian Open, nor the French.
Billie Jean was taking on something far more important,
      attitudes and barriers long entrenched.

The immediate issue was equal prize money for women and men.
She pushed for equality again and again.
She took the position, if not now, when?

In the midst of her fight for female equality, entered the
      voice of Bobby Riggs-
The self-proclaimed male chauvinist pig.
He played the hustler and light-hearted clown-
But his message's upshot was far more profound.

He disparaged women's tennis while spouting that women
      belonged in the kitchen and the bedroom-
Feeding the Big Lie that women were unfit for boardrooms,
      operating rooms, and courtrooms.

At a time that Billie Jean was fighting to open doors
      and break down barriers for all women of every race-
Bobby asserted that women should settle down and
      know their place.

So after Bobby crushed Margaret Court and issued a challenge,
      daring any other female tennis pro to take him on-
Billie Jean knew that she had no choice. It was game on!

Billie Jean was at times amused by Bobby's showboating,
      carnival act-
But now she needed to soundly beat him on the court,
      as thoroughly as Rome was sacked!

While Billie Jean embarked upon serious training,
  Bobby fiddled.
Spouting his nonsense, the words that belittled.

His sense of self was over-inflated-
So Billie Jean King he underrated.
Match day approached as it was slated-
For Bobby Riggs it proved ill-fated.

When the time came to actually play-
When the verbal spouting was put away-
The woman whose game he tried to belittle-
Wore him down, little by little.
In the tennis match that mattered most-
She deflated Bobby and all of his boasts.

Upon completion of the match, Billie Jean and
  Bobby were forever connected as friends-
A friendship which lasted for the remainder of
  Bobby's days, to the very end.

Due largely to his antics, Bobby is mostly remembered
  as the self-promoting, over the hill,
  male chauvinist pig-
Who lost the Battle of the Sexes, big!

Largely overlooked by the general public
  are his world championships
  and titles from the 1930's and 1940's,
  which landed him in the International
  Tennis Hall of Fame.
Perhaps the public's overlooking of his
  achievements is a shame.
But at least as far as I've discerned-
Bobby wasn't the least concerned.

On the other hand, Billie Jean's defeat of Bobby
      greatly advanced the cause of women's
      equality and liberation-
Providing Billie Jean an invaluable platform
      for advancing women's opportunities
      for generations.

So perhaps for all of his championship ways-
It's the Billie Jean match he was born to play.
The match which led to a better day.
Some would take issue but who's to say-
Does God not work in mysterious ways?

WHISPERING PALMS
(Historical Fiction)

Whispering Palms was a grocery store-
Beside an old laundry and a "ghetto" next store.
All kinds of people shopped in that store-
White folks and black folks, rich folks and poor.

All of us kids would rush through the door-
For a bottle of pop and we'd be back for more.
Summers of baseball and after the games-
Whispering Palms was the place we all came.

Ice cream and comics, baseball cards too-
Were post-game desserts, as all the kids knew.
Black kids and white kids were all quite the same-
We wanted our snacks, after the games.

A long sixties summer rushed to end-
By "back to school sales," like an unwelcome friend.
Black kids went to one school, us whites to another-
Only once in a blue moon did we see one another.

Each day at school we proudly stood tall-
And solemnly pledged, "And Justice for All."
Our hands on our hearts, as proud as could be-
In the home of the brave, and the land of the free.

"Quiet down," I whispered, during the pledge-
But Johnny, my friend, had the teacher on edge.
He'd crumpled a paper into a ball-
While the class was reciting, "And Justice for All."

The teacher exclaimed, "For your lack of respect-
Homework this weekend which I will inspect!
Write 500 times so you'll learn what they mean-
The words, 'Justice for All'," boy was she mean!

Saturday morning to help him get calm-
Johnny and I visited Whispering Palms.
We passed by the laundry and folding her wash-
There was our teacher, Oh My Gosh!

Johnny walked over and meekly he said-
"I crumpled a paper into a ball, while we were reciting,
     'And Justice for All.'
I'm very sorry for the lack of respect-
And I'll have all the words for you to inspect."

Our teacher looked cross and sternly she said,
"Justice for All in the land of the free-
Are words to be taken quite seriously."
Then abruptly she turned and continued to fold-
Johnny walked out- he'd really been told!

As we slowly walked off with baseball and bat-
Our teacher was leaving the old laundry mat.
On top of the door as our teacher walked through-
The words, "White Only," faded from view.

A VOICE FOR AUTUMN

(Historical Non-Fiction)

Amid the anger of the day-
A voice of reason showed the way.
A voice which spoke up for a child-
Against the voices shrill and wild.

Amid the meanness of the crowd-
A teacher spoke, her voice unbowed.
Through the dark abyss of fear-
A voice was heard, brief but clear-
And spoke these heartfelt words:

AIDS is such an unfair cross
For any child to have to bear-
So don't make Autumn's burden worse
By barring her from school this year.

With common sense and loving care-
She's not a threat, no need to fear.
Let Autumn stay in school this fall-
Learning much and standing tall.

Her message heard her words complete-
The voice for Autumn took her seat.
Did they listen, did they hear-
Some looked angry, filled with fear.

Fear and reason clashed again
Those warring age-old foes, and so-
In time we'll learn how high or low-
The children's parents choose to go.

YOUNG LIFE IN THE BALANCE
(Fiction)

At 16, over her mom's objections, Hope rebelled, dropped out
    of school, and left home-
To be with her boyfriend and on her own.
At 17, she and her boyfriend had Jackey, a baby boy-
Who filled her with love and filled her with joy.

At first, she saw her boyfriend as kind and gentle;
But over time, he became increasingly temperamental.
She thought he cared for her with a love that was zealous-
Slowly, it dawned upon her he was controlling and jealous.

He wanted an accounting of her every move and visit-
In painstaking detail, complete and explicit.
He insisted upon checking her cellphone contacts on a daily basis-
And he constantly accused her of being flirtatious.

The first physical attack occurred over dinner.
He grabbed her hair, snapped her head back, and called her a sinner.
After that, she limited where she went and who she saw-
Worried about conclusions he might draw.
She treaded lightly and narrowed her path-
Constantly worried she'd incur his wrath.

She wanted to leave him but refused to go home-
She stayed in place with no job of her own;
And no means of supporting her baby alone.

Her boyfriend sold drugs for a living.
She liked it not and had misgivings;
But because baby food and diapers were needed-
Her objections to his drug selling went unheeded.

To increase his level of control, he offered her drugs.
The more she resisted the more he insisted.
Once he coerced her into using-
He went right on physically abusing.

She was hospitalized with two broken ribs and a
      black eye that swelled.
When her doctor asked what happened, she
      responded that she tripped and fell.

Out of misguided loyalty and fear of abuse-
She protected her boyfriend with her bogus excuse.
She thought to herself, "If he's locked up in jail-
Support for our child will diminish or fail."

He began driving her to the scene of his sales.
To diminish his chances of going to jail-
She carried the drugs, he insisted she must-
So she'd be arrested in case of a bust.
As fate would have it, they were both busted for
      a single sale-
Both were arrested and hauled off to jail.

After bailing out, Hope's boyfriend failed to visit her in jail.
Nor did he put up money for her bail.
It was Hope's mom who would visit in her time of need-
And it was Mom from whom assistance with bail was received.

The State intervened on Jacky's behalf. He was placed in the
      custody of Hope's mother.
Hope's boyfriend showed no interest in taking responsibility
      for his child, revealing his true colors.

Hope was ordered by the court to receive drug treatment. In addition,
      she was ordered to participate in parenting, domestic violence,
      and general education classes. The judge informed her that
      she must successfully complete both her treatment and her classes,
      as a prerequisite to her parental rights being restored.
She was forced to face up to the reality that none of the court imposed
      conditions could be ignored.

Toward whom will she gravitate? How will she choose?
There's so much to gain and so much to lose.
Will she opt for a life of drugs and of booze?

Will she obey the Court Order in the best interest of her child?
Or return to her boyfriend's world of broken dreams, violence,
     and drugs, and reconcile?
Which shall it be, the road to redemption or pathway to hell?
Only the years ahead will tell.

JUNE 12TH-DAY OF HATE, HOPE, AND CELEBRATION
(Historical Non-Fiction Essay)

On June 11, 1963, Governor George Wallace stood in front of the
 "schoolhouse door" at the University of Alabama, to block
  Viviane Malone and James Hood, two African-American students,
   from being admitted.
It was a political expression of his support for segregation,
 to which he was committed.

It was a political extension of his mantra, "Segregation now,
 segregation tomorrow, segregation forever!"
Not a shred of respect for the principle that all men are created equal.
 None whatsoever.

It was his way of telling Viviane Malone and James Hood, and all black
 Americans- stay back and stand clear-
You are not permitted here.

It was an expression of contempt for the Rule of Law and the
 law of the land-
A blatantly unlawful stand;
An expression of defiance of the U. S. Supreme Court's 1954 holding in
 Brown v. the Board of Education, that segregation in regard to
 public school education violated the Fourteenth Amendment's
 Equal Protection Clause.
By holding firm to his lost cause, he was lauded by many with
 love and applause.

It was an expression of Wallace's corrupt view of "state's rights"- that
 the big bad dictatorial federal government had no right to interfere
 with Alabama's "right" to discriminate against black citizens
 within its borders-
A twisted view of right and wrong, and law and order.

President Kennedy federalized the Alabama National Guard,
 and deployed it to enforce desegregation at
 the University.
He sent Deputy Attorney General Nicholas Katzenbach to
 stand up to Governor Wallace's perversity.

Katzenbach had been told by Attorney General Robert Kennedy
      that the President wanted him to make Wallace and his
      bigotry look foolish.
Katzenbach made his bigotry look cruel, diabolical, and kinda ghoulish.

Katzenbach and Wallace faced each other down, eyeball to eyeball,
      and Wallace blinked and stepped aside-
It was a moment of triumph for justice, a moment of pride.

That evening, President Kennedy took the next step beyond
      utilizing the power of the federal government to desegregate
      public schools.
During a televised nation-wide address, he proposed Civil Rights legislation
      to eliminate laws unjust and cruel.

Kennedy became the first modern day President to define as a moral crisis the struggle
      for civil rights-
A transformed nation, a fairer country, was the heart of his vision within his sight.
His proposed Civil Rights Bill would eliminate segregation in regard to
      hotels, restaurants, toilets, and all other public accommodations-
Stickin' a fork in the Jim Crow abomination.
For "one brief shining moment," hope cried out for celebration.

The moment was soon desecrated by an act of violence, an act of hate.
During the early morning hours of 6/12/63, veteran of the
      Normandy invasion and civil rights leader, Medgar Evers, was
      gunned down in his driveway by racist murderer, Byron De La Beckwith,
      who was lying in wait.
Evers' wife had allowed the children to stay up late-
To listen to the President's stirring words.
The gunshots that killed their dad, they heard.

In every sense of the word, it was a heartbreaking scene of
      blood and gore.
The bullet had ripped through Medgar Evers' mighty heart. He
      collapsed while trying to reach his family at the front door.

At the time he was murdered by Jim Crow-
By a racist bigot going low-
He was holding in his arms NAACP T-shirts emblazoned with the
      words, "Jim Crow must go."

Despite being a day of hate and loss of hope-
With decency and tolerance on a slippery slope-
6/12/63 marked a new beginning-
To counter our history of racial sinning.

Efforts were launched to pass through Congress the Civil Rights Bill
      of 1963-
So black Americans could at last be free.
While President Kennedy never lived to see the passage of his Bill-
His successor, President Lyndon Johnson, pushed it through on Capitol Hill.

Despite some progress in Civil Rights-
There was a long way to go to reach the light.
Four years later, an interracial couple, Mildred and Richard Loving, were
      sentenced to prison in Virginia for getting married, for a term of one year.
They were convicted as criminals, their good names besmeared.

Eventually, the U.S. Supreme Court held that state laws prohibiting
      interracial marriage were unconstitutional.
The Court's holding overturned the Lovings' convictions, righting
      the inexcusable.
The Court decided the case in 1967 on the 12th of June.
Justice prevailed and none too soon.

As a result, June 12th, the day of Medgar Evers' assassination, the
      day of hate and decency betrayed-
Is also known as Loving Day.

On June 12th, 2016, a man armed with semiautomatic firearms walked
      into Pulse, a gay nightclub in Orlando, Fl., and opened fire.
For those trapped inside who'd been socializing and dancing, the
      situation was deadly and dire.
Hatred and intolerance resulted in a scene of unspeakable horror and gore.
The killer murdered forty-nine innocent souls. He wounded 53 more.

In 1929, a girl was born who proved that ultimately, the pen is mightier
than the sword.
Her words will live forever, and cannot be ignored.

Hitler bragged and boasted that the Nazi Third Reich would last a thousand years.
Through her diary, she outlasted their hatred, sadism, and ugly
and arrogant sneers.

The remarkable young girl, Anne Frank, was born on the 12th of June.
She died in a concentration camp at the age of fifteen shortly before
the end of the War- gone too soon.
She once said, "I wish to go on living long after my death."
And so she has, long after taking her final breath.

Despite being a day of hate and loss of hope-
With decency and tolerance on a slippery slope-
June 12th will forever mark the birthday of Anne Frank,
the very personification of courage, love, and endless hope.

What to make of it?
What might we take from it?
Historical acts of hate and love, good and evil, cowardice and courage,
each converging on a common calendar day:
Is it only coincidence, a case of come what may?
Is there more we can take from it- more we can say?

Anne Frank once said, "I keep my ideals, because in spite of
everything, I still believe that people are really good at heart…"
"What is done cannot be undone, but one can prevent it happening again."
Thoughtful words from her gifted pen.

Perhaps June 12th, in some inexplicable way, validates reason for
Anne's optimism-
Even in the face of Nazi barbarism:
Demonstrating that for every injustice, for every Byron De La Beckwith
who would darken the world and lead it astray-
There is a Vivian Malone and James Hood; a Mildred and Richard Loving;
an MLK and a Nicholas Katzenbach; Medgar Evers and Anne Frank; an LBJ,
JFK, and RFK-
Determined to fashion a better day.

SUFFRAGETTES: TRAILBLAZERS OF JUSTICE
(Historical Non-Fiction Essay)

Before Gandhi and Martin Luther King, Jr. fought for justice and equality-
Before they engaged in peaceful protest while applying techniques
     of nonviolent civil disobedience, there were the suffragettes-
About which, I suspect, far too little is known to many Americans as of yet.

This must change. For when it comes to peaceful protest and civil disobedience
     in the cause of women's rights and racial justice, the ladies paved the way!
Leading to change and a better day.

In 1840, Elizabeth Cady Stanton and her husband, Henry, attended
     a worldwide abolition convention in England. Lucretia Mott
     attended as well-
To support an anti-slavery tide that refused to be quelled.
Even as they intended to elevate abolition as never before-
Wishing only to see it soar-
Due to their gender, Elizabeth and Lucretia were disallowed from
     the convention floor.

Outraged, they were determined to stand up against the treatment
     of women as second-class citizens, to fight it like cancer.
Unwilling to sit back and take "No" for an answer.
Since they were not allowed onto the anti-slavery convention floor-
They would one day fashion their own means of opening doors!

Eight years later, in 1848, Elizabeth and Lucretia teamed up and
     organized the first women's rights convention at Seneca Falls-
Setting sail to brave the waves and knock down walls.

They spoke out at their convention against unjust laws-
Which were morally bankrupt and ethically flawed;
Laws which decreed that upon becoming a bride-
A day when happiness was so alive-
The bride in fact had "civilly died":
Transformed into a legal nonentity-
Losing at once her separate identity-
By unjust laws, a legal obscenity.

She became subject to unchecked power-
Her rights dismantled, destroyed, and devoured.
She was forbidden from owning property; And she had to turn
    over to her husband any money that she earned.
If divorce occurred, she could wind up destitute and burned.
In most cases, the father gained custody of the children.
The laws toward women were cold and reptilian.

At Seneca Falls, Elizabeth declared a Declaration of Sentiments
    which stated, "We hold these truths to be self-evident, that all
    men AND women are created equal"-
Words intended to create upheaval-
To eliminate laws unjust and medieval.
In his anti-slavery newspaper, The North Star, Frederick Douglas wrote-
That there was no reason for denying women the right to vote!

Elizabeth soon met Susan B. Anthony, a Quaker who believed in
    racial justice, equality for women, and nonviolence.
She wasn't interested in being silenced!
They forged a lifelong friendship and alliance-
Taking on sex discrimination with determined defiance.

Elizabeth wrote speeches opposing slavery and supporting women's
    rights which were often delivered by Susan;
But overcoming prejudice wasn't going to be easy, they were
    under no illusions.
In contrast to Elizabeth who had seven young children to raise
    making travel impossible, Susan travelled incessantly
    throughout the country enduring all kinds of weather.
    She delivered 75 to 100 speeches a year-
Delivering her message to all who would hear.

Her speeches sometimes stirred emotions which boiled over like
    a powder keg.
At times she was pelted with rotten eggs.
No matter the intensity of the emotions that were stirred-
She refused to quit or to be deterred.

The egg hurlers were the true rotten eggs.
Though they've long been dead it must be said-
The memory of those abusive misogynists should be
        taken down a peg!

Many other women spoke out against racial injustice while supporting
        women's rights. One such remarkable woman was Sojourner Truth,
        a former slave.
She escaped from slavery with her daughter- risky business and a close shave.
She was gutsy and she was brave.
She stood up for justice through speeches she gave.

Elizabeth and Susan formed The National Woman Suffrage
        Association. Susan decided upon a plan-
To stick it to the man for the unjust ban!
Regarding the 1872 presidential election, Susan persuaded an election
        official to register her to vote. Then, on election day, she voted!
Her vote constituted an act of civil disobedience to which she was devoted.

As planned, she was arrested, put on trial, found guilty, and fined $100,
        a fine she vowed never to pay!
Nor did she, a promise she kept to the end of her days.

Elizabeth and Susan drafted and fought for a proposed constitutional
        amendment granting women the right to vote. It was introduced
        in Congress in 1878.
Its passage faced a long and winding road with many years to wait.

It read as follows: "The right of citizens of the United States to vote
        shall not be denied or abridged by the United States or any
        state on account of sex."
It was rejected out of hand with little respect.

In this context, entered Alice Paul, a suffragette from a family of Quakers-
A dreamer and a doer, a mover and a shaker.
On 3/13/1913, a day before the inauguration of President Woodrow Wilson, she
    organized a parade of 8000 demonstrators with floats.
The demonstrators demanded an amendment to the Constitution granting
    women the right to vote!

In 1917, in an effort to pressure and persuade President Wilson into supporting
    a suffrage amendment, Alice, along with her friend and fellow women's rights
    advocate, Lucy Burns, organized volunteers to picket in front of the White House.
    The picketing continued for months on end.
They courageously defied misogynist trends.

Alice and Lucy refused to call off the daily picketing even after America entered WW1.
Despite spurious attacks upon their patriotism, they resolved not to back off until the
    battle for women's suffrage was won.
As they noted, for women, taxation without representation had never ended.
Nor would it, if the struggle for a woman's right to vote was suspended!

Alice, Lucy, and their fellow protestors became known as the Silent
    Sentinels, as they continued to picket in silence in front of the
    White House while holding up signs.
They refused to allow their message to be silenced by the threat of jail
    or the risk of fines.

Eventually, Lucy, Alice, and their fellow picketers were arrested on charges of
    obstructing sidewalk traffic. They were locked up in the Occoquan Workhouse,
    in Va. They endured unsanitary, horrendous living conditions and inhumane
    treatment over many months of incarceration.
Alice, Lucy, and others went on a hunger strike for the duration.

They suffered physical abuse and brutality. Guards held them down and
    force fed them raw eggs by shoving tubes up their noses or down their throats!
Torture endured for the right to vote!

Finally, in 1/1918, President Wilson announced his support for a suffrage amendment!
It was a long time coming and it felt transcendent.
It took more than two years, but at last, in 8/1920, the 19th Amendment was
        ratified granting women the right to vote!
As for the backward thinking National Association Opposed to Women Suffrage, its
        cause was lost, it was all she wrote!

The wording of the 19th Amendment contained the language originally
        drafted by Elizabeth and Susan in 1878.
The battle was hard and the battle was long, but the outcome was worth the wait!

Elizabeth Cady Stanton, Lucretia Mott, Susan B. Anthony, Sojourner Truth, Lucy Burns,
        Alice Paul (who lived to the age of 92), and many others, devoted their entire lives
        to the struggle for women's rights and civil rights.
It was social justice upon which the ladies set their sights-
And each of their contributions raised equality to new heights.

Alice, Lucy, and others fought for an Equal Rights Amendment to
        the Constitution. To this day it has never been ratified.
The long road to justice is an uneven ride.

In 1864, Swarthmore College was founded by members of the Religious
        Society of Friends.
In the 1970's, through the College's generous grant of financial aid, I was fortunate
        enough to attend.
I learned of the virtuous traditions of religious tolerance and racial and
        gender equality of the Quakers.
And of their tradition of lending support for the peacemakers.

Alice Paul graduated from Swarthmore in 1915. One of its founders
        was Lucretia Mott.
So much change they each have wrought.
So much good they each have brought.
They must never be names that time forgot.
Along with Susan B. Anthony, Elizabeth Cady Stanton,
        Lucy Burns, Sojourner Truth, and many others,
They changed the world through the battles they fought.

So here's to honoring the suffragettes-
Who refused to flinch in the face of threats.
With strength of conviction and uncommon courage-
They refused to give in or become discouraged.

THE TREASURED GLOVE
(Historical Fiction)

In the midst of the 2020 Coronavirus pandemic, twelve-year-old Davey Sullivan spent the first Monday evening in June hunkered down in his bedroom at home in Queens, New York City. Prodded by his mom, he was studying for his year-end virtual history exam scheduled for Wednesday morning. Davey was not a happy camper for a couple of reasons. He deeply disliked virtual learning which had been in place since March due to the threat posed by Covid-19. He had not been able to attend school in person and see his friends for almost three months. In addition, while most teachers at school taught little history, Davey's sixth grade teacher, Mr. Learned, emphasized history. Davey hated history. He abhorred memorizing dates, times, and places. He found himself bored stiff. He told his mom, "History's boring! It's yesterday's news and has nothing to do with me. Those things took place before laptops, video games, or cell phones!" Despite his grumbling, his mom insisted that he focus on the material. Reluctantly, Davey asserted, "I'll learn the material for the test, but that's it. After the exam, I'm gonna forget all about it."

His mom responded, "Well, get busy. I'm going to watch the news with your dad, and then I'll be back to check on you."

As Davey settled in focusing upon the material, he was suddenly startled by the sound of his dad's voice yelling at the television set! Since his dad was normally a very easy going, mild-mannered man, Davey jumped up and ran toward the TV room to find out what was upsetting him. Davey entered the room just as his dad cursed at the TV images he was watching. Davey's mom stated, "Calm down, dear. Look, you've interrupted Davey's studies."

Mr. Sullivan, his face red, looked up and said, "I'm sorry, son. I want you to do your best on your history exam. Go finish your studying." Mr. Sullivan stood up to head for the master bedroom. Before exiting the TV room, he turned, looked back at Davey, and said, "I love you, son."

"What's wrong, Mom? Why was Dad so upset? I've never seen him like that before."

"Go on back now and finish your studying for Wednesday's history test. When you're finished and after you get ready for bed, I'll come in if you'd like and explain what upset him."

An hour later Ms. Sullivan knocked on Davey's door. Davey had just gotten ready for bed, and he was sitting on his bed playing a video game.

"Do you still want to hear about what upset your dad?"

"Yes, Mom, I do."

Ms. Sullivan sat on the rocking chair next to Davey's bed and said, "Close out your video game, Davey, and I'll explain it to you."

"About a week ago, a black man named George Floyd was arrested in Minneapolis for allegedly using counterfeit or fake money to purchase cigarettes from a convenience store. During the arrest, an officer pressed his knee down on top of Floyd's neck while he was handcuffed face down on his stomach. Despite Floyd's repeated pleas that he couldn't breathe, the officer continued to press his knee upon his neck for over nine minutes while three other officers looked on and did nothing to stop it. Shortly thereafter, Mr. Floyd died. His tragic death was part of a larger pattern of police using way too much force, excessive force, against unarmed people of color. There are many dedicated and hard-working police officers who are faithful to the oath they take, to serve and protect the public. They risk their lives fighting crime every day, and they deserve the public's support; But there has also been a pattern of bad apples, bad cops from many different police agencies throughout the country, who have acted toward black people with extreme force and violence. This is simply fact, as proven by so many episodes of extreme police violence having been caught on video. This pattern of excessive and extreme force against people of color, has led to a protest movement which your dad and I support known as Black Lives Matter. The intent of the movement is to bring about reform to police departments in order to bring an end to this pattern of improper violence."

"This evening, black and white people were peacefully protesting together in Lafayette Park across the street from the White House. They were holding up signs against the use of excessive and extreme force by police against black people. The First Amendment to the United States Constitution guarantees all Americans freedom of speech, as well as the right to peacefully assemble, to gather together to speak out against what they see as unfairness, and to call for change to make things better. That's what the protesters were doing in Lafayette Park tonight. Nevertheless, officers, including officers on horseback, forcefully cleared the protesters from the area. Blinding tear gas was discharged upon the peaceful protesters. The President soon walked through the cleared area to a church, where he held up a Bible to express his disapproval of the protestors. When your dad saw the tear gassing of the people, he yelled out in anger and disgust."

"I can see why you and Dad would be mad about peaceful protesters being teargassed. That's wrong, Mom. That's unfair. I can see why Dad was mad enough to yell at the television set; But when I walked into the TV room, I noticed that Dad's face was not only red with anger. Tears were running down his face as well. Why was Dad crying, Mom?"

"Your dad shed some tears because the teargassing of the peaceful protesters upset him personally and emotionally. To understand why, you'd have to learn a little about our country's history, and about how that history has affected our family's history."

"Please tell me about it, Mom. I want to know."

"It's getting late, Davey. Maybe we should talk about this another time. You've got that test coming up Wednesday, and you've got more studying to do tomorrow."

"Please, Mom. Please explain it to me. I promise I'll go right to sleep afterward; And I intend to study hard tomorrow."

"Ok then, Davey. Sit back against your pillow. If you fall asleep, I'll finish tomorrow night. Good, okay, so here goes. The reason why the teargassing of the protesters was so upsetting to your dad goes all the way back to your dad's grandfather, Patrick, your great-grandfather. Grandpa Patrick was born at the turn of the last century, in 1900. Your dad was born in 1969; So Patrick was getting up in years, into his 70s, when your dad knew him as a young boy. Your dad was crazy about Grandpa Patrick and he looked up to him. Patrick used to take him to Rockaway's Playland, an amusement park. Your dad would ride the rollercoaster to his heart's content. When Patrick took him to lunch, he was like a kid in a candy store. Patrick bought him hotdogs, snow cones, and cotton candy. On many weekends, Patrick would join your dad and his parents for swimming and sunbathing at Rockaway Beach. While there, Patrick enjoyed buying pizza and Italian ice for everyone."

"Every summer from the time your dad was six years old, Patrick took him to a number of games at Yankee Stadium to watch Patrick's beloved Yankees. They loved watching "Mr. October," Reggie Jackson, slug home runs into the far reaches of the stands! Patrick told your dad stories about many of the Yankee greats, including Babe Ruth, Lou Gehrig, Joe DiMaggio, Yogi Berra, Whitey Ford, Mickey Mantle, Roger Maris, Elston Howard, Bobby Richardson, and Reggie. Patrick saw them all at Yankee Stadium, from the 1920s through the 1970s."

"In addition to your dad's fond childhood memories regarding those happy times he and Patrick spent together, there's another reason why he still thinks about Patrick with great love and respect. When your dad was about your age, twelve years old, his dad, Jimmy, told him about Grandpa Patrick's military service, his marriage, and the fate of his beloved wife. The time has come for me to tell you about it as well."

"Grandpa Patrick fought in WWI, also known as The Great War. During the Second Battle of the Somme, he pulled two of his fellow soldiers who had been wounded off the battlefield while bullets flew past him. One of the bullets struck him in his right side. Poisonous mustard gas was used during the war which endangered the soldiers' lungs. Battlefield mustard gas seeped through Grandpa Patrick's uniform causing severe blisters in the area of his gunshot wound. That led to serious infection and almost cost Patrick his life. For saving the lives of his two buddies, Patrick was awarded a Medal of Honor for bravery and courage. In light of the serious injuries which he suffered while rendering aid to his buddies, he was also awarded The Purple Heart Medal."

"Is that why Dad got so upset tonight, Mom? Was it because the protestors in Lafayette Park were teargassed, just as Grandpa Patrick was gassed in The Great War?"

"That could be part of it, Davey, but the main reason for your dad's pain cuts much deeper. Let me explain. After Grandpa Patrick was honorably discharged from military service in 1918, he spent two years in and out of the Veterans Administration Hospital recovering from his injuries. As soon as he was physically able to do so, he found work in New York City in an automobile plant. In 1923, he met a woman named Sally Winters at a dance. He fell madly in love with Sally, and a year later they were married. In 2/1930, Sally gave birth to their son, Jimmy, your dad's father. A few months earlier on 10/29/1929, the Stock Market crashed which led to The Great Depression. By 1932, twelve million Americans were out of work. Since people didn't have the money to purchase new cars, Grandpa Patrick's auto plant was forced to lay off many of its employees. Among those who lost their job was Grandpa Patrick."

"Facing unemployment at the same time that he and Sally had a toddler, an additional mouth to feed and care for, Patrick toiled and struggled to provide basic necessities and care for his family. At times, the family was forced to join thousands of other unemployed, desperate, and hungry people at soup kitchens and on bread lines established by charities. After two years of struggling to make ends meet, to pay the bills, Patrick travelled with his wife and child to Washington D.C. in 1932 to join the Bonus Army."

"What's the Bonus Army, Mom?"

"The Bonus Army referred to nearly 20,000 unemployed WWI veterans and their families who set up camps in Washington D.C. consisting of tents and shacks. Based upon their service to their country during The Great War, the veterans had been awarded by the federal government extra payment, or bonuses, which were to be paid to them in 1945; Because of their desperate financial situation, their lack of money to live on resulting from the lack of jobs, the veterans were demanding payment of their bonuses right away. Instead of ordering early payment of the bonus money, President Hoover ordered the U.S. Army to clear out the veterans' camp sites. Army Chief of Staff General Douglas MacArthur was sent in with infantry soldiers on foot and cavalry soldiers on horseback, along with the additional support of six army tanks, to drive out the veterans and their families. Tanks rolled over and crushed many of the shacks. Tents and personal belongings of the Bonus Army veterans were set on fire."

"On top of everything else, the army discharged tear gas upon the veterans and their families. Patrick and his wife and toddler were among those who experienced burning eyes and blurred vision, coughing and choking, and shortness of breath. At one point while holding on tight to baby Jimmy, Sally stepped away from the flames of a burning tent. Still half-blinded by the tear gas, and her hearing impaired by the yelling and noise, Sally stepped directly into the path of an approaching soldier on horseback! At the last minute she spotted the horse bearing down upon herself and Jimmy, and screamed! In an instant, Patrick whipped around and shoved his wife and baby out of the way of the oncoming horse! Sally fell back onto her side, while somehow managing to keep Jimmy's head from striking the ground. Sally, who suffered from a weak heart valve due to rheumatic fever which afflicted her as a child, suddenly went into cardiac arrest, a heart attack! Desperately, Patrick cried out for help to get her to a hospital. A bystander on Pennsylvania Avenue responded to Patrick's cry for help. He and Patrick lifted her into the bystander's car and rushed her to a nearby hospital; But for Sally Sullivan it was too late. She was dead on arrival at the hospital."

"Heartbroken over the loss of his beloved Sally, Grandpa Patrick was left to raise Jimmy on his own. Fortunately, his mom provided day care for Jimmy which allowed Patrick to look for work. In November 1932, Franklin Roosevelt defeated President Hoover in the presidential election. Grandpa Patrick finally found work building roads and sewers under a Public Works Administration program. This jobs program was part of what became known as President Roosevelt's New Deal for the American people. Patrick's mom continued to provide day care for Jimmy."

"Grandpa Patrick was very patriotic. He loved his country and the people in it; But he never got over the pain and anger he felt seeing the U.S. military which he had served so proudly, attacking American citizens, veterans no less, and their wives and children. As for the loss of his beloved Sally as a result of that attack, he was forever inconsolable. He remained heartbroken."

"Over the years, Patrick's son, Jimmy, and later his grandson, Andy (your dad), filled his life with joy and lightened and eased his broken heart. Often as a young boy, your dad spent the weekend at his Grandpa Patrick's home. Whenever Patrick was around Jimmy or your dad, he was always careful not to allow his anger and sorrow over the loss of his Sally to surface; But sometimes in the evenings in the quiet times, while Patrick sat gently rocking on his front porch swing, your dad sensed a deep sadness about him. On more than one occasion, your dad walked over to him while he was rocking on his swing, looked over his shoulder, and saw him looking down at a photograph of Sally which he'd removed from his wallet. Your dad saw Patrick weeping over his lost love so senselessly taken from him. Grandpa Patrick never remarried."

"This evening while your dad and I were watching the news, we saw the peaceful protestors being tear gassed and driven out of Lafayette Park by officers; Just as General Douglas McArthur tear gassed the veterans and their wives and children, and drove them out of their camp sites. The Lafayette Park attack was kind of like history repeating itself in a different context or situation. As your dad watched the Lafayette Park attack take place and unfold, the past tragedy experienced by his beloved Grandpa Patrick, the senseless loss of his wife, Sally, due to the actions of the military, rushed in and filled his senses. He felt anger, sadness, and pain that cut deeply. That's why your dad shed some tears."

Ms. Sullivan paused. For the next 10 or 15 seconds there was dead silence. She looked carefully to see whether Davey had nodded off; But Davey had not fallen asleep. He had listened intently to his mom's words, all of them. His heart was deeply moved by those words. The impact of the story upon young Davey had left him uncharacteristically speechless. Finally, his mom broke the silence: "Davey, do you remember those baseball catches you and your dad used to have last year? Davey, are you listening?"

"Oh yes, Mom. Dad still nags me sometimes to play catch with him on the weekends. I wish he wouldn't. I've told him over and over that I'm a soccer player now."

"Dad never wanted to say anything, Davey, but those baseball catches the two of you used to have meant a great deal to him. They were part of an ongoing Sullivan family tradition between fathers and sons passed down from one generation to another, going all the way back to Grandpa Patrick. It was Patrick who started the tradition. The glove your dad used whenever the two of you played catch remains one of his most treasured possessions, because it once belonged to Grandpa Patrick."

"When Patrick's son, Jimmy, your dad's father, turned seven years old in 1937, Patrick took him to his first major league ballgame at Yankee Stadium. At the end of the game, Patrick called out to the great

Yankee first baseman, Lou Gehrig, and asked him to autograph his glove. Lou always remained Grandpa Patrick's favorite, or first among equals, on his list of beloved Yankee players. He loved to tell the story of what happened next: 'I told Lou that I intended to pass on my glove one day to my son, Jimmy. Lou smiled at Jimmy and said, 'That's wonderful. If I'm lucky enough to have a son or daughter of my own, I'm gonna pass my glove onto my child as well.' Lou then autographed the glove, To Jimmy from Lou Gehrig. He handed the glove to Jimmy with a broad smile and said, 'Take good care of this glove, Jimmy. Whether it's your dad wearing it or whether it's your own hand filling it out one day, I hope you and your dad have some wonderful catches together for many years to come.'"

"Davey, Jimmy did take good care of that glove right up to the day he passed away from cancer in 2013 when you were five years old. Jimmy played catch with his dad, Patrick, and later on with his own son-your dad, Andy- all the years of his life; And while the hand filling it out changed at different points in time, Patrick's autographed glove was included in all of those family catches from the 1930s on."

"Well, that's an awful lot for one night, Davey. Time for you to get some sleep."

"Thank you, Mom, for explaining everything to me."

Ms. Sullivan hugged Davey and said, "Goodnight, dearest." She turned out the light as she left the room.

The next evening after Davey had gotten into bed, his mom stepped in to his room for a moment and asked if he was ready for his history test in the morning. Davey responded, "Yes, Mom. I intend to ace it."

"Great, son!"

"Mom, I'd like to learn more about the things that affected Grandpa Patrick's life, and affected the rest of our family as well: The Great War, the Great Depression, the Bonus Army, and the past Yankee greats, especially Lou Gehrig."

"Well, Davey, if you take a break from those computer games, you'll find that Wikipedia, if used wisely, is an excellent tool for beginning to learn about history. When your dad and I had history reports to research in school, we had to go to the city library to use resources such as the Encyclopedia Britannica; And if we were researching fairly recent history, the topic might not even be included within the outdated encyclopedia. If someone had told us that within 25 years or so, much of the world's knowledge would be accessible and available in the palm of one's hand, we would have said they were nuts! But Wikipedia accessed through a cellphone, does place much of the history of the world at one's fingertips as a starting point. If you would like, later this week after your history exam, I can help you get started accessing some material about the things you mentioned. We can order you up some books on Amazon."

"Thanks, Mom, I would like that very much."

"You know, Davey, as it seems like you've begun to understand, the heart and soul of history isn't dates, times, and places. History is the stuff of humanity, of people. It's a record of the lives lived by our family members, their joys and sorrows, from one generation to the next. It's a record of how people have chosen to treat each other along the way, for better or for worse. It's a record of the manner in which people and countries have chosen to treat others of different backgrounds, different religions, and different economic circumstances, whether rich or poor. History serves as a kind of roadmap. If used wisely, it provides guidance for deciding whether we should remain on the same path, or whether we should choose a different path. In either case, people must live with the consequences, the results of their decisions, for better or for worse."

"Well, goodnight, Davey. Get some sleep."

"Goodnight, Mom."

Davey's mom walked toward the door and prepared to turn out the light.

"Mom?"

"Yes, Davey."

"Was Lou Gehrig lucky enough to have a son or daughter of his own who he could play catch with? And who he could one day give his glove to?"

"No, son. Lou never got that chance. He had a loving wife, Eleanor, but they never had any children. In 1939, only two years after he autographed Grandpa Patrick's glove, Lou was diagnosed with an incurable, rare disease known today as Lou Gehrig's disease. Lou died in 1941 at the age of 37."

On Saturday morning, like most Saturday mornings, Davey planned to meet three of his friends at 8:00 at the nearby city park, where they were going to practice their soccer skills. They had each promised their parents that they would practice social distancing in light of the pandemic. At 7:15, while Davey was still sleeping in, his dad knocked on his bedroom door and called out to him: "Wake up, Davey. If you want to eat breakfast and get to the park by 8:00, you better get moving." Davey was still sleepy and he had trouble getting out of bed. By the time he joined his parents at the breakfast table, it was 7:45.

"Maybe you ought to call your buddies, Davey, and tell them you'll be a little late for soccer practice."

"That's ok, Dad. We've decided to meet at 8:30."

"Oh. I wish you'd mentioned it, Davey. I wouldn't have knocked on your door so early."

"Don't worry about it, Dad. It's ok."

After a quick breakfast, Davey walked back into his bedroom and reappeared a minute later. In his right hand he was holding his cellphone while speaking to one of his soccer buddies, Billy. In his left hand he was squeezing his baseball glove which he hadn't picked up for nearly a year. Inside the mitt of the glove was a baseball.

"I'll be a little late, Billy, but I'll be there."

"What's with the glove, Davey? Did Billy and the other boys talk you into throwing the baseball around a few minutes while at soccer practice?"

"No, Dad, that's not it."

"So what's with the glove and the baseball?"

"I was hoping to have a catch with you, Dad."

"A catch? Really? But you've told me many times since you've become a soccer player not to bother you anymore about having catches."

"Well, I've changed my mind about that, Dad."

"How come, son? What changed your mind?"

"Family tradition. It's just something we should do together. I love you, Dad."

Upon hearing those words, Davey's dad stood up from the breakfast table, hugged Davey, and walked into the master bedroom. He emerged a minute or so later with his autographed glove. He had also put on a baseball jersey which he'd had custom-made. Emblazoned on the back of the jersey was the number 4, the same number which was retired by the Yankees on 7/4/1939. It was Lou Gehrig's number. Davey took a close look at his dad's glove.

"This glove, Davey, once belonged to your great grandfather, Patrick. If you look real closely, you can still see Lou Gehrig's autograph which he signed for Patrick's son, Jimmy, my future dad, when he was a young boy. It's mostly faded away now. Tradition, however, can last forever. Let's go outside and have a catch to celebrate family tradition and Lou Gehrig, the Iron Horse!"

"The Iron Horse?"

"Yes, Davey, the Iron Horse. That was Lou Gehrig's nickname."

"Why'd they call him that, Dad?"

"Come on outside, son, and I'll explain it to you during our catch."

As Davey and his dad headed out the door, Davey yelled out, "See you in a bit, Mom." Ms. Sullivan walked over to the window facing the backyard, and gazed outside just in time to see her two ballplayers begin their catch. As she watched Davey's pitched ball land squarely in the mitt of the mothballed, autographed glove brought back to life, she beamed from ear to ear.

"Hey, Dad?"

"Yes, son."

"Once the pandemic is finally behind us, maybe next summer, do you think we could go to the Yankee Stadium and see the Yankees play?"

"Why sure son, we'll definitely go!"

"Do you think Mom would like to go?"

"I don't see why not. Why don't we go ask her after our catch?"

"Ok, great. Let's do that."

"You know, Davey, if we get to the ballpark early enough, we can visit Monument Park which contains a collection of monuments, plaques, and retired numbers honoring the Yankee greats."

"I'd like that, Dad! Is there a monument or plaque there to honor Lou Gehrig?"

"Why, of course! He's the Iron Horse, ain't he?"

"So tell me, Dad. Why was Lou Gehrig known as the Iron Horse?"

"Well, son, as Grandpa Patrick used to say, it had a lot to do with Lou's character and his courage; And with his grit, durability, and staying power, his ability to go right on playing game after game without taking a day off no matter how tired and bruised up he was. Those qualities made him an outstanding role model for children and adults alike, right up to the present day. Pitch it in here, son."

"Hey Dad?"

"Yes, son?"

"Can we have another catch tomorrow morning? I don't have soccer practice then so we'll have more time."

"Absolutely."

"Tomorrow, can I try catching a few with your Lou Gehrig autographed glove?"

"Sure you can, son. It might be a little big for your fingers to fill out right now; But you'll surely grow into it. After all, I'm but a temporary guardian or caretaker of this treasured glove. One day the tradition will carry on, and the glove shall be yours."

"WADE-IN" ON BLOODY SUNDAY
(Historical Non-Fiction Essay)

It wasn't the "Bloody Sunday" which took place in Selma in 1965.
It wasn't D-Day, when Americans stormed the beaches of France to ensure
　　that freedom survived.
It was Sunday, 4/24/60, in Biloxi Mississippi, where Jim Crow laws
　　continued to thrive.
Despite the D-Day crusade, blacks were freedom deprived.

On this particular Sunday, Black Americans stormed the beaches armed
　　not with rifles, revolvers, or pistols, ready to shoot or brawl-
But with sunscreen, food, umbrellas, and beachballs!

Dr. Gilbert Mason, a black family physician and scoutmaster, had
　　organized a "wade-in," a day of nonviolent civil disobedience
　　against Jim Crow laws barring black people from the public beach.
To pull it off, Dr. Mason relied heavily upon community outreach.

About one hundred and twenty-five black people, mostly women, teens, and
　　young children, stormed the beaches in peaceful protest
　　in a family event filled with sun, surf, and sand-
All in the cause of taking a stand.
Many black men were breadwinners and risked retaliation from their bosses-
So they avoided the protests to avoid the losses.

The protestors gathered on three sections of a 26-mile shoreline-
On a beautiful day that was brimming with sunshine.
White property owners upland claimed the beaches as their own.
They had turned the beaches into black forbidden zones.

In reality, the beaches had been fortified to stem seawall erosion
　　by the U.S. Army Corp of Engineers, financed by taxpayer funds.
No one should have been banned or shunned;
But blacks were relegated to small, segregated sections of sea and sand.
The time had come to take a stand.

Violence was not anticipated, for it hadn't occurred during the first
      two wade-ins which took place a week earlier on Easter Sunday
      and a year before that on 5/14/59.
On those occasions, the results had been relatively benign.
The participants, including Dr. Mason, had simply been arrested.
The protests and responses had been tried and tested.

But 4/24/60, turned into another story-
A day of hate, bloody and gory.
For demanding and exercising access to public beaches-
The protestors were attacked, history teaches.

They were attacked by a white mob-
That was primed for violence and ready to rob.
To execute the violence they wished to inflict-
They came armed with brass knuckles, clubs, pipes,
      chains, 2x4s, tire irons, and bags of bricks.

Some of the white supremacists, like Klan members throughout history,
      undoubtedly viewed themselves as God-fearing Christians-
Who professed to believe in religious traditions.
Only one week earlier on Easter Sunday, churches had
      celebrated the life, death, and resurrection of Jesus Christ,
      the Prince of Peace, to atone for humanity's sins-
Through which believers might seek their better angels within.

Nevertheless, one week later, the attackers abandoned God's teachings
      on Biloxi Beach-
With satanic fury they assailed who they reached!
Their attack upon women, children, and teens-
Was horribly cruel and tragically mean.
Despite the lessons of Easter Sunday-
Their assault turned into Bloody Sunday.

As the unarmed beachgoing protestors were beaten,
      the police did nothing, they stood by and watched.
They seemed to approve as the beat-downs were notched.

One of the protestors who had eagerly joined the wade-in after
      learning about it from his scoutmaster, Dr. Mason, was
      Clemon Jimerson, a fourteen-year-old boy scout.
He didn't hesitate, he had no doubts.
His family joined the wade-in as well-
To take a stand, to at last rebel.

Clemon, who lived only two miles from the beach, had always
      wanted to go swimming with his friends, and he resented
      that they were banned.
It was time to peacefully take things into their own hands.

On countless occasions he had endured the idiocy after stepping
      onto a bus to pay the fare, of being required to exit the bus for
      the sole purpose of using the backdoor to re-enter the bus.
The indignity and stupidity of this procedure stirred within Clemon's
      soul feelings of anger and complete disgust!
On some occasions, before he could re-enter the bus, it drove away-
One more gesture of moral decay.

All of his feelings were magnified by his natural angst which
      came with being a teen.
He'd had it with the entire stinkin' segregationist scene!
His dreams and horizons forever constrained-
Dragging him down like a ball and chain.
It was high time to stick it to the segregationist laws-
Clemon was in a rebellious state of mind, a rebel with a cause!

On the day of the wade-in after the barbarity broke out-
And the sand turned red with blood near the cookout-
Clemon ran for his life-
To escape from the violence and the mindless strife.
One of the racists cried out, "You better get that nigger! You better
      not let him get away!"
The mob pursued him like hunter's prey.

Clemon crossed a seawall and raced down the road parallel to the beach.
He was fleet of foot, and stayed out of his pursuers' reach.
He was cornered in an alley by a member of the mob. He threw a punch
    which ended the stand-off.
His pursuer, a closet coward, immediately backed off.

At the end of the day, the mob's attack resulted in dozens of injuries
    and shootings. Two of the peaceful protestors fell dead on the beach.
In this racist hate-filled climate, justice remained far out of reach.

The "law enforcement" officers who had done nothing to stop the beatings,
    swung into action, executing arrests:
In a manner akin to deputies, gone bad in the wild wild west.

Most of the criminals, the members of the violent white mob, went about their
    business, remaining scot-free-
While the black victims, the peaceful beaten-up protestors, were arrested
and given the third degree.
Many were charged with trespass upon the beach.
It was Alice in Wonderland justice-a moral and ethical breach.

Violence by the mob continued deep into the night-
To terrorize further and foster fright.
Shots were fired into a black community church:
Extra helpings of Jim Crow "hospitality," decency besmirched!

The April 24, 1960 wade-in on Bloody Sunday, and the other wade-ins
    to desegregate public beaches and swimming pools, were courageous
    landmark efforts in the struggle for civil rights-
Demonstrating that seizing the moral high ground could one day result
    in right over might.

While the wade-ins were in some ways overshadowed and obscured by
    sit-ins, boycotts, freedom rides, and demonstrations yet to come-
They sounded the alarm and beat the drum-
For non-violent attacks on discrimination yet to come.

By getting their feet wet and testing the waters, courageous people like
    Dr. Gilbert Mason and Clemon Jimerson, turned
    the early wade-ins into a litmus test for future challenges
    to segregation-
To tear the roots from its very foundation.

They demonstrated that the waters to be navigated were as
    treacherous as a flash flood-
Exacting a price to be paid in blood.
They showed us that courageous souls we'll always need 'em-
To reach for the treasure-trove of freedom.

TAKING ON THE PURVEYORS OF HATE
(Historical Non-Fiction Essay)

Their hearts filled with racial prejudice, venom, and hate.
Their minds closed, their capacity for change, too late.
Their attitudes set in stone-
Lacking the slightest ability to atone.

Their openness to challenging their own thinking,
       to self- reflect:
As futile as looking into a shattered window in which all
       clarity of sight has been compromised and wrecked.

Their eyes reflecting rage, "the windows to their souls."
Their mouths spewing hatred, divorced of self-control.

Waiting for a demagogue whose ugly tropes are spewed-
Racist and religious hate for Muslims, blacks, and Jews.
Emboldened by the demagogue who makes them feel secure:
They post and chant their venom, while feeling self-assured.
While casting off their robes and hoods perhaps forevermore-
No longer hiding who they are or what they're calling for:
A land of white supremacy, an all-out racist war.

Social media platforms constitute the new town square, a free
       market of ideas:
On the one hand, a miraculous means for tolerant people of goodwill
       and all backgrounds to come together.
Where there's no obstacle or storm they cannot weather.

On the other hand, an unregulated and expedient means for intolerant people
       of bad will to peddle and spread pernicious lies; Where
       anything goes, unaccountability reigns, anonymity lives,
       and hatred oozes like sludge-
To be spewed and slung like mud-
Across the terrain like a runaway train;
A high-tech whistle-stop tour-
For spreading lies as never before.

Tweeted lies and tweeted hate-
Replace ideas through reasoned debate.
Tweedle dumb and tweedle dee-
Dumbing down to the nth degree.

Unchecked lies and abject hate-
What does that say for our country's fate?
Will tolerant voices commit to a stand-
For a "more perfect union" in a more just land?
Repudiating bigotry at the nation's polls-
In a do-or-die battle for the nation's soul?

Will we break at last the demagogue's spell?
Shoot an arrow through-it like William Tell?
The passage of time will surely tell-
If we rise toward heaven or plunge toward hell.

PUERTO RICO- FORSAKEN BUT UNBOWED
(Historical Non-Fiction Essay)

Oh Puerto Rico we failed you so-
We cared too little and we moved too slow.
In your darkest hour, in your time of need-
The U.S. government failed to take heed.

Mayor Cruz's desperate pleas for assistance in the
      wake of Hurricane Maria, fell on deaf ears-
The response to your plight offered little care.

Like a voice crying out in the wilderness,
      your mayor spelled out your need for food,
      clean water, medicine, shelter, repaired roads,
      and repaired electric grids to support dialysis
      and other critical care.
She tried to make sure that America was made fully aware.

She pleaded that people were dying, that lives
      were at stake-
She appealed to our country's compassion and empathy, to jar
      it awake.

Her pleas for help, for greater assistance-
Were met with cold and callous resistance.
In the midst of your crisis and terrible pain-
Her pleas were met with dismissive disdain.

Oh Puerto Rico, due to Maria's relentless path of destruction,
      almost three thousand of your people died-
A death toll the former President flat out denied.
He made light of your crisis, remarking, "I hate to tell you
Puerto Rico, but you've thrown our budget a little out of whack"-
He failed to commit to having your back.

The government's response- half-hearted and wrong-
Our country has failed you for far too long.
Treated you poorly like you don't belong.

As dark clouds block the sun from shining-
Somewhere there breaks a silver lining.
Not from the sky but from deep inside-
Your peoples' hearts full of dignity and pride.

Stirring within, a fervent drive-
To ensure that justice comes alive.
A dream of Statehood- full citizenship, the right
        to vote, a New Day-
No longer a territory without a say.

If Maria was the price you had to pay-
To bring about that brighter day-
Then all of the loss and all of the pain-
Was not without meaning or all in vain.

A FEISTIER VOICE OF THE PEOPLE
(Historical Fiction)

The young and feisty reporter, Edward, had a reverence for journalism.
He had no intention of being cowed by any sort of
        employment paternalism.

In journalism school, he developed a love for
        The Constitution and The Bill of Rights, especially
        The First Amendment-
He vowed that upon becoming a journalist, he would champion
        and defend it.

He was born into a family of journalists, who named him after
        Edward R. Murrow, perhaps the greatest journalist of them all.
Unearthing and uncovering the truth was Murrow's protocol.

As a radio correspondent in 1940, Murrow had literally broadcast
        from the rooftops to report upon Germany's bombing of London
        during The Blitz.
To maintain his safety, he lived by his wits.

Edward admired Murrow's commitment to relentlessly reporting
        the truth, and his unbridled courage.
And his refusal to back down or become discouraged.

Edward learned about Murrow's reporting from the Korean War
        on his weekly radio program, Hear It Now-
With as much depth as the length of his program would allow.

Edward studied that in the 1950's, Senator Joseph McCarthy engaged
        in smear tactics against American citizens which destroyed
        many innocent lives. Few people took him on, they didn't dare.
In that context, Murrow stepped up and went on the air.
He broke through the cowardice of silence, and called out Senator McCarthy
        for his irresponsible red-baiting- his "Red Scare."

Edward read about Murrow reporting on the plight, poverty, and exploitation of
America's migrant workers in the documentary *Harvest of Shame*.
Opening America's eyes to the suffering of the migrant worker was its aim.

Edward also studied the issue of freedom of the press versus alleged
national security concerns in the landmark Pentagon Papers case of 1971.
He learned that freedom of the press had resoundingly won.
The New York Times and *The Washington Post* could publish the classified
Pentagon Papers without being censored, punished or attacked-
The Founding Fathers intended the free press "to serve the governed and not
the governors," wrote Justice Hugo Black.

He studied the tenacity of Woodward and Bernstein in the face of President
Nixon's vicious attacks upon the press.
He was inspired by their bull-dog determination and refusal to acquiesce-
As they sounded the alarm over threats to our Constitution like the issuance
of an SOS-
While they doggedly worked to uncover the crimes of Nixon's Watergate mess.

He learned about Dan Rather's willingness to stand up to
Nixon during a news conference.
Nixon asked, "Are you running for something?"
Rather replied, "No Mr. President, are you?"
Rather wasn't there to be trifled with, he had a job to do.

The intrepid journalists he studied inspired Edward and lit a flame.
Uncovering the truth, defending the First Amendment, and holding
politicians' feet to the fire would be his aim.

When freedom of the press was under attack-
He'd refuse to refrain or hold himself back.
When leaders tried to deflect and distract-
He'd refuse to allow the obscuring of facts.

Working for a newspaper, he was initially assigned at the state level.
He found himself immediately annoyed and bedeviled-
By the failure of legislators to speak out against presidential attacks
        upon the independence of the press, the courts, the Justice Department,
        and the FBI.
The legislators behaved as if they were gagged, as if they were tongue-tied.
As if they were powerless, frozen with cowardice.

Edward's next assignment was covering Capitol Hill.
It was more of the same, an absence of shame and a lack of will.
He confronted legislators with their failure to defend the Constitution-
Or to stand up for American institutions.
Their silence spoke volumes: attacks by the President they wouldn't redress-
The smear of the press they refused to address.

Edward was next assigned to the White House Press Corp-
A position he'd long been hoping for.
At a press conference, the President repeatedly attacked the press as,
        "The enemy of the people."
Edward immediately stood up and replied, "Mr. President, the press is
        the Voice of the People.
Attacks upon the press as the enemy of the people-
Constitute an undemocratic, damnable lie, as well as a clear and
        present danger to the freedom of the people."

"Like it or not, sir, Edward continued, we intend to fact check you
        In The Moment, throughout your presidency.
Any attacks upon the press or other lies, will be immediately and
        consistently called out, without a moment's hesitancy."

Who is Edward, this young reporter who unflinchingly stands up,
        In The Moment, to political leaders-
Some of whom are liars and cheaters?

Who is this intrepid reporter who relentlessly defends,
        In The Moment, the role of a free and independent press?
Against all attacks, from the President no less?

Alas, young Edward is but a figure of hope and aspiration-
A figment only of my imagination.
But a Walter Middy I would not be-
This tale is but an urgent plea:

For a feistier press that challenges power-
In the moment of truth, in the midnight hour.
So the First Amendment is always protected-
And the Constitution forever respected.

THE DIAMOND BOYS AND THE GOLDEN GIRL
(Historical Fiction)

Seventeen-year- old Davey Armstrong's prized possession was his leather glove.
He played third base with a passion, and baseball was like a religion, his deepest love.
He studied the history of the game.
He was well-versed in Major League Baseball's Hall of Fame.

He played ball for the Missouri Bluebirds of Truman High.
With his strong arm, powerful bat, and first-rate defensive skills, he was ready to fly.
He dreamed of advancing one day from the Missouri Bluebirds to the
	Baltimore Orioles to follow in the footsteps of his hero, Brooks Robinson, the
	"Human Vacuum Cleaner."
Davey studied his form, his class, and his professional demeanor.

His best friends were the other highly talented members of the Bluebird's infield-
	LeBron Davis at shortstop, Ariel Simon at second, and Ali Abbas at first,
	positions they were born to play.
Each of them dreamed of playing ball in the Big Leagues one day.

Davey was white, Lebron was black, Ariel was Jewish, and Ali was Muslim. They
	constituted an All-American melting pot, some liked to say;
But ominously, some viewed them in a much darker way.

They viewed themselves not through the lens of race or religion, but simply
	as teammates and trusted friends.
On the ballfield, by any measure, their friendship and loyalty to each other paid
	endless dividends.
They called themselves the Diamond Boys.
They excelled in teamwork, trusting each other and playing with poise.

Prior to the spring baseball season, October meant the upcoming High School
	Halloween Dance.
The Diamond Boys were not going to miss it, not a chance!
But very soon, the days leading up to Halloween resulted in a horror story-
A Nazi "Kristallnacht" came to Missouri.
The Diamond Boys were targeted as if they were quarry.

Their homes, both windows and doors-
Were spray painted with racial slurs, impossible to ignore.
The slurs were accompanied by Nazi swastikas to be sure.
Symbols of hate they each deplored.

Their parents implored them not to go to the Halloween Dance.
But they refused to be intimidated, not a chance!
No one backed out, they all attended-
Just as they all originally intended.

Davey had long had a crush on Lebron's sister, Tanesa, and he was
        looking forward to taking a chance-
Of finding the nerve to ask her to dance.
He had worshipped her from afar-
Especially at the track meets where she starred.

She ran like the wind and was smart as a whip. He viewed her as
        the Golden Girl: talented, beautiful, and graceful in every way-
He had longed to meet her, somehow in some way.
Each time he had thought about asking Lebron to introduce him to her, he
        chickened out and shied away.
Racial slurs were not going to intimidate him from trying to meet her
        at last, come what may.

Upon his arrival at the dance, he awaited slow dance music as the lights
        went low.
He approached in her direction, though kinda slow-
As he gazed upon her beautiful glow.
He searched for words to say, but he hadn't a clue beyond, "Hello."

Finally, as he stood before her sweating but frozen, the words popped out, "I'm
        Davey, would you like to dance?"
He awaited her answer in endless silence in a frozen trance.
Finally, sound broke through as he heard, "Yes." He was
        deliriously happy he had taken the chance!

He looked into her eyes and smiled, then gently took her hand while resting his
        other hand upon her back-
Beginning a trip to heaven and back.

The dance floor was extremely crowded.

Suddenly, voices screamed while others shouted!

In a flash, Tanesa was grabbed by the back of her dress by two figures wearing
    satanic masks, and forcefully shoved into a wall!

Upon her knees impacting the wall-

Her legs buckled and she began to fall.

One of her attackers yelled out, "So much for your being able to race!

Stick to boys of your own race!"

As Davey, stunned and shocked, desperately tried to go to her rescue, he
    was grabbed from behind by two more attackers wearing similar masks.
    One of the attackers screamed at him, calling him a traitor to his race.

As he did so, he targeted Davey's throwing arm, twisting it out of place!

At the moment of the attacks, the other three Diamond Boys were standing
    off from the dance floor, over by the punch bowl.

The second they heard screaming and commotion and spotted Tanesa
    on the floor, Lebron exclaimed, "My sister needs us, let's roll!"

As they reached the dance floor, they themselves were grabbed from behind
    by several more attackers and thrown to the floor-

Blind-sided like in a guerrilla war!

Their attackers wore similar masks as well.

All of the assailants belonged to the same white supremacist cell.

As the stunned crowd moved forward to assist the victims and confront the
    attackers, one of the attackers gestured toward his pocket and screamed out
    that he had a gun!

The crowd stopped in its tracks, and many turned and began to run!

As the crowd backed off in a state of panic-

Faced with the hate of all things satanic-

The attackers bolted in a state of flight-

Vanishing into the black of night.

The aftermath wasn't pretty.
The perpetrators had taken no pity.
Upon the disappearance of the assailants-
The students and teachers who remained behind served
       as angels of mercy, that was apparent.
They called 911 and comforted those who were harmed-
To lessen their pain and diminish alarm.

In the days that followed, Davey and his friends experienced difficult
       moments while their bodies were weak.
Their pain was deep and their spirits bleak.
Davey's throwing arm was badly twisted out of place. Ariel and Ali
       suffered concussions, and Lebron's throwing arm sustained a break.
The Diamond Boys believed their dreams of baseball glory were at stake.

Tanesa suffered from a fracture to her right knee and bruises to her arms.
The Diamond Boys and Tanesa each suffered a degree of post-traumatic
       emotional harm.

Even as they dealt with their own injuries and struggled to cope-
       Lebron, Davey, Ariel, and Ali felt supportive and protective
       of Tanesa. They tried to raise her spirits and her sense of hope-
To help along her ability to cope.
Davey gave her a locket containing a symbol of hope and faith,
       a four-leaf clover-
After carefully selecting and looking it over.

He asked Tanesa if they could work through their rehabilitation together.
Like two recovering birds of a feather.
His romantic feelings for her were not the order of the day.
He simply wanted to help her, supporting her recovery in every way.
He was happy and pleased when she said, "Ok."

Thus began for the Diamond Boys and the Golden Girl, a long and arduous
       road of treatment and rehabilitation-
Requiring deep reserves of effort and motivation.

Meanwhile, the perpetrators were rounded up in a matter of weeks-
As a result of standard police techniques.
Davey thought he recognized the voice that called him a traitor to his race.
He informed the police it was the voice of Billy Ray, a town bully
     and self-proclaimed white supremacist. Davey viewed him as a disgrace.

Davey also provided police with the names of a number of Billy Ray's white
     supremacist friends-
Whose liberty would soon be drawing to an end.

Their plastic masks were located stashed beneath a city grate-
Which cemented the case and sealed their fate.
Fingerprints and DNA lifted off the masks matched the fingerprints and DNA of
     each of the assailants, including Billy Ray.
The fingerprint and DNA evidence spoke volumes and had its' say.
And now it was going to put them away!

They were each charged with aggravated battery. The charges were enhanced by
     their designation as hate crimes.
In addition, they were charged with criminal conspiracy, one and all.
Now it was their turn to take a fall.

It wasn't long before Christmas and Hanukkah arrived.
The victims' parents gave thanks that their kids had survived.
Their arduous recovery stretched on into months of continuous rehabilitation-
As they struggled through pain and ongoing, post-traumatic stress and debilitation.

Another spring, followed by another Halloween, Hanukkah, and Christmas
     came and went-
The supremacists were unremorseful, failing to repent.
Facing lengthy years in prison, they each pled out shortly after Christmas
     to the State's offer of three years' probation tacked on to ten years prison
     "up the road."
Prison would become their new abode.

As part of the prosecutor's negotiated deal, a special condition was imposed.
During their sentencing hearings, each of the Defendants would be required to view
     photographs and recordings which the State Attorney disclosed.

The State Attorney projected onto a large screen within the courtroom,
photographs of the swastikas and racial slurs which the Defendants
had spray painted upon the Diamond Boys' homes. Right beside
those images, the State Attorney displayed a blow-up of a newspaper
headline from the past spring which read, "Rehabilitated Diamond Boys,
the Comeback Kids, mount triumphant return to the diamond!" Next
to the headline was a blow-up photo of the Diamond Boys back on the
field, as the student body stood and cheered!

The State Attorney pointed to each of the infield positions to make clear a
notable point. Because Lebron and Davey had suffered diminished
strength in their injured arms, they'd switched positions from shortstop
and third base to second and first.
In turn, Ariel and Ali had switched positions to shortstop and third. They
weren't coerced.
Helping their buddies had clearly come first.

Next, the State Attorney projected onto the screen the following words screamed
at Tanesa during the attack: "So much for your being able to race!
Stick to boys of your own race!"
Right next to those words on the screen was a blow-up of a newspaper
headline which read: "Rehabilitated Golden Girl, Tanesa Davis, the
Comeback Kid, wins Spring Conference 100 and 200- meter sprints!"
Next to the headline was a blow-up photograph of Tanesa breaking the
tape ahead of the pack, as the student body stood and cheered!

The final exhibit displayed by the State Attorney on the large screen which each
of the Defendants was required to watch, was a DVD.
It began with the image of a Christmas Tree.
The tree was located at the High School Christmas Dance, held one month
earlier in December.
The DJ opened the dance by announcing to the student body that there was some
"Unfinished business to remember."

"Fourteen months ago, he stated, five of our own were attacked at
      the Halloween Dance.
By the Grace of God, along with the support of each other and of the entire
      student body, their dreams were not broken by their attackers, not a chance!
Rather, their endless hours of rehabilitation resulted in the rebuilding of their
      dreams, as well as the beginning of a beautiful romance."

At that moment, the Diamond Boys and the Golden Girl opened the door to the dance
      hall and were seen at a glance.
They entered to the accompaniment of wild applause as they slowly advanced.

The DJ announced, "For the sake of completion of 'unfinished business' interrupted
      fourteen months ago at the Halloween Dance-
And for the sake of all who believe in the enduring triumph of love over hate and the
      magic of romance, we reserve for Tanesa and Davey, The Very First Dance."

The slow-dance music began to play-
They held each other and began to sway.
And the lights went low-
As they reclaimed a moment from a year ago.

As Davey gazed into her eyes and smiled while holding
      her close, his hand gently resting upon her back-
They soared on a trip to heaven and back.

THE CONTEMPTIBLE SIN OF VOTER SUPPRESSION
(Historical Non-Fiction Essay)

It's hard to conceive of a worse transgression-
Than willfully engaging in voter suppression.
Undemocratic, un-American, and unconstitutional, rolled into one.
Tilting elections before they are run.

Regarding the 2020 presidential election, the incumbent was soundly defeated.
Despite the fact that at least sixty-three lawsuits alleging voter fraud were dismissed or
dropped due to the courts' findings of a Lack of Evidence to support
the allegation, the President went right on publicly spouting the conspiratorial,
baseless Big Lie that he'd been cheated.
He exhibited autocratic contempt for democracy by refusing to concede he'd been
defeated.
And by refusing to respect the peaceful transition of power-
Which plunged democracy into a perilous hour.

Like a sore loser from hell, he incited a racist mob to storm Capitol Hill-
On a twisted mission to stop the certification of the election results- to
suppress the people's will.

By any other name, the violent storming of The Capitol, including the violent
attack upon the Capitol Police, by white supremacists and far right militants
bent upon nullifying the results of a presidential election, constituted
insurrection and sedition-
Predicated upon The Big Lie of voter fraud as the rationale for overturning
democratic principles, norms, and traditions.

While the insurrection failed, numerous states immediately picked up where
the insurrection left off, by passing laws of voter suppression.
They did so with alarming speed, and a kind of single- minded obsession.
The enactment of such undemocratic state voter suppression laws was enabled
by *Shelby v. Holder*, a 2013 U.S. Supreme Court decision-
Which set back years of progress in regard to voting rights with ruthless precision.

The 1965 Voting Rights Act required states with a proven history of voter suppression
based upon race, to obtain "preclearance" from the Justice Department
before implementing changes to their voting procedures and laws.
In *Shelby*, the Court struck down the preclearance requirement, a decision that was ill-
advised and deeply flawed.

The Court's holding released an evil genie from the bottle-
Allowing states such as Georgia, Mississippi, Alabama, Florida, and Texas, with a
history and track record of racial discrimination and voter suppression,
to implement voter suppression provisions at full throttle.

In 2021, numerous states from across the country utilized the factually vacant
conspiratorial claim of widespread voter fraud, as their rationale for enacting
a myriad of laws making it more difficult for minorities and young people to
vote. They passed bills prohibiting automatic voter registration, Election Day
voter registration, and no excuse absentee ballot mail-in voting. They enacted
laws reducing the number of polling sites, drive through voting sites, and mail-
in ballot drop boxes.

They also enacted laws shortening the early voting period, and reducing the
hours for in- person voting. Despite the fact that such limitations upon the sites
and hours for voting created the inevitability of long lines, some states passed
bills making it a crime to provide food and water to those waiting on such
lengthy lines in order to exercise their right to vote! It amounted to the
double-whammy by the voter suppressers:
Long lines and a made-up "crime"-
And the added threat of doing time!

Some states passed bills restricting or eliminating Sunday morning voting, which
stymied the well-known practice of "souls to the polls" within the
black community-
One more blatant and shameful effort at suppressing minority voting opportunities.

Most insidious of all, Arizona passed a bill which would allow the state legislature by
	majority vote, to overturn the formal certification of a presidential election vote
	count conducted by its Secretary of State and Governor. Such a nullification law
	would empower the Arizona legislature to substitute its own decision as to the
	outcome of a presidential election! It could do so by appointing its own slate of
	electors as a replacement for the electors selected by Arizona voters as a
	consequence of casting their votes! If enacted, the Arizona law could open the
	floodgates to state legislatures across the country overturning election results and
	the will of the people. If the day comes when the people no longer choose the
	President through the exercise of the ballot, that day will mark the death knell of democracy-
The death of freedom and the birth of autocracy.

The 2021 state voter suppression laws amount to the greatest attack upon voting rights
	since the bad old days of poll taxes, literacy tests, and the counting of jelly beans
	in a jar.
Is this the essence of who we are?

Congress has the power to pass federal legislation which would preempt these
	nefarious state voter suppression laws in their tracks. The John Lewis Voting
	Rights Act would restore teeth to the 1965 Voting Rights Act by
	reimposing the federal "preclearance" requirement which the court tragically
	struck down in *Shelby*. The For the People Act would expand voting rights
	by providing for automatic voter registration and Day of Election voter
	registration. It would also prohibit the practice of partisan voting district
	gerrymandering, which is being utilized to dilute the voting power of minorities.
	Yet Congress fiddles and does nothing! Both bills remain dead in the water-
While democracy's shredded like lambs to the slaughter.

Those who recognize injustice, including the dismantling of the right to vote,
	while choosing to do nothing to stop it, are themselves enabling the
	decline and twilight of democracy-
The destruction of freedom and the birth of autocracy.

The systematic enactment by state legislators of voter suppression laws,
　　　constitutes a Sun Tzu-inspired insidious plot-
To win elections before they are fought.
Suppression here, some cheating there-
Destroying the principle of fair and square-
Targeting minorities most everywhere.

Suppressing their votes at all opportunities-
Doing the deed with outright impunity-
And an arrogant sense of blameless immunity.

They have no fear of retribution-
They won't be seeking absolution;
For they don't distinguish wrong from right.
It's suppress the vote and win the fight.

Rather than playing by the rules, attempting to offer a superior message
　　　on the issues, and working hard-
They prefer to ensure victory and the seizing of power through
　　　cheating, by playing the voter suppression card.

Voter suppression laws constitute a slap in the face to the memory
　　　of our heroes, to the memory of all those who fought and died
　　　overseas to preserve freedom, the right to vote, and our very democracy-
By standing up to the twin evils of tyranny and autocracy.

Voter suppression laws also constitute a betrayal of our civil rights heroes, a betrayal
　　　of all those who paid the price in blood, sweat, and tears in the struggle for
　　　equal justice, including the right to vote-
A betrayal which sticks like a bone in the throat.

If We the People allow voter suppression to go unchecked, the democracy
　　　which our heroes fought to preserve will wither away-
Consumed by apathy and moral decay.
Despite their sacrifice of life and limb-
The light of freedom will fade and dim.

THE ENDURING EVIL OF INSTITUTIONAL RACISM
(Historical Non-Fiction Essay)

The truth, of course, is that America was only partially conceived in liberty. It was
     also conceived in institutional racism, known at the time as slavery.
Institutional racism has persisted to this very day, due to a lack of political bravery.

On 7/4/1776, the day the United States was born as an independent nation, the slave trade
     upon which the economy of the South relied, was alive and well. From the
     time they first arrived in Jamestown upon slave ships in 1619, slaves were
     utilized to harvest, among other crops, "King Cotton."
The dehumanizing, evil institution of slavery continued on and on, vile and rotten.

The transatlantic slave trade of the United States was finally abolished under the
     presidency of slave owner, Thomas Jefferson, in 1808.
But for those enslaved black people already within the United States whose lives were
     devastated and or destroyed by the slave trade, it was too little, too late.

It took a bloody Civil War before slavery was abolished by the Thirteenth
     Amendment in 1865.
Yet institutional racism remained very much alive.
Southern states immediately began passing "Black Codes" to ensure that the newly
     freed former slaves were treated as second class citizens earning a
     second-class wage.
So on continued the moral outrage-
And on continued the ethical stone-age.

In 1876, in order to ensure that the presidential election swung his way, Rutherford B.
     Hayes entered into an unscrupulous backroom deal, an unwritten agreement
     with Congressmen to pull Federal troops engaged in Reconstruction out of
     the South. This deal with the devil, this institutional sell-out of principle for
     power, led to the unchecked rise of the KKK-
To murder and lynchings and moral decay.

In 1896, the U.S. Supreme Court in *Plessy v. Ferguson*, twisted and perverted the heart
  and soul of the Fourteenth Amendment's Equal Protection Clause, into the
  shame and heartbreak of "separate but equal"-
A legal abomination that remains in many ways unequalled.
The decision tightly fastened legal bootstraps onto the jackbooted enforcers
  of racial segregation-
Enforcers who ruled with an iron fist, ensuring that the South remained for well over a
  half-century, an apartheid Nation.

Over the course of that half century, with institutional checks out of the way-
Racist violence and terror continued to rule the day-
The disgraceful practices of the KKK.

In Wilmington, N.C., in 1898, white supremacists engaged in a coup d'état, utilizing
  violence to remove duly elected black government officials. Many black
  people were murdered. Property and businesses of black citizens were destroyed
  or robbed-
Destruction unleashed by the racist mob.

In 1921, the wealthiest black community in America, known as the "black Wall Street,"
  was located in Tulsa, Oklahoma. The community had lifted itself up by its
  bootstraps even in an era in which black people were continuously kicked in
  the shins by Jim Crow.
Jealous, angry white mobs decided that this successful black community must go.
They utilized guns and explosives to murder black residents, and to target their
  businesses and their homes.
More than 35 square blocks of the district were destroyed until there was little
  left to own.

In 1/1923, to avoid being lynched or shot by a white mob, the black citizens of
  Rosewood, Fl. were forced to flee through an untamed swamp. Rosewood,
  a self-sufficient black township, was set afire and burned to the ground.
No compensation of any kind was ever paid to the black citizens of that town.
No remunerations were paid regarding the land of which they were divested.
None of the white supremacists who murdered and destroyed the town were
  held accountable. None were arrested.

The past destruction of black homes and businesses constituted an obliteration of
future intergenerational wealth. This destruction of wealth has been
further exacerbated by various forms of present- day institutional racism.
Despite the Fair Housing Act of 1968, statistics reveal that many banks
and mortgage companies have continued to engage in discriminatory "red
lining," denying loans needed by black people to rebuild, purchase, or
renovate homes, or to invest in start-up businesses. In many cases, all other
things being relatively equal, homes owned by blacks have been appraised at
lower property values than similar homes owned by whites. Such
discriminatory practices have shaped demographic and wealth patterns
between blacks and whites within communities. By any other name, these
red lining practices constitute a form of institutional racism, figuratively
and literally keeping many black people "in their place"-
Relegated to second class citizenship based upon race.
So on continues the moral disgrace, and on continues the fall from grace.

In 1955, for allegedly flirting with a white woman in her family's Mississippi grocery
store, a fourteen-year-old black teenager, Emmett Till, from Chicago, was
savagely brutalized, tortured, and murdered. His body was thrown into the
Tallahatchie River, weighed down by a large cotton gin fan blade. The murder
was committed by the woman's husband and his half-brother.
At his funeral, Emmett was displayed in an open casket by Mamie Till, his
loving Mother.

Photos of Emmett's brutalized and deformed body were taken and appeared in *Jet*,
a black owned magazine. Ms. Till wanted the world to bear witness to the
brutal consequences of racist hate-
Which was alive and well within Mississippi, an apartheid state.

The two killers were acquitted by the criminal justice system's all-white jury.
Afterward, knowing they were forever shielded by Double Jeopardy,
they arrogantly admitted in an interview with *Look* magazine to having
done the deed.
They admitted that they were the murderers that the jury freed.

Between the post-Civil War Reconstruction period and 1950, approximately
6500 black people were lynched.
In most cases, the criminal justice system did little or nothing about it. The racist
murderers got away with it scot-free. It was a cinch.

On 8/28/1963, MLK delivered his I Have a Dream Speech in front of the Lincoln
Memorial in Washington D.C.
Only two and a half weeks later, on September 15, 1963, four members of the KKK
blew up the Birmingham 16th Street Baptist Church. The church was left
full of debris.
Tragically, the bombing of the church killed four black school children. It was intended
to send a message that black people would never be free.

After more than fifty years of terror and legalized racial discrimination in the wake
of *Plessy,* the pillars of institutional segregation finally began to crumble. In
Brown v. the Board of Education, the U.S. Supreme Court held that in the area
of public education, segregated schools violated the Fourteenth
Amendment's Equal Protection Clause.
The Big Lie, the fiction of "separate but equal" public schools, was at last rejected as
a lost cause.

The Civil Rights movement of the 1960's resulted in further advances in the struggle
for racial justice. Racial segregation in regard to all public accommodations-
toilets, water fountains, restaurants, hotels, swimming pools, beaches, and
movie theaters, was prohibited by the Civil Rights Act of 1964.
It broke down barriers and opened doors.

Poll taxes, literacy tests, the counting of jelly beans in a jar, and other barriers to minority
voting, were prohibited by the Voting Rights Act of 1965.
For a time, it appeared that sinister measures of voter suppression by southern states,
would fail to survive.

Some have cavalierly insisted that the civil rights legislation of the 1960s
delivered a death knell to institutional racism. They have maintained that
the legislation established an instantaneous level playing field of equal
opportunity for all people regardless of race. They have argued that those who
continue to call out systemic racism are playing the victim card, making an
excuse for their own personal failings. Such assertions constitute spurious
ad hominem attacks-
Lacking truth and devoid of fact.

Case in point: In 2013, the U.S. Supreme Court in *Shelby v. Holder* extracted the teeth
from the 1965 Voting Rights Act. Sections 4b and 5 of the Act required that
those states with a history of targeting minorities for voter suppression, and
who wished to implement changes to their voting procedures, were subject
to oversight by the Justice Department. They were required to obtain
federal "preclearance" before implementing changes to their voting laws
and practices. The Supreme Court in *Shelby* struck down the preclearance
requirement. As a result, in 2021, numerous states with a long history of targeting
minorities for voter suppression, states such as Georgia, Mississippi, Florida,
Texas, and Alabama, began erecting new barriers to suppress minority voting
unchecked by federal oversight. They passed laws reducing the number of polling
places in and around minority neighborhoods. They reduced the days and hours
for voting. They required expensive voter IDs.
By any other name, these state voter suppression laws targeting minorities constituted
blatant institutional racism, predicated upon undemocratic sleaze.

Thanks to video cameras, institutional racism, rampant within far too many police
departments, cannot so easily be buried and hidden from sight-
Within the shadows, beyond the light.
In 1991, following a high-speed chase, four officers brutally and savagely beat Rodney
King while he was on the ground being arrested for DUI.
The entire vicious attack was captured by the camera's eye.

In 2015, Walter Scott ran from an officer after being stopped for a non-functioning
brake light. As he ran away, he was shot in the back by the officer and killed.
For running away, his blood was spilled.

In 2014, Eric Gardner pulled his arms away while being arrested by the NYPD for selling
cigarettes illegally. He was placed in a chokehold and pinned face down onto the
sidewalk. The chokehold had been banned by the NYPD since 1990. Eleven
times Mr. Gardner pleaded, "I can't breathe." Eleven times his pleas were
ignored by the officers. Mr. Gardner lost consciousness, and in just over an
hour he was dead. They ignored his pleas and cut off his air-
Without regard, like they didn't care.

In 2020, George Floyd was arrested after allegedly passing a counterfeit $20.00 bill at a
grocery store to purchase cigarettes. During his arrest, a Minneapolis officer
pressed his knee into Floyd's neck for nine minutes and twenty-nine seconds
while Floyd was handcuffed face down on the road. Two other officers
restrained Floyd as well. Over and over, Floyd pleaded that he couldn't
breathe; And over and over he was ignored. For the last three minutes of those
nine minutes and twenty-nine seconds, Floyd was motionless. No attempts
were made by any of the officers to revive him. Soon he was dead. They ignored
his pleas and cut off his air-
Without concern, like they didn't care.

The list of killings caught on video goes on and on. By any other name, this pattern of
police brutality directed against people of color, constitutes institutional
racism. Police departments throughout the country have a responsibility to
institute training and strict standards regarding the use of force, and to
rid themselves of bad apple cops who take the law into their own hands.
Consent Decrees, whereby police departments with a history and pattern of targeting
minorities for racial profiling and excessive use of force, consent to oversight
by the Justice Department to ensure that reforms are instituted, would constitute
a constructive plan.

Some have argued that if the victims of police brutality had avoided violating the law
in any manner, they wouldn't have wound up beaten or dead.
Such assertions are a form of blame the victim that's being fed.
Officers do not have the right to play judge, jury, and executioner. They are
forbidden from doing so.
They don't get to mete out punishment or pass sentence, as if they were replicating
the "incident at Ox-Bow."

In light of these unrestrained and unjustified incidents of excessive use of force by
law enforcement caught over and over again on camera, why do so many
people deny that institutional racism exists?
How many more videos must be viewed before people acknowledge that systemic
racism persists?
How many people of color must die-
For people to trust their ears and their eyes?

In 2017, in Charlottesville, gun-toting white supremacists and Neo-Nazis marched while
holding up tiki torches and chanting, "Jews will not replace us!" In reference to
the white supremacists and neo-Nazis, as well as those who were protesting
against them, the former President asserted that there were some "very fine people
on both sides."
When the Chief Executive Officer of the United States asserts such a moral equivalence,
the inescapable conclusion is that institutional racism and anti-Semitism is
alive and well. It hasn't died.

In the shadow of the 1896 *Plessy v. Ferguson* "separate but equal" decision, statues of
Confederate Generals were erected as monuments to white supremacy and
Jim Crow.
The statues were a further means of going low-
Of dealing blacks a dirty blow.
The statues were yet another form of institutional racism, a means of cementing within
the South a symbolic and enduring message infamously expressed a half
century later by Governor George Wallace in 1963:
"Segregation now, segregation tomorrow, segregation forever"- a message to blacks that
they'd never be free.

Some assert, "They're just statues," and that black people should "calm
down and get over it." One shouldn't lose sight of the fact that the statues of
Confederate Generals require tax money to be maintained. Should black
people be required to pay taxes for the preservation of monuments to their own
oppression? Should a person of color who approaches the footsteps of the
courthouse door seeking justice-
Be confronted by symbols of racial injustice?

Statues of Confederate Generals should be preserved as part of the historical
record of what they represented- monuments to white supremacy and the
enduring destructive legacy of Jim Crow-
Museums are the places they ought to go.

Some insist that statues of Confederate Generals constitute monuments to
        "Southern heritage." But given the context in which they were erected,
        they symbolize the dehumanization of people of color by Jim Crow-
The second-class citizenship and the violent blows-
That's why it's time for the statues to go.

On the other hand, of course, there are many wonderful aspects of
        "Southern heritage" and southern culture which deserve to be celebrated
        and honored. Why not replace statues of Confederate Generals with statues
        celebrating southern literature and southern music? Statues of writers such
        as Harper Lee, William Faulkner, Ralph Ellison, Thomas Wolfe, and
        Richard Wright; Statues of country singers such as Hank Williams, Patsy
        Cline, and Johnny Cash; And statues of great jazz musicians such as
        Louis Armstrong, Dizzy Gillespie, B.B. king, and Muddy Waters-
Great figures who inspire adults and their sons and daughters.

Why not replace statues of Confederate Generals with statues of unity? Statues
        displaying a union and confederate soldier laying down their arms together at
        the end of the Civil War, accompanied by an inscription of Lincoln's
        generous words, "With malice toward none, with charity for all." Or statues of
        whites and blacks engaging in sit-ins together at segregated lunch-counters; Or
        boarding buses together as freedom riders; Or engaging in wade-ins together to
        desegregate public swimming pools and beaches; Why not statues of
        Goodman, Chaney, and Schwerner working together to register blacks to vote
        in Mississippi during Freedom Summer in 1964, before they were
        murdered together by the Klan?
Why not statues like these to unify our land?

Each new generation of school children in America begin their day by pledging
        allegiance to the American Flag. It is a pledge which describes America as a
        nation which stands for "liberty and justice for all." In order to live up to
        those words, in order to bury institutional racism once and for all, America
        must do far more then remove statues of Confederate Generals who fought
        to preserve slavery. Changes in the law of the land will be needed-
To combat injustice engrained and deep-seated.

Congress must reinstate the preclearance provision of the 1965 Voting Rights Act,
    requiring states with a proven history and pattern of targeting minorities for voter
    suppression, to once again obtain "preclearance" from the Justice Department
    before implementing changes to their voting laws and procedures. Congress must
    also pass legislation prohibiting partisan voting district gerrymandering intended to
    dilute the voting power of minorities. Until such safeguards are put in place,
    systemic voter suppression personified by Jim Crow, will continue to rear its
    ugly head-
From the depths of hell like the walking dead.
And moral outrage will continue on-
And the ethical stone-age, on and on.

Yad Vashem is Israel's memorial to the murdered victims of the Holocaust. In a section
    of Yad Vashem known as The Garden of the Righteous Among the Nations, the names
    of non-Jews who selflessly put their lives on the line to protect
    Jews from the genocide are honored. Among the names honored are Miep
    Gies, her husband, Jan Gies, Bep Voskuijl, Victor Kugler, and Johannes
    Kleiman, all of whom worked together to protect Anne Frank and her family
    while they were in hiding in Amsterdam from the Nazis. Also honored in
    the Garden is Raul Wallenberg, the Swedish Diplomat who saved tens
    of thousands of Hungarian Jews from the Nazi gas chambers and crematoria.
    He did so by issuing them protective passes and by sheltering them in
    buildings within Hungary which he designated as neutral Swedish territory.

In the years to come, Americans will choose who they wish to be. Will
    they be swayed by the cynical, racist tropes of demagogues intent upon
    stoking hatred and division by appealing to age old racial resentments
    and grievances? Or, will they choose a path inspired by the one located in
    Yad Vashem's Garden of the Righteous Among the Nations- a path which
    honors and embraces those who exemplified courage, righteousness, and
    tolerance toward all people, regardless of race, religion, gender, or class? If
    the American people are courageous enough, and righteous enough, and
    tolerant enough to step toward the light and away from the darkness, they
    will reaffirm that the lives of the very best among us, the Anne Frank's and Raul
    Wallenberg's of this world, were not lost in vain; And that the humanity
    they displayed and the example they set, will not be forgotten, and won't be
    erased from the human heart.

GRINDING IT OUT AS AN APD

(Personal History)

Thirty-one years as a Public Defender-
At times I was mocked as a "Public Pretender"-
By clients who thought they got what they paid for:
If little was charged than little was paid for.

So many were dealt a weak losing hand-
Abused by their parents, punished and tanned.
Raised in poverty as kids without dads-
Meagerly fed and shabbily clad.

Parents on drugs who left them neglected-
And left them feeling completely rejected.
As they grew into teens, they felt disrespected-
While turning to drugs, they felt disaffected.

Remaining in school was seen as uncool.
They felt disconnected so school was rejected.
As they dropped out of school, their future was shot.
Some made a living, others could not.

Racial profiling was alive and well-
Unfounded stops with a fishy smell;
Excessive force and harassment as well.

Motions to Suppress were the means to fight back-
Crossing the cops with a plan of attack-
Again and again to develop the knack.

For thirty-one years, I worked the caseload, grinding it out-
Taking the depos, trying the cases, going all out.
Talking to clients in the office and jail-
Putting them in for reductions of bail-
"Pounding the rock" and racing the clock.

One night at jail on a break between clients-
Somehow there seemed an unusual silence.
Inmates battled in a fierce game of chess-
I followed the game I readily confess.
Perhaps in the moment it broke all the stress:
A vacation was needed is all I can guess!

The duty owed by attorney to client-
Whether easy to manage or mostly defiant-
Representation unfailingly zealous-
The duty that drives us and always compels us:
To champion their cause and fight without fail-
Fight for them always, but don't go to jail!

In one of my trials in which we prevailed-
I was the one left looking at jail.
The trial was delayed no more than a day-
To transport a witness from miles away.

Upon his arrival his story had changed-
He behaved like a person completely deranged.
If called as a witness, just as I'd planned-
He'd lie on my client, right from the stand.

In light of the change, the sheer double-cross-
His value to us was hopelessly lost.
The Judge was convinced I'd falsely delayed-
He refused to believe the words I conveyed.
He'd consider contempt when the verdict was in-
And perhaps lock me up in the Jailhouse Inn.

Attempted Murder in the Second Degree-
The verdict came back and my client was free!
While happy my client had beaten the rap-
I was the one now facing the rap.
Played by the witness like a double-crossed sap.

Our Chief Trial Director provided support-
In regard to my hearing for Contempt of Court.
My investigator verified the "stab in the back"-
So I too beat the bogus rap!
Instead of a one-way ticket to dine as a jailhouse sinner-
I joined our Trial Director and Boss for a barbeque dinner!

Surrounded by colleagues who believed in the Mission-
They fought for our clients no thought of submission.
I learned from them all and I owe them a debt-
The best group of people I ever met.

While learning the ropes as I started out-
I found myself filled with many a doubt.
An old friend counseled when my future seemed blurred-
Clearing my path with the following words:
"Public Defender service is like working in the Peace Corp,
        'The hardest job you'll ever love.'"
So here's to my friend who's in heaven above.

At the end of the day if I'd just walked away,
        it would have been kind of like falling-
For the privilege of working in the Office I loved,
        became my life and my calling.

LAKE WORTH PIER
(Personal History)

I like to visit the old Lake Worth Pier.
It's far away, but in my heart it's near.
The surfers hang-ten, and the fishermen eye
     where the pelicans dive-
To help their fishing to thrive!

Return to the land of the sand and sea-
So much joy, the place to be.
A scene of pure festivity.
Swimming and music, catching some rays-
So much fun and so much play-
And people out to seize the day!

Gazing upon the beauty of the sea-
Its power and its sweeping enormity-
For a time, one feels trouble-free-
Realizing that what will be, will be.

And when I walk out to the end of the pier-
Visions of those I've loved and lost, they appear:
And give me a smile-
Say stay for a while-
So nice you could be here-
Back on your home-town pier.

I think about Dad
And the walks that we had.
And once more, he's alive as before-
With his love and rapport-
And we walk it once more.

The old pier, a kind of promised land-
Where old friends graced the sea and sand.
The pier that stands above the sea-
Where Dad spoke words to guide me:
To teach me to soar, and lead me to shore.

When life brings us to our knees-
It is a symbol of strength for us to see.
It has weathered storms, been battered and repaired
       but never broken;
Withstood the test of time-
Like a mighty keepsake that shines.

And when it's time for me to leave-
I hear Dad's words, I do believe:
Don't stay away, come back for a stay-
Where it's A-OK!
Don't steer clear, come back to this pier.

Drop by now and then-
You *can* come home again.
And we'll watch the surfers hangin' ten.

FATE, DESTINY, OR SIMPLY LUCK
(Personal History)

To this day, my thoughts about it run amok.
Was it fate, destiny, or simply luck?
My friend was nine years old, and I was but eight-
That cold winter morning we tempted our fate.
The weekend was upon us, we just couldn't wait.
We got up quite early, and beelined toward our favorite lake.

We were tempted by an old wooden rowboat moored to the shore.
We climbed aboard, unmoored the boat, and rowed away from shore.
Something we'd never tried before-
Like mariners, setting off to explore!

Techniques for rowing were surely ignored:
Like learning the method to paddle with oars;
Balancing weight on both sides of the boat-
Ensuring that rowboat was staying afloat.

Suddenly, in an instant, the rowboat flipped!
We fell in the water so poorly equipped.
My friend swam his way to the safety of shore-
But I was in trouble as never before.

Wearing no life jacket- my heavy winter coat, lengthy blue
     jeans and sneakers, all waterlogged, were
      weighing me down.
I treaded water, desperately fighting not to drown.

The water was cold and heavy, murky and dark-
Within the quiet of that empty park.
For a moment, as I struggled to remain afloat-
My chance for survival seemed remote.

My friend cried out for help, but no one was there.
Suddenly, an old man appeared out of thin air!
He threw off his jacket, swam to my rescue, and towed
  me to shore.
I will be thankful forevermore.

But I never thanked him, though I owed him my life.
After making quite sure that I was alright-
He walked away like a gallant knight.
He disappeared from my line of sight-
There was never a chance to reunite.

I didn't know his name, nor where he lived.
Our contact was fleeting, so very short-lived.
As I treaded water above death's door-
He saved my life, then disappeared forevermore.

As a kid, I sometimes wondered-
Who was that masked man, that Lone Ranger-
That total stranger-
Who saved my life and then was gone-
Like Superman, who came to earth from planet Krypton.

I've gone on to live a charmed life-
Blessed by my son and my beautiful wife.
For 31 years, I tried to improve the lot of others as a
  Public Defender-
Regardless of race and regardless of gender.

My son played intercollegiate tennis for a great University.
Now he's studying law, and standing up to all adversity.
For him, a wonderful life is clearly in store-
Of this I am certain, entirely sure.

I think of all he's achieved, and all he'll become,
  and the blessing of his very existence.
And I hope that on my better days, some have gained
  from my assistance.
So thoughts and questions still arise, and nag with real persistence.

I recall my almost fatal mistakes-
And those dreadful moments in the murky lake.
My future son's destiny, the lives I might touch,
        all was at stake:
Hanging in the balance in my early youth-
In a dicey and desperate Moment of Truth.

And I think of my friend, with his presence of mind
        in his early youth-
Who delivered me help in that Moment of Truth.
He cried out for help and he saved my life-
That I might meet my future wife.

But what if my anonymous guardian angel, had not been
        around to fearlessly tread-
To keep me alive and away from the dead-
While destiny hung by a slender thread?

Why was he there in the critical moment-
To answer the call in his act of bestowment?
Was it fate, destiny, or nothing but chance?
The truth eludes me, I have no answers, no definite stance.

For truth lies in the eye of the beholder-
But clearly my fate was upon his shoulders.
But for him, I had no future, no destiny, and
        no destiny for my son.
He salvaged it all, he was the one.

So here's to your soul my Superman-
My eternal thanks for your helping hand.

THE GAME THAT NEVER STOPPED GIVING
(Personal History)

When I was a kid one summer day-
The wind was blowing and the sky dark gray.
But in my mind's eye it was the sunniest of days-
Under a magical rainbow, many years ago.

As I looked across the net, hitting his shots in
     business shoes and argyle socks-
There stood Dad. Boy did he rock!

On that carefree day with Dad, he taught me
     as he taught himself to play;
And he taught me the meaning of fair play-
A code from which to never stray.

The years passed, and I squared off against
     competitors across the net.
What lasts? The memory of friends and rivals I met.
And my affection for them all, and deep respect.

And to my amazement the game I adored-
Unlocked and opened an unlikely door-
Where a Swarthmore education was in store.

While I was a young lad at S'more, I looked across the net-
And saw a beautiful girl who I'd never met.
I stood for a time and watched her play-
The girl I was blessed to marry one day.

When I was middle-aged, I looked across the net to see-
My precious little boy hitting tennis balls at me.
It was a joyful day to a degree that words cannot convey.

Never would I have dreamed beforehand-
That he'd develop a sledge-hammer forehand-
Which unlocked and opened a faraway door-
Where a UNCG education was in store.
My wife and I are blessed that he played the sport-
Which turned him into a champ on and off the court.

Many years have passed and I am older now.
But due to the conditioning demands of the game,
       perhaps 60 is the new forty somehow.

Looking back through the years-
A simple fact is crystal clear:
Every dream I've dreamed, every door that's opened,
       all that I've loved, is tied to that day
When the wind was blowing and the sky dark gray.

But in my mind's eye it was the sunniest of days-
When "dear old Dad" taught me to play-
The Beloved Game-
Under a magical rainbow, long, long ago.

REACHING BACK FOR GRANDPA JOHN
(Personal History)

I was thirteen years old when he passed away-
I miss him so much to this very day.
When he died, so much was lost-
His love, his laughter, and the knowledge of my roots,
    such a painful and priceless cost.

Each year from the time I was a young child, he traveled
    from the Bronx to Lake Worth by way of train-
He hated to fly, so he never visited by plane.
He'd hop off the train in his hat and his snappy yellow suit.
I'd spot him waving and smiling. He was the most delightful hoot!

To celebrate his arrival, Grandpa, my folks, and I headed directly to H. J.'s
    as I laughed and beamed-
While looking forward to my scrumptious ice cream supreme!
Sometimes we'd feed popcorn to seagulls up at the ocean-
As the gulls gathered and screeched, while hopping in great commotion.

He always made sure he returned to N.Y. with a Florida tan. It wasn't hard.
All it took was a little sunbathing while making me laugh in our backyard.
He always threw in the story about limburger cheese and how it stinks!
I'd laugh as he held his nose and gave me a wink!

Grandpa, Dad, and I made trips to the ballpark to see the West Palm Beach Braves.
While the team and the old ballpark are long gone, those were times of joy which my
    memory has forever saved.

So little I knew at the time that he passed-
So much do I yearn to go back and ask.
He loved the Yankees and he saw the greats, from the earliest to the latest:
Ruth, Gehrig, DiMaggio, Berra, Mantle and Marris; Oh that I could ask him
    who he rated as the very greatest!

He loved tennis. Did he see Bill Tilden, Bill Johnston, the Four Musketeers,
      Don Budge, Fred Perry, Ellsworth Vines, Bobby Riggs, Jack Kramer, Pancho
      Gonzalez, Pancho Segura, Althea Gibson, Maureen Connolly, Tony
      Trabert, Ken Rosewall, Lew Hoad, Rod Laver, or Billie Jean King battle at
      Forest Hills?
And which matches gave him the greatest of thrills?

He loved and admired the great Joe Louis, and he followed each of his fights.
What was it like listening on radio to Joe Louis knocking out Max Schmeling, while
      landing a blow against Hitler in Yankee Stadium that night?
Did Grandpa follow the triumphs of Jesse Owens in Berlin in 1936 as he
      won four gold medals-
Blowing away the myth of Aryan Supremacy that Hitler peddled?

Born in 1900 of Irish Roots, he grew up in the Bronx. How was he affected
      by a legacy of signs that read, "No Irish Need Apply?"
What prejudices did he face, and what opportunities passed him by?
Why the name- change from McGinnis to Mack?
Did Grandpa or his dad feel that the name, McGinnis, was holding them back?

What was it like for Grandpa and his loving wife, Rose, raising Dad through
      the Great Depression?
How difficult were the times and struggle, and what were his lasting impressions?

How did he cope in 1940 when his beloved Rose passed away?
How did he and Dad endure the sadness and get through the day?
What was it like raising Dad, his only child and the apple of his eye, on his own-
On a bank teller's salary, 'til Dad was full grown?
How did he cope in 1945 when Dad enlisted in the service?
How alone did he feel, and how sad and how nervous?

Grandpa's dad, Edward, was born in New York City in 1861.
Which leads me to believe that Grandpa's grandpa was my ancestor
      who escaped the Irish potato famine on a ship setting sail-
For America, the land of milk and honey, to succeed or to fail.
But who was Grandpa's grandpa who sailed from Ireland so long ago-
I never asked him and I so wish to know.

Grandpa John passed on to Dad something akin to a priceless baton-
Inscribed with a message to never stop reaching for his dreams, and to carry on.
Dad passed it on to me. I in turn passed it on to Danny, my son.
I wonder who passed it on to Grandpa John- was his dad, Edward, the One?
I suspect that the baton was first set in motion-
By the man with the Dream who sailed from Ireland and crossed the ocean.

When Grandpa John died, so much was lost-
His love, his laughter, and the knowledge of my roots,
      such a painful and priceless cost.
So little I knew at the time that he passed-
So much do I long to go back and ask.

MY ENCHANTED FOREST
(Personal history)

It was an Enchanted Forest from my distant past-
The kind of place that forever lasts-
Close to one's heart and deep in one's mind-
And deep in one's memory, forever enshrined.

I was a child aged six through ten-
I thought it would last forever back then.
The woods were located in Lake Worth, Florida,
  where I grew up-
I'd visit often, soon after sun-up.

They were located parallel to Lake Osborne, on the
  other side of the street-
And close to my home, just down the street-
The woods where us kids would excitedly meet.

The woods were beautiful and foreboding-
Which intensified our desire for knowing-
Their many secrets and rumored lore-
Stories we'd heard quite often before.

Just beyond the beautiful Lantana located at the entrance
  to the woods-
Was a long and winding pathway cutting deep into the woods.
The path opened a gateway to explore- all to the good!

Rumor had it that unfriendly "Teenagers" sometimes occupied an
  old deserted tree-fort, midway down the path.
We feared our being spotted, and incurring someone's wrath.
So we never dared to dawdle, we quickly walked on by-
All the while we dreaded, hidden evil eyes!

As we forged on deeper into the woods-
Resolved to keep on going, but wondering if we should-
Another danger filled our minds we peered around each tree-
For a threat that we had heard of, but one we'd yet to see.

Legend held that a "Bobcat" prowled within the deeper grounds.
We lowered our voices and froze in place, listening for the
      slightest sound.
At times we sensed a danger, stalking us from behind a bush.
We'd tell each other quiet down and hurry up and Shush!
Had we spied a fearsome Lynx, we simply couldn't say-
Perhaps we were in jeopardy of falling Bobcat prey!

Right across from the woods and just above the street
      where I lived, stood a deserted rickety two-story house-
The "Haunted House on the Hill!"
An ominous thrill which filled me with chills!

When temptation grew too strong, we crawled our way inside.
Through layers of dust and spider webs, above us, below us,
      and to our sides.
We began exploring while wishing to hide-
We stayed together, side by side-
Praying we'd make it, out alive!

As I recall in my mind's eye- the floors squeaked,
      the stairs creaked, shutters slammed,
        furniture shifted, forks floated, our blood curdled,
        shadows were cast, footsteps were heard-
And we came within inches of being interred!

On those occasions when we pressed on deeper into the woods, the
      very end of the path led to "The Old Car." It was located
      twenty yards back from the road which separated the woods
      from the lake.
I was frightened by that beat-up, damaged old car, make
      no mistake!

Discretion being the better part of valor-
My drive to explore it always soured!
For reasons that may seem inexplicable or vague-
I avoided "The Old Car" like a deadly plague.

Getting down to the nitty-gritty-
My uneasiness was intensified by the fact that it remained there
      for years on end, without being claimed by person or City.

On a weekend morning when I was ten-
Or somewhere close, right about then-
We began building a fort near the pathway into the woods. Doing
      so necessitated our cutting down a smaller pine.
We believed that doing so was perfectly fine.

We were approached by two disgruntled neighbors who
      threatened to call the police if we took another whack on that tree.
We stopped, looked at each other, and all agreed-
To abandon our mission, to let it be.

Sometime later that year, an important City Commission Hearing was held.
      The commissioners voted to enter into a construction contract which
      resulted in the total destruction of the woods to be replaced by retirement
      apartments, The Lakeside Point Gardens.
No one ever said to us kids, "We're sorry about bulldozing the woods, we
      beg your pardon!"

My friends and I were devastated as we watched our beloved woods disappear
      before our eyes.
I, for one, walked away, entered my home, and "cried me a river" while
      wondering, "Why?"

Looking back upon that terrible deed, I often wondered whether
      the neighbors who'd complained about us kids chopping on
      that single tree-
Showed up at the City Commission Hearing to voice their objections to the
      complete destruction of the woods, by zealously asserting,
      We Don't Agree!
Perhaps they did so, addressing an outrage they couldn't ignore.
But deep in my heart I'm not so sure.

The woods were the glue that bound my neighborhood friends
     and me together.
When they vanished, we were no longer quite the birds of a feather.
We slowly began to drift apart-
Not abruptly, but in bits and starts.

Eventually, each of us went our separate ways.
Some of us simply moved away.
For those of us who happened to stay-
It was never the same as in previous days.

It made me sad the loss of those days-
But sooner or later, we had to grow up and find
     our own way.
I've made many new friends along the way.
Still, looking back over the years, few moments have
     filled me with greater happiness than those carefree
     days hanging out with my childhood band of
     sisters and brothers-
Exploring the Enchanted Forest, and looking out for one another.

PLANET BETRAYED
(Historical Non-Fiction Essay)

I walk alone within the crowded city-
Upon the scorching streets of cracked cement-
Taking in my nature-stripped surroundings-
A world we all may one day soon lament.

For miles around the buildings scrape the sky.
Smoke stacks belch their waste into the air-
Emitting fumes of toxic clouds of smog-
Which burn our throats and cause our eyes to tear.

The burning of fossil fuels and carbon emissions trap the heat.
In an endless, poisonous cycle- rinse, repeat.
Air pollution, climate change, and environmental decay-
Are denied, ignored, or written off as a fated price to pay-
For the acquisition of enormous wealth-
At the planet's expense and our people's health.

Must a global warming doomsday, be the price our kids must pay-
For money and greed and profit, and our planet's health betrayed?

TIME TRAVELING
(Personal History)

I've yearned to engage in travel through time-
Back to the past to stop on a dime.
At least as pleasant as a perfect tea-time-
Perhaps something more, something sublime.

Reaching back for a time in my past-
To a moment and place that's beyond my grasp.
Shrinking the distance to a stone's throw away-
Back through the years not a moment's delay!

Mom, Dad, Rusty the cocker spaniel and I,
    moved to Florida when I was but four.
We've returned only twice I'm practically sure.
I find myself longing for past days of yore.
New York draws me as never before.

My New York relatives who remained behind-
Are firmly entrenched so deep in my mind.
Due to the dictates of Father Time- Mom, Dad, Grandpa John
    and Grandma Rose, Grandpa Hymie and Grandma Bessie,
    Uncle Gershon and Cousin Mark, Uncle Sidney, Aunt May
    and Uncle Bill, have passed away.
I wish to go back and connect in some way-
Connect with them all on a beautiful day.
Wishing to know what came before-
There must be a key to unlock the door.

I've yearned to engage in a flight of time travel-
With a judge's conviction when striking his gavel!
Before my old memories dim and unravel-
Backward through time with some huge razzle-dazzle!

Backward through time while in search of my roots-
In tattered old clothes or a pin-striped suit.
Slung from a slingshot, landing on Wall Street
      right on a dime!
And spotting my dad in the midst of his prime.

Like a fly on a wall, I watched him toil through his whole
      working day-
Grinding it out and earning his pay.
Tracing his path on his drive home to Yonkers-
As he listened to Chopin his working day conquered.

I watched the greeting at the wide-open door-
Of the house we moved from when I was but four.
Dad hugged Mom who he truly adored-
While Rusty, our doggie, leaped from the floor!

We took a stroll down Kathwood Road-
It gave Dad a chance to relax and unload.
Laughter was intermixed with chat-
While Rusty was eyed by the neighborhood cat!
And time stood still on Kathwood Road-
For a walk such as that could never grow old.

My thoughts turned to my Grandpa John-
A man for whom I've always been fond.
I dropped on a dime in front of his place.
Where he'd lived in the Bronx on old Phelan Place.
We perused ancient family photographs-
As he pinpointed faces while making me laugh.

Grandpa John's grandfather, I believed, was my blood line
      ancestor on Dad's side of my family tree-
Who escaped the Irish Potato Famine on a ship which
      sailed on the wide- open sea.
I asked, who was that ancestor of our family tree-
At last, a name was provided to me.

The others I've listed who'd passed away-
I yearned to know them somehow in some way.
People so dear who we long left behind-
Who'd remained in my heart and deep in my mind.

Out of the blue a thought came to mind-
A tea-party in Central Park would be so sublime!
In the twinkling of an eye in a mysterious way-
They appeared together without delay-
On a beautiful, blissful, and magical day.
We strolled to the middle of Central Park-
As ducks were scattered by Rusty's bark.

To those who know me, it's not a mystery-
I've long had a love of American History.
So I asked about living through two World Wars
        and the Great Depression;
And I wanted to hear about their impressions-
Of Babe Ruth and Lou Gehrig; Mickey Mantle and Roger Maris;
        Don Budge and Pancho Gonzalez; Jack Dempsey and
        Joe Louis; and Jackie Robinson and Joltin' Joe.
All these things I wished to know.

But I didn't ask questions for very long-
That wasn't the reason I'd come along.
I'd traveled more with my heart and less with my mind-
I'd followed my heart far back into time.

So we watched Rusty play, and picnicked beneath the
        brilliant blue sky-
And we portioned out the delicious blueberry pie-
While sharing laughter and sipping tea;
And for "one brief shining moment," it felt as good
        as life could be.

As I savored these moments while sipping tea-
I was filled with a dream that came over me.
When I returned to the present, to the land of the living-
I'd set aside doubts and any misgivings.
I'd seek out my relatives from long ago-
Who I'd kept in my heart and so wished to know.

Aunt Lila, Aunt Ellen, and each of my cousins: Iris, Gary, Amy,
       Ayala and Paul- I'd search for them all;
And tell them I love them, one and all.

Upon awakening from my dream, I spent some final
       moments in Central Park with those family members
       who had passed-
Wishing the moment would forever last.

But all good things must come to an end-
In a New York minute my Now became Then.
I was transported back to the present, though I'm
       not sure how and I'm not sure when.

Things are not always as they seem-
Was my time travel real or only a dream?
My heart says it was real and mustn't be ignored-
For I'm connected to my family from the past and
       present as never before.

My mind is skeptical, it has its doubts-
For the identity of my blood line ancestor eludes
       my memory, it's blotted out.

As I mulled it over while sipping tea-
That "brief shining moment" returned to me.
That felt as good as life could be.

So I'll trust in my heart to the end of my time-
And I'll choose to believe in something sublime.

STOLEN HOMES AND DESPERATE JOURNEYS
(Historical Fiction)

In 1839, fourteen-year-old Nokomo Summerhill lived in a wooden house with his Cherokee family in New Echota, the capitol of the Cherokee Nation in western Georgia. The site was located at the junction of the Coosawattee and the Conasauga Rivers. Like many Cherokee families of the time, Nokomo's parents owned a family of black people as slaves. While it was taboo, Nokomo had, in recent months, formed a close friendship with one of those slaves, fourteen- year-old Jamar Johnson. Jamar lived in the small wooden slave quarters with his fifteen-year-old sister, Tanisha, and their parents and grandparents.

Nokomo saw Jamar and his family as people, not slaves. For months after Jamar had toiled away in the field along with his sister, parents, and grandparents, he and Nokomo began hanging out late at night by the woods and river after the others were fast asleep. They talked and laughed, engaged in foot races, fished from the river shore, and occasionally took Nokomo's family's canoe out onto the river. When a full moon lit up the night, Nokomo began teaching Jamar to read. He confided in Jamar that he had a crush on his sister, Tanisha, who he worshipped from afar.

One summer evening upon returning from a canoe ride up the river, Nokomo and Jamar began walking back in the pitch dark toward Nokomo's house and Jamar's slave quarters. Suddenly, when they were about twenty feet from the canoe, without warning, the quiet and stillness of the night was broken by a large animal which sprang out of the woods! It was a panther! In an instant, the big cat knocked Nakomo over, bit onto his left arm, and began dragging him toward the woods! Jamar immediately and repeatedly punched the panther on its head in an effort to force it to release its mouth from Nokomo's arm! The cat released its bite and attacked Jamar, knocking him over! It sank its claws deeply into both sides of his chest as he shielded his face by crossing his arms. Nokomo ran over to the canoe, picked up an oar, ran back over, and with all the strength he could muster given his wounded arm, struck the panther across the back! The panther immediately released Jamar and ran off into the woods. Nokomo ran for help.

When Nokomo arrived back home yelling for help, his mother immediately wrapped a tourniquet around his injured arm to stop the bleeding. He then led both sets of parents, Jamar's grandparents, and Tanisha to the spot where Jamar remained lying on his back. Jamar's mom wrapped his chest with bandages to stop the bleeding. Tanisha leaned over her brother, smiled, and softly whispered "Don't worry, Jamar, you're gonna be ok." There was something about his big sister's reassuring words and smile that comforted him and allayed his fears, as they always had before.

After they all arrived back home, the boys thanked their moms for dressing their wounds. Nokomo told his mom that he hoped to one day study medicine to help others. The next day, both boys were seen by a doctor. Nokomo received stitches to his injured arm. Jamar received stitches to both sides of his chest. While each of the boys fully recovered, Jamar was left doubly and vertically scarred on both sides of his chest.

A few days after Nokomo's arm was stitched up, his father said to him, "Nokomo, you had no business hanging out with Jamar. He is a slave boy."

"Father, Jamar got mauled while coming to my rescue. He repeatedly punched the panther on its head at a time it was dragging me off toward the woods. He saved my life, Father." Nokomo pleaded with both of his parents to allow him to continue being friends with Jamar, and to hang out with him for a time after the day's labor was done.

Nokomo's mother opposed slavery. It had once led her to consider ending her marriage; But she was unwilling to risk losing her son. This time, however, she spoke up and persuaded her husband, however reluctantly, into acceding to Nokomo's request, provided that it did not interfere with Jamar's daily output of slave labor.

The boys were thrilled that they would be able to continue on with their friendship. Having saved each other's lives, they viewed themselves as blood brothers for life; But their time together would not last much longer.

While Jamar was still bedridden to keep from loosening up his numerous chest stitches, his parents, grandparents, Tanisha, and Nakomo took turns keeping him company as much as they could. His grandparents liked to teach him Bible stories. On one occasion, his grandmother said, "Jamar, Moses led the Jewish people out of slavery in Egypt. Eventually, he led them to the Promised Land, to the land of milk and honey. Someday, our people will be freed as well. No matter how badly white people, Indians, or anyone else treats you, don't ever allow anyone to make you feel like a slave inside of your mind or your heart. Everyone is equal in God's eyes." His parents taught him the Golden Rule and other lessons from Jesus. "Jamar, his dad asserted, slavery is an ungodly, man-made evil. All people are equal before the eyes of the Lord, regardless of their skin color and regardless of their riches or station in life." Often, Tanisha added, "That 'equal' thing includes girls as well as boys! And just to prove it, I'm gonna whip you in a footrace just as soon as you are healed up!" That challenge never failed to cause a big grin to appear upon Jamar's face.

One evening after Jamar's stitches were removed and after he had regained his full strength, he confided in Nokomo a secret that he was not to share with another soul. Jamar related that he and his family were planning an escape during the darkness and cover of night. They were intending to head north toward freedom. Jamar asked Nokomo to do a couple of things to assist in the escape. Nokomo agreed to do so. He snuck some supplies into the slave quarters which Jamar and his family could take with them as they began their journey. In addition, on the evening of the planned escape, Nokomo checked to make sure that his parents were fast asleep. Just before Jamar and his family set off into the dark, he and Nokomo embraced, promising each other that no matter how long it took, they would one day find each other and renew their friendship.

Not long after the escape, Nokomo and his family received devastating news. They were to be forcibly removed from their home and their land by the federal government pursuant to the Indian Removal Act. They were to be relocated to the Oklahoma Indian Territory west of the Mississippi River. Thus began their arduous and deadly thousand-mile trek, accompanied by other Southeastern Native Americans being relocated as well, along the Trail of Tears.

Nokomo, his parents, and the other Native Americans travelling with them, suffered from exposure to the elements as well as malnutrition due to the meager rations that were provided. After a while, sheer exhaustion set in as they marched endlessly onward wearing worn-out shoes and scant clothing to protect them from the bone chilling cold, made worse by the howling winds. Flu, typhus, and dysentery set in among the large number of those being forcibly removed. Over time, Nokomo's parents grew weaker and sicker. Nokomo, often light-headed himself from the near starvation conditions, begged those who were fitter to help along his parents. Thankfully, many who were healthy enough to do so took turns answering the call.

At the same time that Nokomo and his parents were suffering through hardships on the Trail of Tears, Jamar and his family were desperately fleeing north by means of the Underground Railroad. They were taught by "conductors" to travel mostly at night while following the North Star. They were instructed to look for safe houses along the way, where they would be welcomed by other abolitionist "conductors" who would offer a warm meal and a decent night's lodging out of the elements. The safehouses could be identified by a candle in the window. Fleeing slaves and conductors were to identify each other through the words, "Friend of a friend." Jamar and his family counted upon those safehouses to provide desperately needed respites from the elements and from the ever-present dread of being caught!

Jamar and his family experienced many close shaves along the way. Before they left Georgia, Tanisha almost leaned right into a hornet's nest which was located on a tree branch against which she was resting. Jamar spotted the nest, grabbed his sister, and pulled her out of harm's way! In South Carolina, Jamar's grandparents, walking side by side, came within a few feet of stepping on a rattler! Tanisha grabbed each of them by an arm and pulled them away at the last second! On a number of occasions as the family plodded through swampy areas in North Carolina, they spotted treacherous looking gators peering at them with greedy eyes without twitching a muscle. The gators were far too close for comfort!

As they forged ahead into Virginia and then on into Maryland, it wasn't hornets, rattlers, or gators that did them in. It was the bloodhounds! Maryland was crawling with slave catchers utilizing bloodhounds to track slaves who were attempting to reach the free state of Pennsylvania. As Jamar and his family headed in the direction of a Maryland safehouse, they heard bloodhounds barking! Even as they beelined toward the safehouse as fast as their feet would carry them, the incessant barking of the bloodhounds grew louder, and louder, and louder! And then, suddenly, they heard the command, "Hands up, don't move!"

Four months after their thousand- mile journey through wilderness and mountain ranges began, Nokomo and his parents made it to the Oklahoma Indian Territory alive! Nokomo felt blessed and thankful that his parents had pulled through and survived the journey. Many others were not so fortunate. About four thousand Cherokee perished from disease, starvation, the freezing temperatures, and exhaustion along the Trail of Tears. At the end of the day, Cherokee, Creek, Chickasaw, Choctow, and Seminoles were "ethnically cleansed" from their native lands and homes in the southeastern United States. Their forced removal by the government was prompted to a large extent by greed for their arable land, and for gold. In the case of the Cherokee, gold had been discovered on their land near Dahlonega, Ga. In short, the government wanted the Cherokee out of the way.

Immediately following their capture, Jamar and his family were marched by the slave catchers into a Maryland public auction in chains. Jamar watched helplessly as his parents, grandparents, and Tanisha were inspected for the quality of their muscle tone and teeth, and then split up like cattle to be sold to different slave owners. As they were marched out of his presence one by one, Jamar had no idea whether or not he was gazing upon each of his loved ones for the very last time.

Jamar was sold and transported to a Virginia plantation where he lived under a cruel master. For the next eleven years of his life, from 1840–51, he was worked to the bone picking cotton while enduring beatings and whippings at the pleasure of the master's sadistic whims and impulses. During this time in hell, Jamar coped by reflecting upon the stories his grandparents and parents had taught him about Moses and Jesus, and about how all people were equal in God's Eyes. Despite the steady diet of inhumane and cruel treatment which he was forced to endure, his spirit remained unbroken! He never stopped thinking about escape, and he never stopped dreaming about one day reuniting with his loving family.

During that same eleven-year span from 1840–51, Nakomo and his parents learned to endure the hardships of living on the Oklahoma Indian Reservation. Land on the Reservation west of the Mississippi was largely unsuitable for the regular farming practices of the southeastern part of the country, including Ga. Farming on the Reservation required expertise such as the implementation of complex irrigation systems. This was specialized knowledge that Nakomo and his parents, and most Cherokee, did not have. There were many other hardships as well. Disease spread rapidly on the Reservation. There were also threats imposed from hostile tribes that were in the area from time to time.

In 1851, Jamar decided once and for all that he was going to escape the cursed slave plantation or die trying! He devised a plan which relied upon the assistance of a number of other slaves in whom he trusted. The master had recently purchased a mare for his eight-year-old daughter as a birthday present. He planned to provide her with horseback riding lessons. The mare was kept in a stable on the west side of the plantation, the same side on which Jamar was assigned to pick cotton. Each day around 5:00 p.m., there was a shift change between plantation overseers. The overseers routinely met out in front of the master's house to exchange notes about the work of the various slaves. On the day Jamar planned for his escape, shortly after the overseers began conferring, six slaves on the east side of the plantation broke into a feigned fight. As the overseers' attention was drawn to the melee, Jamar stealthily crawled west through the field of six-foot-high cotton stems. He then entered the stable, mounted the mare, and galloped off toward the woods to the north of the stable without looking back! One of the overseers spotted him and opened fire! One of the bullets creased Jamar's left arm. Despite losing some blood, he made his escape. He rode on about seven miles until he recognized a safehouse by the candle in the window. The safehouse conductor and abolitionist, Jane Fryer, dressed Jamar's wound. She then served him a nourishing hot meal of meatloaf and potatoes and a salad. While Jamar was eating, Jane asked where he was headed. Jamar responded, "To freedom in the free state of Pennsylvania."

"Jamar, Ms. Fryer stated, The Fugitive Slave Act of 1850 was passed by Congress last year with the approval of President Millard Fillmore. The law authorizes slave catchers to capture any and all escaped slaves and return them to their former masters, even if they are captured in a free state. The law also greatly ups the penalties for assisting or harboring slaves. Abolitionists have nicknamed it the Bloodhound Law after the dogs utilized by slave catchers to track escaped slaves anywhere in the country. As a result of this notorious law, Jamar, escaped slaves like you will no longer be relatively safe upon reaching a free state such as Pennsylvania. To reach the Promised Land, you must now follow the North Star all the way into Canada. In contrast to America, the moral cesspool of slavery was abolished in Canada back in 1834. Canada is welcoming escaped slaves from America."

Even as Ms. Fryer explained the need for Jamar to greatly increase the length of his journey, she recognized that due to his recent injury as well as his compromised condition attributable to years of physical abuse suffered upon the slave plantation, he lacked the physical strength and stamina to endure such a formidable journey on foot. So after Jamar thanked her for the fine meal and retired for a good night's sleep, Ms. Fryer thought long and hard and came up with an idea to assist him in reaching Canada. She remembered that in 1849, another slave, Henry "Box" Brown, had successfully escaped from Virginia into Pennsylvania by arranging to have himself placed by friends into a wooden crate and "mailed" by way of train to abolitionists in Philadelphia. Over the course of the next day or so, Ms. Fryer got word to a number of fellow abolitionists who devised a similar plan to ship Jamar aboard a steam locomotive to Philadelphia while hidden inside a wooden crate containing air holes. The crate would be accompanied by an undercover abolitionist. Upon arrival in Philadelphia, Jamar would be removed from the crate. He would then travel by means of a series of stagecoaches and wagons headed for upstate New York to the Niagara River. From there, he would board a ferry and cross the river into Canada, the Promised Land of freedom!

Once the plan was arranged, it was set into motion immediately. Jamar's crated journey aboard the steam locomotive to Philadelphia, went according to plan. He then made it safely into New York while hidden under straw and wares in a wagon driven by David James, a "conductor." The trouble began after he reached upstate New York. While travelling by wagon on a moonlit night, David suddenly spotted a group of men blocking the path a couple of hundred yards up ahead! David immediately warned Jamar telling him to jump off the back of the wagon and head for a safehouse about five miles away. Jamar did so just in the nick of time! The men up ahead turned out to be a group of ruthless slave catchers ready to seize their prey. Instead, they searched a wagon which contained only an empty wooden crate and supplies.

The next morning, David made his way to the safehouse and picked up Jamar. They journeyed on toward the Niagara River. When they got within a few miles of the river, David stopped the wagon. He advised Jamar to get inside the empty wooden crate which David would nail shut. Jamar was reluctant to get crated a second time! David explained that since the passage of the Fugitive Slave of 1850, the slave catchers were well aware that many slaves were heading for freedom in Canada. David suspected that the banks of the Niagara River would be crawling with slave catchers ready to seize slaves by gunpoint and place them into chains. That was all the convincing Jamar needed! He followed David's advice and climbed inside the wooden crate.

Sure enough, the banks of the Niagara River were crawling with slave catchers! As they intensely eyed the lengthy banks of the river like birds of prey ready to swoop down and strike, David calmly enlisted help in carrying the wooden "supply" crate onto the local ferry. Very shortly after the ferry began its crossing, two slave catchers yelled for the ferry operator to turn back so they could check the crate! They yelled to the operator that there was some money in it for him. As the ferry operator began to slow down in preparation for turning back, David pulled out a revolver, stuck it in the operator's side, and said, "Don't say a word. Just keep going straight ahead!"

The ferry made its way across the river into Canada. Upon reaching the Canadian shoreline, David opened up the crate. Jamar climbed out of the crate and for the first time in his life, stepped onto soil as a free man!

Over the course of the next eight years, from 1852–60, Jamar utilized his skills as a blacksmith to earn a living in Canada. He loved the dignity of working for wages and of experiencing self-sufficiency. He also loved the Canadian people who viewed him as a human being as opposed to an item of chattel to be enslaved, humiliated, and exploited. Canada offered the liberty and dignity that had been unavailable to him in his own country which professed to believe that "all men are created equal." And yet, despite the relief and joy that Jamar felt living his life as a free man in Canada, deep within him was a feeling of discontent and of regret- a terrible ache. He missed his family something awful.

Jamar had no idea whether his parents, grandparents, or sister, Tanisha, were still alive. He had no idea whether they were still suffering as slaves under the evil sadism of a master. In addition, while he loved the Canadian people, he had not yet found a woman to love. He had no children. There was no responsibility to others to keep him from moving on. These thoughts filled his mind as he heard the news that Civil War had broken out in America in 4/1861.

Many Cherokee on the Oklahoma Indian Reservation who were slaveholders or former slaveholders, joined the Confederacy when the Civil War broke out. Among those who did so was Nokomo's father. Nokomo, on the other hand, intended to join the Union Army. This decision made his father furious. Ever since that night in 1839 in Georgia when Jamar and his family escaped, Nokomo's father suspected that he had assisted in their escape. Shortly after the escape, he had confronted his son about it. Nokomo denied helping in the escape. He lied because he was afraid that the truth would cause a permanent rift with his father. He loved his father, and he feared losing his father's love. Now, twenty-two years later, his decision to join the Union Army was creating the very rift that he always dreaded. Once again, his father brought up his suspicions that he had assisted Jamar and his family in making their escape; And once again he denied doing so. His father said, "Nokomo, if you insist on following through with joining the Union Army, you are no longer my son."

Nokomo was extremely upset by his father's words. He asked his mother what he should do. She took hold of both of his hands and said, "You are your own man now. You must do what you think is right. I have never agreed with slavery. If you wish to fight on the side of the Union, you should do so. It will take time for your father to accept your decision. Perhaps as long as it takes the country to fight this war; But in time, your father will come around to accepting and respecting your decision. I will see to it that he does."

Jamar remained in Canada biding his time and staying informed of developments in the Civil War. He learned that following the Union's victory at Antietam, Maryland, in September 1862, President Lincoln issued the Emancipation Proclamation which went into effect on January 1, 1863. The Proclamation freed all slaves in the states that had seceded and were in rebellion against the Union. Jamar clearly understood that the Proclamation turned the Civil War into something much more than a struggle to save the Union. It turned the war into a moral crusade to abolish slavery! Upon hearing this news, Jamar resolved to leave the refuge and safety of Canada and its good people. He began making plans to return to America, where he would join the Union Army to fight for the freedom of all black people. In addition, he was determined to learn the fate of his loving family no matter how long it took him to do so, and to reunite with those who were still alive.

Ever since his family members had been sold at auction, separated and scattered to the four winds, Jamar had no idea where they were or how to locate them. He thought of his old friend, Nokomo. He guessed that in all likelihood, Nokomo and his family had been forcibly relocated to the Oklahoma Indian Territory along with other Cherokee, by order of the Indian Removal Act. He decided to volunteer to fight for a Union regiment in the Oklahoma Territory in the hope that he might also reunite with his friend.

On July 7, 1863, a few months after Jamar joined the Union Army in the Oklahoma Indian Territory, he and his battalion saw action in what became known as the Battle of Honey Springs. This battle was also known as the Gettysburg of the Civil War in the Indian Territory. It was considered a unique battle of the Civil War in the sense that white soldiers fighting for the Confederacy and for the Union were in the minority. Native Americans made up a significant portion of each of the opposing armies. In addition, African Americans fought on the side of the Union forces. The Union Army emerged victorious.

During the battle, a white Union soldier, Private Joe Brady, was struck in the leg by multiple bullets and knocked off his feet! Jamar ran through gunfire to reach him! As Jamar carried him out of harm's way to a makeshift medical station, Jamar himself was shot! An enemy bullet struck and penetrated his right shoulder near his chest. As a medic examined Private Brady's wounds, his medical assistant rushed over to Jamar. Upon removing his blood-stained shirt, he recognized the unique double vertical scars on each side of his chest. "Jamar!" he exclaimed. For the second time in his life, Jamar's well-being was in the hands of his long-ago but eternal friend, Nokomo! Nokomo applied a tourniquet to stop the bleeding. With Nokomo's assistance, the medic performed double duty, tending to the wounds of both Jamar and Private Brady. Both soldiers survived their wounds.

By war's end in April 1865, Nokomo remained estranged from his father due to his decision to side with the Union Army. When Jamar informed him that he was heading back east in an effort to locate his family who he'd last seen twenty-five years earlier in 1840 on a Maryland auction block, Nokomo offered to join forces to find them. Jamar was thankful to have his help. They boarded a train headed for Washington D.C.

During the ride, Jamar informed Nokomo that he had heard that Congress, with the encouragement of President Lincoln, had recently passed a law creating The Freedmen's Bureau. "The Bureau, Jamar explained, was created to help former slaves begin a new life as free men and women. I've heard that it is providing former slaves some essential supplies such as food, dry goods, and clothing. It is planning to build lots of schools to provide freedmen the opportunity to learn to read and write. It is taking steps to make sure that newly hired freedmen are paid a living wage, and that employers are prevented from once again exploiting them as a source of slave labor. Most importantly, the Bureau is offering assistance to former slaves in their efforts to locate and reunite with their families. And that, Nokomo, is how we're going to locate my loved ones!"

Upon reaching Washington D.C., Jamar and Nokomo made their way to the Bureau. The only good news for Jamar was that the Freedman's Bureau provided some answers. The bad news was that most of the answers were heartbreaking. They learned that Jamar's parents and grandparents had succumbed to disease and death as a result of being physically abused and worked to death by cruel masters. Jamar was devastated and crushed by the news. He entered into a dark place, a deep depression. For a time, he practically stopped eating and he spoke little.

In Jamar's darkest hour, Nokomo stepped up and kept pressing the Freedmen's Bureau to provide information concerning the fate of Tanisha. A few weeks later, agents of the Bureau provided information that years earlier, Tanisha, while living on a slave plantation in Maryland, had married a man named Denzel George with whom she had a daughter, Cleotha. Tragically, a deadly strain of influenza had taken the lives of Denzel and Cleotha. There was still no word regarding the fate of Tanisha.

The agents explained that Maryland's slaves had been declared free on 11/1/1864, a few months before Congress, urged on by President Lincoln, passed the Thirteenth Amendment abolishing slavery throughout the United States. Upon being informed of the same, Jamar and Nokomo resolved to travel to Maryland in the hopes of finding Tanisha. They were prepared to search till hell froze over to locate her or to learn of her fate.

They didn't have to search long. A short distance from the plantation where Tanisha's husband and daughter had died, was a lodging room for the poor and homeless. Upon entering the sitting room, Jamar and Nokomo observed an emaciated looking woman sitting by herself in the corner. They walked over to her. At first, she was barely recognizable. But when she glanced up at them, her lifeless expression of despair slowly transformed into that bright smile that had so often comforted Jamar when he was a boy. "Tanisha!" he exclaimed. They hugged each other in a moment of pure joy. But soon, in a cruel twist which typified the destruction of almost all moments of joy in an age of slavery, bloody war, and its aftermath, Jamar was forced upon his sister's inquiry, to disclose that their parents and grandparents had lost their lives. In an instant, Tanisha's tears of joy were extinguished, replaced by tears of utter despair.

Tanisha, Jamar, and Nokomo remained in Maryland and soon found work on a plantation as share-croppers. The working conditions were extremely difficult and the wages were terribly low. Still, as God-awful as their situation was, it was a step up from slavery which Jamar and Tanisha had known all their lives. They continued on as sharecroppers for the remainder of 1865 and throughout the first half of 1866.

Over time, the affection that Nokomo had felt for Tanisha from afar when they were young teens welled up within him once again; And to his surprise and joy, this time his feelings were requited. They began seeing each throughout the summer of 1866. One evening after a long day of sharecropping in the scorching sun, they went for a short walk together. Suddenly, Nokomo dropped to his knees. For a moment, Tanisha thought one of his legs had given out as a result of squatting all day in the field; But then she heard the words, "Please, Tanisha dear, will you marry me?" When her shocked expression changed into a joyful smile accompanied by the word, "Yes," Nokomo was overwhelmed with happiness and gratitude. Upon the couple breaking the news to Jamar, he too was filled with great joy.

Nokomo had received word that during that summer of 1866, the federal government had negotiated treaties with the five tribes of the Oklahoma Indian Territory including the Cherokee, abolishing slavery within the Territory forever. He began thinking of the future- of love, family, and reconciliation in ways that had seemed impossible in a world filled with slavery and war. He resolved that since Tanisha had graced his life by accepting his proposal of marriage, he would ask her to consider a second proposal of a different nature but of great import.

The very next evening after work, Nokomo took Tanisha out for dinner.

"Tanisha, I would like for you to carefully consider what I have to say; But please, dear, don't feel that you must agree to what I have in mind if you cannot. I won't love you any less. As I've explained before, my father disowned me over my decision to join the Union Army. I deeply wish to reconcile with him. Slavery has been abolished in the Oklahoma Indian Territory. I would like to marry you in the presence of my parents on the Oklahoma Indian Reservation with my father's blessing; But first, I wish to ask both my parents to apologize to you and Jamar for having enslaved your whole family. It is only right that they should do so. While Mother opposed slavery in her heart, you and Jamar lived under both my parents as slaves. You have each told me that Father never physically beat the two of you, your parents, or your grandparents; Nevertheless, all of you endured the evil, the indignities, and the humiliation of being worked to the bone as slaves. As evil and cruel as slavery was, President Lincoln spoke of a post-war reconciliation between all Americans, 'with malice toward none, with charity for all.' He also spoke of binding up the nation's wounds.' In the spirit of Lincoln's vision, I am asking whether you feel that upon receiving an apology from my parents, you would be able to find it in your heart to forgive them for the unforgivable. We are all orphans in need of family and of healing."

After only a few moments, Tanisha smiled, took hold of Nokomo's hand, and gently replied, "Yes, Nokomo, because you have won my heart and in the spirit of our late President's vision, I am willing to forgive, just as you have asked." Tanisha and Nokomo tenderly embraced. When the two of them later shared the nature of their wedding plans with Jamar, he immediately responded, "I'm in. It's off to the Oklahoma Indian Territory we go! After all, Tanisha is my beloved sister; And you and I, Nokomo, are blood brothers for life."

A few days later, the three of them boarded a steam locomotive and journeyed to the Oklahoma Indian Reservation. Upon arrival, Nokomo, initially by himself, sought out his parents. To his surprise and great relief, the rift between his father and himself almost immediately began melting away like so many snowflakes upon winter's end meeting early spring. Perhaps it was because his father as well as his mother were relieved and overjoyed beyond all measure to learn that their son had survived the deadly war. Perhaps it was because slavery in the Oklahoma Indian Territory had been abolished. Perhaps it was because sometimes absence does make the heart grow fonder. For a time, Nokomo and his parents said almost nothing, simply enjoying the precious moments of their reunion compared to which all words paled in comparison.

Nokomo was the one to break the sweet silence. "Father, Mother, after so much misery, I have a chance for happiness in this world by marrying my true love, Tanisha, the very same Tanisha who was our family's slave so long ago at our home in Georgia. I reunited with her brother, Jamar, by chance, in The Battle of Honey Springs when I was called upon as a medic's assistant to tend wounds upon the battlefield. Jamar had volunteered to fight for the Union in the Oklahoma Territory in an effort to end slavery. He also hoped to find me so that we could renew our friendship after so many years. He was wounded while carrying a wounded soldier, a Private Joe Brady, to a makeshift medic station. While the medic examined Private Brady, I tended to Jamar. I utilized a tourniquet to control his bleeding. In some strange way, my parents, it seems like divine intervention played a role in placing me in position to come across Jamar and to control his bleeding in the critical hour. My assistance led to the renewal of our friendship. That, in turn, led to our teaming up in an effort to locate Jamar's family following the end of the war. We located Tanisha living in a lodging room for the homeless. We rescued her from a life of utter poverty and despair. Tanisha and Jamar have only recently learned that their parents and grandparents, our former slaves, died at the hands of abusive and cruel slave masters. They had all been sold at public auction after falling into the hands of ruthless slave catchers following their escape from our Georgia property. They were separated and sold off to different slave plantations. Tanisha married long ago. But her husband and young daughter succumbed to a deadly strain of influenza which broke out on the plantation."

"Slavery and the Civil War, my parents, have divided not only our family, but the Cherokee people as a whole. Cherokee fought on opposite sides of the war, just as Father and I chose opposite sides. The curse of slavery and the violence of war have wounded and scarred all of us in one way or another. We cannot afford to wait any longer for 'time to heal all wounds.' We are all in need of family. It's time for our family and the Cherokee people as a whole to heal by coming together. I would like to marry Tanisha right here in your presence on this Reservation. Tanisha and Jamar have accompanied me here in the hope that you would give your blessings to our being wed.

Jamar waited anxiously for his parents' reaction to his words. At first, there was only silence; But he wasn't to be disappointed. In lieu of words, both of his parents broke into smiles and the three of them affectionately embraced.

"I have one more thing I wish to ask of you, my parents. I would like for you to apologize to Tanisha and Jamar for the years you held their entire family as slaves." His parents asked him to have Tanisha and Jamar join them. He went for them right away and brought them back.

"Tanisha and Jamar, my wife and I are very happy that you are here. We ask for your forgiveness for the years we held you and your family as slaves. We are so very sorry that you have lost your parents and your grandparents; And we are truly sorry to hear, Tanisha, that your husband and young daughter lost their lives on a slave master's plantation. My wife and I would be honored for you and our son to marry upon this Reservation; And if you and Jamar will allow us, we would like to be a loving family to you for all the years left to us in this life."

Tanisha and Jamar were moved by those words, and they warmly embraced Nokomo's parents. Nokomo rejoiced in these moments of reconciliation which he had dared to envision in his mind, but which his heart had feared was almost an impossible dream.

The wedding was delayed for a time pending the arrival of Jamar's friend, Private Joe Brady, the white soldier whose life Jamar had saved in The Battle of Honey Springs. The two of them had provided moral support for each other while they recovered from their wounds. They had become close friends. Upon learning of the upcoming marriage, Private Brady was excited about attending the wedding out of friendship to Jamar, and because he wished to honor the marriage of Jamar's sister and her fiancé. Unfortunately, Private Brady had developed some complications attributable to his wounds, rendering him unable to attend the wedding. When Jamar advised Tanisha and Nokomo of the same, the couple decided that they wished to postpone the wedding until Private Brady recovered and was able to attend. Six weeks later he arrived for the wedding.

And so it was that on a bright and beautiful late summer day under a deep blue sky, a joyous wedding ceremony took place on the Oklahoma Native American Reservation. Gathered together for the occasion were Tanisha and Nokomo, the happy bride and groom; Nokomo's parents, Tanisha's brother, Jamar, and Jamar's friend, Private Joe Brady. Also attending to honor the loving couple were hundreds of Cherokee, many of whom were veterans of opposing Confederate and Union armies. Tanisha and Jamar and their former slave masters, Nokomos's father and mother, were for the first time joined together within family as equals; And after so many years of misery and war fought over the evil institution of slavery, the multi-racial wedding party offered if only for a fleeting moment in time, a symbol of hope for a better future and a better country filled with understanding and tolerance between the races.

THE PROMISE
(Historical Fiction)

As enemy gunfire rang out and broke the silence, fear mounted within Sammy O'Riley's heart with each passing second. Sammy was as afraid for Tommy Benson as he was for himself. Tommy had been his best friend since childhood, and they were next door neighbors. They had each been assigned to the same battalion upon arriving in Vietnam in 1969. They had survived many desperate battles and skirmishes fighting side by side within the jungles of Vietnam; Now, as a result of President Nixon extending the war into Cambodia in 1970, Sammy and Tommy were under fierce fire from North Vietnamese and Viet Cong forces which had established bases of operation in the eastern border region of Cambodia.

Tommy's big brother, Donny, had tragically lost his life two years earlier during the 1/68 Tet Offensive. Tommy's distraught mother, Helen Benson, had begun to develop heart problems soon after Donny was killed. It had worsened to the point that she could no longer work full time at the General Store. After a while, she wound up collecting Social Security Disability Benefits. When Tommy and Sammy were preparing to board their flight to Vietnam, Mrs. Benson pleaded with Sammy to watch over Tommy while they were in Vietnam together. Sammy had given her his word he would do so. More than anything else, Sammy was determined to see to it that he and Tommy came home together alive.

In the midst of the gunfire, a scream rang out and everything turned crimson! For a split second, Sammy thought he was shot! But then he realized that he was covered in Tommy's blood! Tommy had been shot in the chest and he was struggling desperately to breathe! Sammy cried out, "Medic!" Gasping for air, Tommy pulled Sammy closer. He strained to whisper the following words as Sammy cradled his head in his arms: "My little brother, Billy, will come of age to be drafted next year. Please promise me that you will do whatever you can to keep him out of the war. He's always been gung- ho to fight for his country. If Mom were to lose Billy, her only remaining child, it would destroy her. Please, Sammy."

Through his tears, Sammy reassured him, "Yes, Tommy, I promise."

Tommy nodded as his face took on a peaceful expression and he slipped away.

Despite the fact that he was devastated over the loss of Tommy, Sammy was forced to carry on in a daily struggle to survive. Three months after Tommy's death, Sammy's leg was seriously injured when the soldier beside him stepped onto a land mine! The blast caused permanent nerve damage in Sammy's right leg requiring lifelong use of a walking cane. As a result of his injury, he was awarded the Purple Heart, honorably discharged, and sent home a little before the end of his tour.

On his long flight home, Sammy could not stop thinking about Tommy and about his promise to do all he could to keep Billy out of the war. He fell into a dream-state back into his past:

"It's not a war worth fighting or dying for, son. You wouldn't be fighting Nazis or Fascists. Vietnam is a civil war which America should have avoided getting drawn into in the first place. Robert Kennedy was intending to get us out of this terrible war; But he's dead and gone now."

"But Dad, while Kennedy intended to get us out of the war, he asserted while campaigning in Oregon that it was wrong for some to avoid the war through college deferments, while others less academically inclined or too poor to attend college, do the fighting and dying in their place. When Lincoln's draft law was passed in 1863, wealthier young men who had the means to pay a $300 fee to hire a substitute in their place, could legally buy their way out of the draft. Many draftees referred to the Civil War as, 'Rich man's war, poor man's fight.' A college deferment is just another way of buying one's way out of the draft."

Sammy's mom gently placed her hands on his right forearm and his shoulder. "Please dear, she said, "you are our only child who we dearly love. Please utilize a college deferment to stay out of this terrible, bloody, God-awful war."

As he continued on in his dream-state, Sammy's mind drifted further back into his past, to the carefree and happy days of his childhood growing up in a suburban neighborhood in Wamego, Kansas. He was next door playing in the backyard with Tommy and his brothers, Donny and Billy. Mrs. Benson had baked a tray full of her delicious homemade oatmeal cookies while also putting out for the boys a pitcher of Kool-Aid.

"Sammy, can I speak with you a moment, Mrs. Benson asked. I'd like to ask a favor of you. Sometimes my boys play pretty hard out there. It looks like things get a little rough between the brothers from time to time. Tommy is the littlest in size and he seems to look up to you. Watch over Tommy for me, won't you, Sammy?"

"Yes, Mrs. Benson, I sure will. I promise. I'll watch out for Tommy."

"Thank you, Sammy."

Still back in his childhood, Sammy's mind drifted to thoughts of Donny. Donny was a natural leader with a great throwing arm even as a little boy. He played quarterback, called the plays, and devised patterns for his receivers (Sammy, Tommy, and Billy) to run within the backyard. The boys were always joined in the backyard by the Benson family dog, Skippy, the Golden Retriever. Skippy playfully chased after the boys and practically served as a fourth wide receiver. The boys started referring to her as "The Golden Receiver!" They devised out of cloth a soft head covering to serve as her "helmet." They'd gently stick it on top of her head at the beginning of each passing session; And each time Skippy shook her head and flung it off within seconds. She seemed to take great joy in the ritual!

"Come on in for oatmeal cookies and milk, boys," Mrs. Benson called out. It was the very first Saturday that Sammy met her boys and joined them for play in their backyard after he and his parents moved in next door.

"Where is your daddy?" Sammy asked Billy on their way inside.

"He died. Let me show you something, Sammy."

They walked into the study where Billy showed Sammy the medals that his dad had received for his service in WWII. "My daddy was a hero, Sammy. Mom and my brothers will tell you the same thing. We all want to be like my daddy."

Sammy's mind drifted to his memories of the boys trying to round up neighborhood kids for a sand-lot baseball game on a nearby ballfield. If there weren't enough kids around for a ballgame, Tommy often asked Sammy to throw the baseball around with him in Tommy's backyard. Tommy's prized possession as a kid was his leather baseball glove. He loved to walk around the backyard pounding his fist into the mitt to loosen it up. He liked to play catcher while having Sammy pitch to him in an effort to strike out imaginary batters. "Hey batter batter, Tommy exclaimed! Pitch it in here, Sammy. You got 'em. Strike him out, Sammy!"

Sammy's next retreat into the past landed him in the kitchen of his home when he was eight years old. It was a day that Tommy was staying over for dinner. Sammy accidentally knocked over an open can of tomato sauce that his mom had left on the kitchen counter. Herman, Sammy's cocker spaniel, began slurping up the sauce while stepping in it. Herman then tracked the tomato sauce stuck to his paws all over Sammy's mom's brand-new wall- to-wall carpet! To avoid getting into trouble, Sammy convinced Tommy to shoulder the blame for knocking over the tomato sauce.

Later that evening, Sammy's dad called him into his study. "Sammy, I want you to look me in the eye and tell me the truth. Was Tommy really the one who knocked over the tomato sauce?"

Sammy hesitated and then said, "No, Dad, it was me. I'm the one who accidentally knocked it over. I'm sorry I lied about it. Are you angry with me?"

"No, son, I'm not angry, just disappointed; But I'm proud of you for telling me the truth now. I believe, Sammy, that there is a simple code of conduct that we should live by. It's just a matter of choosing to live our lives by doing the right thing, including being honest. Just now you did the right thing by telling me the truth; And by doing so you did right by Tommy. I was also taught that a man's word is his bond. That means that if a man gives his word or promise to do something, he ought to keep his promise and do it. There is an easy test for knowing whether we've done the right thing. We can't hide our actions from ourselves. When you put your head down on your pillow at night and you're all alone with your own thoughts, you will know deep in your heart whether you have behaved fairly and honestly and kindly toward others, and whether you have kept your word. If the answer is No, you'll probably have some trouble getting to sleep. If the answer is Yes, you'll usually sleep soundly without much trouble. Do you understand?"

"Yes, Dad, I think so.

"Good, son. So why don't you and I do the right thing and turn ourselves into tomato sauce, stain busters! Let's make it our mission to clean up those rug stains the best we can. Is it a deal?"

"Yes, Dad, let's do it."

Sammy was abruptly startled out of his dream state and back into the present by the announcement that his plane was coming into the airport. Waiting to greet him were his ecstatic parents. Tears of joy and sadness were shed as they embraced their son while taking in the limp which he'd written about, requiring the use of a walking cane.

On the ride home they stopped off for a homecoming BBQ dinner, Sammy's favorite. At dinner, Sammy's parents asked more about how he was doing and about how much pain he was experiencing. Sammy told them that the pain from his leg injury had diminished significantly in the last couple of weeks. He revealed that what was distressing him the most were his nightmares and flashbacks regarding all the violence and sadness he had experienced, including the death of Tommy who had died in his arms. His parents suggested that he meet with a psychologist to help him deal with his experiences. Sammy agreed that he would do so. His parents also asked if he would like to take some day trips with them to visit some beautiful outdoor areas of nature, as a counter to all the ugliness he had experienced for so long. Sammy responded that he would like that very much.

Sammy shared that while he wasn't yet ready, as soon as he felt up to it he was intending to enroll in college under the GI Bill. He told his parents how right they had been about the brutality of the war. He asked how Mrs. Benson and Billy were holding up over the loss of Tommy. Sammy's mom responded that Mrs. Benson was still grieving and that her tears continued to flow at the drop of a hat. Both parents expressed that they were quite worried about the effects of Tommy's death upon Mrs. Benson, especially in light of her heart problems. His mom mentioned that Mrs. Benson had expressed how very grateful she was for the condolence letter that Sammy had written her from Vietnam. His mom then asked, "Is it true, Sammy, did Tommy's death come quickly without suffering?"

"He died very quickly, Mom. But before he did, his last words were to ask me to promise that I would do all that I could to keep Billy out of the war. I agreed to do so. Since Tommy's death, has Billy changed his attitude about wanting to fight in Vietnam?"

Sammy's dad responded, "No, son, he hasn't. His mom says he's full of anger and more resolute than ever about fighting for his country as his brothers did, and as his dad did before them. You're gonna have a hell of a time, son, trying to talk him out of fighting over there. Maybe you should start by speaking with Mrs. Benson."

"That's what I'll do, Dad. I'll call her and arrange a time to speak to her alone."

Sammy met with Mrs. Benson at her home the very next morning after Billy had gone to work. He was greeted at the door by Mrs. Benson and by Skippy. Mrs. Benson gave him a warm hug. While Skippy had slowed down and didn't see or move as well as in the past, she greeted Sammy with the same unrestrained tail-wagging and joie de vivre she had displayed each and every time he had dropped in as a kid. Sammy reciprocated in the love fest with Skippy. In addition to putting up some hot coffee, Mrs. Benson surprised Sammy with a tray full of her homemade oatmeal cookies which he'd savored so much in years past.

After they sat down in the living room, Mrs. Benson asked Sammy how he was doing and how his leg was feeling. Sammy told her that he was recovering pretty well from his injury and that his pain and discomfort had already significantly diminished. She thanked him for the condolence letter he had sent her. Sammy reassured her that Tommy had died instantly without experiencing pain. That brought tears to Mrs. Benson's eyes. After a time, Sammy asked if Billy had changed his mind since Tommy's death about serving in Vietnam.

"No, Sammy. Billy's full of anger and rage. He speaks of getting even, of exacting revenge for the death of his brothers."

Mrs. Benson placed her hands upon Sammy's right hand, and said, "I don't want Billy going off to war. I'm not sure I could hold up to the anxiety and terror that I'd feel in my heart, worrying about him losing his life over there. Is there anything you can do to keep him from going?"

"While Tommy and I were together in Vietnam, he asked me to promise that if he didn't make it back home alive, that I would do all I could to keep Billy out of the war. That's exactly what I intend to do. I will try my very best, Mrs. Benson. I promise."

Later that evening, Sammy called Billy who was very happy to hear from him. Sammy invited Billy out to a local watering hole for a brewski. They greeted each other with a warm embrace and sat down for the brewski and chips. Billy asked Sammy about his injury. Sammy responded that he was doing ok. The subject soon turned to Tommy. Billy wanted to know how Tommy died. Sammy told him exactly what he had told Billy's mother- that Tommy died instantly and experienced no pain. Sammy asked Billy if he was still intending to fight in Vietnam.

"Damn right, Sammy! I'm gonna make those commies pay for killing my brothers."

"Your mom, as I'm sure you know, has told our family that she doesn't want you to risk your life in Vietnam. She is terrified that she'll lose you just as she has lost Donny and Tommy."

"I understand that, Billy responded, but it is just something that I have to do."

"Billy, let me speak plainly. The war is an unspeakable horror story. Whether one lives or dies or is seriously wounded is to a large extent nothing but sheer luck. I've suffered nerve damage to my leg which has left me with a permanent limp. I shall be forced to utilize this cane for the rest of my life; And I'm one of the lucky ones. My folks and I think of you and your mom as family. We deeply care about you both. We don't want to see you risk your life in Vietnam. We're also concerned that if your mom were to lose you, her sole surviving son, to that bloody war, the loss would destroy her as well."

"It's not up to me, anyway, Sammy. Unless the war comes to an end, I'm going to be drafted by Uncle Sam."

"It doesn't have to be that way, Billy. You could obtain your GED and then enroll in community college in order to receive a college deferment from the war. Thousands of young people are doing so."

"Sammy, I remember your telling me and my brothers that you intended to seek a college deferment from the war; But later you told us that you'd changed your mind because you had decided it was wrong to have another boy fight and perhaps die in your place. You went and served your country. Donny and Tommy did their duty. My dad fought in WWII in the Battle of the Bulge. How can you ask me to do any less?"

"Listen, Billy, I was wrong. In Vietnam we're not fighting Nazis and Fascists like your dad did in WWII. I can't figure out what we're doing in Vietnam. We're on their land caught in the middle of a bitter and bloody civil war. I was wrong not to seek a college deferment. One shouldn't decide the right thing to do in a vacuum. One must consider very carefully the impact that one's decision will have on the people dear to him. I've always been very close with my parents and I am their only child. If I had died in this war, it probably would have devastated their lives. After your dad passed away, your mom put her heart and soul into raising you boys on her own. When we were kids, it was clear as day to me that you boys meant the world to her. And now you're her only surviving son. Think what it would do to her if you were killed in Vietnam."

"Billy, Sammy continued, when I was in Vietnam with Tommy, he asked me to promise that if he didn't make it back alive, that I would ask you on his behalf to stay out of the war. He wanted you to go on living to carry on the family name and legacy. Most of all, he wanted you to take care of your mom. He told me that if she were to lose all three of her sons to the war, it would destroy her."

Almost a full minute went by during which no words were spoken. Sammy held his breath and prayed that he'd gotten through to Billy; But then, Billy lifted up his head which had been cradled in his hands with his elbows upon the table. "Ok, Sammy. You've satisfied your commitment to Tommy. You've told me his wishes. You've explained everything. But I'm going to be drafted and there's nothing to be done." With that, Billy stood up from his chair and walked out of the pub.

The next day, Sammy met again with Mrs. Benson. "I thought I'd convinced him. I really did. He seemed to listen to what I had to say; But in the end I failed to change his mind. Before I spoke with Billy, I went to the law library. I got some help researching whether he would be considered exempt from the draft as the sole surviving son whose brothers were killed in the war. During WW11, there were a number of families in which multiple siblings were killed in the course of their duty. As a result, in 1948, Congress passed a law exempting from the draft in wartime or peacetime, the sole surviving son of a family in which one or more sons or daughters had died as a result of military service. Unfortunately, however, in 1961, Congress, realizing that the post WW II baby-boomers were soon to come of draft age, revisited the sole surviving son draft exemption. The bottom line is that Congress included within the 1961 law a peacetime only exemption from the draft. The sole surviving son exemption from the draft in wartime was eliminated!"

"A lawyer on Billy's behalf could make a very technical argument that he should be exempted from the Vietnam War under the sole surviving son peacetime exemption. The lawyer could argue that the peacetime exemption applies because Congress has never formally declared war on North Vietnam and the Vietcong! However, with blood spilling and thousands of boys being sent home in body bags, I think it would probably be pretty darn tough to convince a court that we're in the middle of 'peacetime.' It would certainly not be the argument on which one would want Billy's fate to rest. Therefore, when I spoke to him, I suggested that he obtain his GED and enroll in community college in order to obtain a college deferment from the war. To me, that makes the most sense. But as I've said, he rejected my suggestion. I'm truly sorry, Mrs. Benson, but I don't know what else I can do."

"Sammy, Billy would not be able to pass the GED exam or attend college because he can barely read. He has tried to hide it from the world all his life. He did very poorly in school and dropped out early. He used to play the class clown and he got into trouble a lot in school to hide the fact that he couldn't read. As you know, he's a bright boy. He's gifted with his hands. He can repair cars, home appliances, or most anything without reading the directions or instructions; But he always hated to be around books."

Two days went by as Sammy pondered Billy's secret. He kept thinking about his promise to Tommy; And he thought about the fact that for a moment during their chat in the pub, Billy had a look on his face which seemed to reveal that what he was hearing was sinking in.

On the evening of the second day, Sammy invited Billy to have dinner with him at an old truck stop restaurant where they had loved to eat as kids. When they were finished eating, Sammy said, "Look, Billy, I want to ask you something. I would like you to be completely honest with me. I promise you that I would never bring it up if it wasn't critically important. I know how gifted you are with your hands. I remember even before you were a teen, if something needed repairing in our home, Dad would call me over and say, "Go get Billy!" On the other hand, I cannot fix a darn thing. Practical things like that are Greek to me. I've had to stick to book learning. I remember that you hated school and avoided books like the plague. Is that because you are unable to read?"

Billy stared back at Sammy and hung his head in his hands without saying a word.

"There's nothing to be ashamed of or embarrassed about, Billy. We all have things we haven't learned to do or believe we are unable to do. For all my love of playing sports, when it comes to dancing, I have two left feet. When we spoke in the pub the other day, it appeared to me that for a moment, it was making sense to you that given all your mom has suffered with the loss of your dad and your brothers, that you ought to stay out of the war. Am I right?"

Billy nodded his head, "Yes."

"Suppose I was to help you learn to read while also preparing you to pass the GED exam, so as to enable you to enroll in community college and obtain a deferment from the war. Would you agree to do it?"

"Sammy, Billy responded, that would involve an insane amount of work and would almost surely end in failure. I don't believe that I can ever learn to read much less pass the GED exam and attend college. That's just a pipe-dream."

"No, I don't think so Billy. If you were to truly commit to the effort, there isn't a doubt in my mind about your ability to learn to read and to pass the GED exam. It wouldn't be easy, and you would need to treat it as your second job. We would need to work together at least four hours every evening after you get home from work. There would be little rest for the weary. Under state law, a person is allowed to take the GED exam up to three times a year. Given the time frame that you're likely to be called up for military service under the draft, you would have about 18 months to learn to read, prepare for the GED Exam, pass the GED Exam, and enroll in college in time to obtain a college deferment. If we throw ourselves into the effort like we're prepping you to climb Mt. Everest, then you will reach the mountaintop."

"I couldn't let you commit all that time to me."

"I want to do this, Billy. It's important to me. I truly want to do this for you, for your mom, and for Tommy. So what do you say? Are you in?"

Billy sat there expressionless for at least ten seconds without saying a word. Then, his face broke into a smile and he said, "Ok Sammy, I'm in!" He extended his hand, and they heartily shook on it.

"Get a good night's sleep, Billy, for tomorrow we go to work!"

The next day, and during the weeks and months to follow, they went to work with a vengeance! They worked on developing Billy's reading skills utilizing phonics, word recognition, and memorization. No matter how tired Billy felt after his eight -hour work day as an auto mechanic, he diligently worked to develop his reading skills four hours a night with Sammy by his side guiding him all the way. When the tediousness and frustration of slowly and painstakingly learning to read began creeping into Billy's psyche from time to time, Sammy would say, "Cool down, Billy, Rome wasn't built in a day." Eventually, Billy would cool off and they'd forge ahead.

After Billy had spent over eight months developing basic reading skills, he and Sammy began studying language arts, science, social studies, and math, the subjects that were going to be tested on the exam. At one point, Billy exclaimed, "It's too much material for me to learn in too little time! It's impossible!"

"It's not impossible, Billy! Just keep on working at it. Keep on keeping on. You'll slowly but surely learn the material, brick by brick."

The first time Billy took the GED exam, he fell 10 points short of passing. After studying for a few more months, he took the exam for a second time within the calendar year. This time he fell 5 points short of passing. Given that he'd failed the test twice, Billy was required under state law to wait 60 days before taking the exam for the third and final time within the calendar year. As it turned out, the earliest he could take the last exam fell only three days before the deadline for Billy to be enrolled in college in time to avoid reporting for military service. Billy and Sammy continued studying together feverishly, right up to the day for Billy to take his third and final exam. This time after Billy walked out of the exam, he felt confident that he had passed it. One day, two days went by, and Billy did not receive the results of his test. By the noon hour of the third day, a Friday, and the last day for Billy to get enrolled in college in time to obtain a college deferment, he still hadn't received the results of his GED exam.

Even as the situation was looking hopeless, Sammy was haunted by Tommy's last words imploring him to do whatever he could to keep Billy out of the war. Billy's commitment and dedication to learning over the last eighteen months had been nothing short of miraculous. As all of this weighed heavily upon Sammy's mind, a possible solution suddenly dawned upon him! He recognized that it was a longshot, but that it was a chance worth taking. They had to move on it immediately! Excitedly, he ran over and knocked on Billy's door. He asked Billy and his mom to get dressed like they were going to church. He asked them to be ready in twenty minutes to take a short drive with him. He emphasized that there was no time to lose! They got ready quickly and they all jumped into Sammy's car. During the drive, Sammy filled them in on his plan. He laid out exactly what they each needed to be prepared to talk about.

Twenty-five minutes later they pulled into the local community college, and the three of them walked directly to the office of the Dean of Admissions. Sammy went up to the receptionist and requested a short meeting with the Dean. He explained that his friend, Billy, needed to enroll in the college that day! He told her that Billy had lost two brothers in Vietnam, and that there were special circumstances they needed to explain to the Dean.

The receptionist listened carefully, stood up, and said, "One moment, please," before entering the Dean's office. To their great relief, the receptionist soon returned and admitted them into the office to meet with Dean Johnson.

Sammy introduced himself, Billy, and Mrs. Benson to the Dean. "Dean Johnson, he said, my friend, Billy, needs to enroll in the college today. Over the past eighteen months, he has worked incredibly hard to learn to read. He has developed the proficiency necessary to take the GED exam. I've watched him study four hours a night over that eighteen- month period after putting in eight- hour days as an auto mechanic to help provide support for his mom and himself. He fell short the first two times he took the exam, but each time he improved his score; And each time he continued to study even harder! Two days ago, he took the exam for the third and final time he was eligible to take it within the calendar year. This time he's confident he passed it. However, he did not receive his test results by today as expected; And the problem, Dean Johnson, is that Billy needs to enroll in your college today if he is to avoid being drafted into military service."

Mrs. Benson then spoke up. "Dean Johnson, my son and I are a tax- paying, law abiding family, and we have been members of this community all our lives. My husband fought in WW II. He passed away a number of years ago. Two of my sons were killed in Vietnam. Billy is my last remaining child. He is a hard-working and talented auto mechanic and provides critical income to our family. I am on a fixed income receiving Social Security Disability Benefits due to heart problems I've recently developed. Billy is a wonderful and loving son."

Dean Johnson looked at Billy and asked, "Billy, given your work as an auto mechanic, would you have sufficient time to attend classes and to keep up with your studies in college?"

"Yes, sir. My boss is quite happy with my work. I am certain that I can alter my work hours accordingly; And now that I've labored so hard to learn to read, I find myself wanting to learn everything! I'm prepared to work even harder in school."

At that moment, Sammy set forth the bottom line. "Dean Johnson, we're asking you to conditionally enroll Billy in college today. Doing so would allow him to meet today's deadline for obtaining a college deferment from the draft. Billy's test results are certain to arrive by early next week."

The room grew quiet as Dean Johnson reflected for a time upon the request. He then asked, "Is there anything else that any of you wish to tell me?" When no one offered anything more, Dean Johnson rose from his chair and said, "Please excuse me, folks, for a few minutes." He then stepped out of his office.

Sammy, Billy, and his mom sat there for a time in dead silence, the tension so thick you could cut it with a knife. Suddenly, Dean Johnson reentered the office. He looked directly at Billy and asked, "Billy, how certain are you that you passed the GED exam this last time?"

"Well, sir, I've received enormous assistance, encouragement, and support from Sammy. I've put my heart and soul into learning to read. I've studied as hard as I possibly could to pass the GED exam. Each time my test score has improved. I truly believe, Dean Johnson, that this time I'll pass."

"Well, Billy, since you have refused to give up on yourself, this college is not going to turn its back on you either. You will be conditionally enrolled in school today. Of course, everything now depends upon the results of your GED exam which you'll receive next week."

Billy, his mom, and Sammy excitedly thanked Dean Johnson for the chance. Billy then sat down and completed the college enrollment paperwork. Afterward, Sammy drove Billy and his mom directly home so that Billy could immediately complete the Selective Service draft deferment paperwork, documenting that he had met the deadline for enrollment in college.

Monday arrived and with it, the envelope containing the results of Billy's GED exam was delivered to his mailbox. It arrived late in the day. Billy and his mom went right over and knocked on Sammy's door. Billy had the unopened envelope in hand. He and his mom wanted to share the moment of truth with their friends. Sammy, his parents, and Herman, as well as Billy and his mom, all gathered together in the living room.

"Sammy, you've brought me this far. Please, if you would, open the envelope for me."

For a few moments which felt like an eternity, the room was filled with deadly silence, racing hearts, and sweaty palms. Sammy opened the envelope and gazed at the letter. As everyone stared at him in prolonged agony, Sammy calmly lifted his eyes from the letter, looked directly at Billy, and then shouted, "You did it, Billy! You passed the exam!"

Everyone broke into cheers! Herman, feeling the excitement, joined in with high decibel barking!

In a split second the future course of Billy's life changed forever. The Benson family would not be losing a third son to that bloody war; And Billy's lifetime of frustration, fear, secrecy, and shame over his illiteracy melted away, replaced by a moment of triumph!

"Sammy, I could never find a way to repay you."

"You already have, Billy. The truth is that you've helped me every bit as much as I've helped you. You see, our intense focus on the task at hand helped keep my mind off the horrible images from the war that have haunted me. You might say that working with you served as therapy for me; And now, thanks to our working together, I feel that very soon I'll be ready to enroll in college myself!"

They all decided to go out to dinner to celebrate. Before they left, Billy pulled Sammy aside. "You know, Sammy, neither limp nor cane nor stumbling blocks will keep me from teaching you to dance!"

Sammy smiled and replied, "Right on, Billy."

The next day, Mrs. Benson and Sammy met and spoke together. "For so long, Sammy, I have not been able to find any meaning or make any sense out of the deaths of Donny and Tommy. I have come within a slender thread of losing my faith; But now I have begun to understand that Donny and Tommy were tragically sacrificed so that their little brother, Billy, might live. I believe that you have served as God's instrument for ensuring that Billy will go on living far from that terrible war. I want to thank you for what you have done for Billy, and for me, from the bottom of my heart."

With those words, Mrs. Benson reached out and gently hugged Sammy. They embraced for almost a full minute without saying a word as they stood above Tommy's headstone within the quiet of the cemetery. All the while, the small American flag set above the flowers placed upon the grave, blew gently in the wind.

That evening when Sammy laid his head down upon his pillow, he had no trouble falling off to sleep; And for the first time in a long time, he slept soundly and peacefully, his mind free of the terrible images of war. He was no longer haunted by images of Tommy's mortally wounded body in the final moments of his life. Instead, as he fell into a deep slumber, the image of Tommy all grown up in the prime of his short life, rose up before him. Tommy was back in his small hometown of Wamego in his backyard where he and Sammy had played catch so often as kids. Tommy was punching his left fist into the mitt of his prized leather baseball glove, the very glove which he'd worn and loved as a boy. He called out, "Hey Sammy, pitch one in here. Throw me a perfect strike. I know you can do it."

Uncertain whether he could pull it off but determined to try, Sammy focused hard in his pitching stance, went through his wind up, and released the baseball with all of his might. It travelled through the air in a beeline and landed smack dab in the middle of Tommy's glove with a thud!

Tommy trotted over to Sammy, threw his arm around him, and said, "Great job, Sammy, I knew you'd come through!" As he spoke those words, Tommy looked directly into Sammy's eyes and smiled upon him reassuringly, and most approvingly.

"ARE THESE THE HANDS OF A THIEF?"
(Fiction)

Jose Rodriguez was born and raised in El Paso, Texas, the first-born son of migrant worker parents. As a young boy, Jose, along with his younger brother, Marcos, worked part time in the fields to help the family eke out a living. As teens, Jose and Marcos had no opportunity to seek higher education as a steppingstone to the American Dream. They each dropped out of school upon reaching their sixteenth birthday to join their parents full time in the fields. Into their mid-twenties, each brother had known only the dead-end tedium of endless days harvesting crops for slave wages, beneath the debilitating heat of the burning Texas sun.

Despite the hardships of his life, Jose struck a high note on two occasions. He married Maria, the woman he loved. She worked part time as a cashier at Walmart. The second high note took place two years later when Maria gave birth to their beloved daughter, Marianna. Jose and Maria yearned to provide a better life for Marianna, filled with opportunities which had been inaccessible to themselves. From the time she was a little girl they encouraged her to dream big and to work hard in school. They taught her values of honesty, fair play, and kindness toward others. They tried to set a good example by the honest, hard-working manner in which they lived their lives.

When Marianna reached her seventh birthday, she was skinny and diminutive of size but sharp of mind. She made top marks in her second-grade class. One day upon returning home from school, she excitedly told her parents that she wished to join the school's after-hours chess club. She explained that the chess club activities began immediately after school, and that she would only have to be picked up an hour later. "Mama, Papa, can I join up? Can I? Please! I really want to play chess!" They each held a straight face for a few moments before breaking into huge smiles. Maria answered, "Yes, Marianna, you can join up and play chess after school." Jose grabbed his daughter and whisked her straight up into the air with the greatest of ease! She shrieked with laughter from the time he launched her until she landed securely in his sure and sturdy hands.

Because Marianna had such a quick, curious, and active mind, her teacher challenged her by assigning extra reading material. Marianna devoured the books her teacher assigned. She loved reading about medieval times, including stories about Arthur and Guinevere, the Sword and the Stone, and Excalibur. She also loved reading biographies about famous people from the Renaissance period, including Galileo, Leonardo da Vinci, and Queen Elizabeth the First.

Over the course of the school year, Marianna became the top chess player in the school chess club. She began entering some inter-school competitions. She quickly rose to the top in those chess competitions in her age group.

A little over three weeks before Marianna's eighth birthday, Jose visited Toys R Us to pick out a birthday present for her. He spotted on display the perfect gift, a beautiful Renaissance chess set! He thought to himself, "She can use it to play chess with friends at home; And as she grows older, she can use it to study the games of the great chess grandmasters." When Judy Doan, a sales lady, asked if she could help, he launched into his proud Papa mode. He said to her, "My seven-year-old daughter, Marianna, is a top student at Loma Verde Elementary School. In addition, she is also the top chess player in her school's chess club. I wish to purchase this beautiful Renaissance chess set as a birthday present for her. Will you check the price for me? I don't see it listed on the display set." She led him over to five boxed Renaissance chess sets sitting on a shelf. The boxed chess sets were priced at $40.00 each. Jose told her that the $40.00 was above his price range, but that he believed he could raise the money in about two weeks, in time for Marianna's birthday. Ms. Doan mentioned that the Renaissance chess sets were a popular item and that Toys R Us had been selling them at a rapid pace. Jose asked if she could place one of the chess sets on layaway for him. Ms. Doan responded that she could not, but that hopefully at least one of the five boxed chess sets would still be available in two weeks' time.

Two weeks later, Jose returned to the store, spoke to Ms. Doan, and learned that only one Renaissance chess set remained in the store for sale! All the others had been sold. Jose said to her, "My daughter's birthday is a little over a week away. I'll be back in four or five days to purchase the chess set."

Two days after Jose's second visit to Toys R Us, an event occurred which had the effect of turning his whole world upside down. Toys R Us was burglarized! The break-in took place late at night after the store had closed for the evening. The point of entry was determined to be a broken window at the back exit of the store. Upon rounding the corner to the back of the store after hearing the window break, the nighttime security officer observed a shadowy figure with his or her back to him, racing away from the back exit of the store. The officer immediately took off after the figure while yelling, "Store security, stop!" As the fleet-footed officer gained ground, the thief dropped an item from his or her arms while continuing to run off. The thief ducked into some woods behind the east end of the store and got away. The security officer recovered the dropped item, a Renaissance chess set. The set was collected by police. No fingerprints were located at the point of entry and exit. No prints were located on the boxed-up chess set. Upon arrival, Officer Tony Thomas concluded, based upon his training and experience, that a burglary tool such as a hammer was utilized to break out the store window.

The next day, Judy Doan was questioned by Officer Thomas and his partner, Officer Warren, concerning possible suspects. She told the officers about Jose's interest in a Renaissance chess set which he had not yet been able to afford. While she didn't know his name, she provided his description: light skinned Hispanic male in his thirties, muscular build, about 5'7", dark black hair, and a mustache. She told the police that when he pointed to the Renaissance chess set on display, she noticed that he had a heart-shaped tattoo on his right arm mid-way between his elbow and his wrist. She also told the officers that he proudly related that his daughter, Marianna, attended Loma Verde Elementary School where she was the top player in the school's chess club.

After completing their interview of Judy Doan, the officers retrieved from the store security officer three of the store's 24-7 security recordings. One camera had been trained upon the area of the store where the chess sets were located. The video recording revealed the thief lifting the stolen chess set off the shelf while wearing a mask to conceal his identity. The thief appeared to be a short male with a muscular build. He had dark black hair and a mustache which extended a bit beyond each side of his mask. His skin color was consistent with that of a light skinned Hispanic male. In addition, the video revealed a round-shaped tattoo on the thief's right arm midway between his elbow and his wrist.

The officers next made their way to Loma Verde Elementary School where they verified that a little girl named Marianna was the top player in the school's chess club. The school's front office provided them with the names of Marianna's parents along with the family's address. Two days later, the officers showed up at the family's home on a Saturday morning with an arrest warrant for Jose. They knocked and announced, "Police, open up!" Within a few seconds, Jose opened the door. Despite Jose's assertions of innocence, the officers seized and cuffed him in front of his wife and daughter! He made no effort to resist or struggle. Maria screamed that there must be some mistake! Marianna burst into tears at the sight of her Papa being cuffed and taken away. The officers placed him into a police car and hauled him off to the county jail.

"Please, Mr. Tanner, Jose begged his court-appointed attorney, you've got to put in for a Bond Reduction Motion right away! I've got to get back to work to support my family. Otherwise, very soon, my wife and our seven-year-old daughter, Marianna, will not have enough to eat! My wife won't be able to keep the electricity on!" Mr. Tanner assured him that he would file the Bond Reduction Motion right away, and that he would get the hearing on the motion set as soon as possible. He then said to Jose, "Please tell me exactly what happened."

"Mr. Tanner, I did not break into or steal from Toys R Us. I only shopped there to pick out a present for Marianna's eighth birthday. That's all. Marianna is not only a top student, she is also the top chess player in her school's chess club. Her teacher recently got her excited about reading biographies about famous people from the Renaissance period. When I spotted a Renaissance chess set at the toy store, I knew that would be the perfect birthday present for her. I asked the sales lady if it could be placed on layaway. She said, 'No.' I told her that it would take me some time to earn the money to afford it. Mr. Tanner, my wife and I earn very little. It's a month to-month struggle just to make ends meet. But I am no thief. There is very little I wouldn't do for my daughter. But I wouldn't steal. My wife and I have taught her to be a good honest person. It's important to me to set a good example for her. I would never risk messing that up. The worst part of being arrested was seeing the look on my wife's face as well as the hurt and disappoint in my daughter's eyes, as I was led away."

At that moment, Tanner could see Jose holding back tears. "Mr. Rodriguez, I have a young child of my own, so I can sense what a painful moment that must have been for you. Are you up to continuing? I have a few more important questions I need to ask you."

"Yes, Mr. Tanner, I'm ok. Go ahead and ask your questions."

"Do you remember where you were on Monday, 3/20/2017, at 10:00 p.m., the date and time of the burglary as listed in the complaint affidavit?"

"Yes, sir. I was out fishing on the Rio Grande with my friend, Pablo Torres. Pablo worked the fields picking crops with me. We had taken to fishing on Monday and Tuesday nights after our young children were asleep. It was a way of making sure there was enough food to last the entire week for our families."

"Mr. Rodriguez, Pablo constitutes an important alibi witness since he was with you on the Rio Grande at the time of the burglary. Do you have his address and phone number?"

"Yes sir, I do. But I must tell you something. Pablo is a good person. He is an honest, hard-working family man. However, he and his wife, Anita, are undocumented immigrants from Mexico. Their two young children were born in El Paso. Pablo follows the news. He is aware that the federal government, by threatening to withhold funding, has been pressuring local officials into investigating the immigration status of people of Hispanic heritage who become involved in the criminal justice system as defendants, victims, or witnesses. During our fishing trips, Pablo told me that if he and his wife were placed into custody by INS and deported, their two children would wind up living in El Paso with their aunt who is in poor health. Pablo was very worried that she would be unable to take proper care of the children. You can talk to Pablo, Mr. Tanner. But if he tells you that he cannot be involved, we'll have to respect his decision. I won't see him forced to risk the well-being of his wife and children in order to help me."

After listening intently while taking notes, Tanner concluded the interview by saying, "I'll work hard for you, Mr. Rodriguez. I will begin by filing that Bond Reduction Motion right away. I hope to have you before Judge Chandler for a hearing on that Motion sometime this week.

At the Pretrial Release Hearing later that week, Tanner addressed the Court as follows: "Judge Chandler, I'm asking you to place Mr. Rodriguez on pretrial release without having to post bond. He and his family have lived in El Paso all of their lives. Mr. Rodriguez is not going anywhere. He has no criminal record. He's never before been arrested or in trouble with the law. Along with his fellow migrant workers, he puts in long hours in the field, six days a week, harvesting the crops which feed the people of our country. He supports his wife, Maria, and their seven- year- old daughter, Marianna, on the meager wages he is paid. As Maria testified today, while she works part time at Walmart, the family relies heavily upon her husband's income to make ends meet. She is struggling to keep food on the table and to keep the electricity turned on. In addition, as she explained, Mr. Rodriguez has a very strong bond with their daughter, Marianna. Marianna's grades have suffered since her Papa went to jail. She needs his love and guidance back in her life on a daily basis."

Judge Chandler refused to place Jose on straight Pretrial Release. He chose instead to reduce his bond to $1000 cash or surety. He held that in the event that Jose bonded out, he would be required to call in to Pretrial Release Services three times a week. Despite the reduced bond, Maria was unable to raise the money needed to bond her husband out. Every penny she earned went toward basic necessities of daily life for her daughter and for herself.

Marianna's birthday came and went while Jose sat in jail. Marianna was so upset about her Papa being locked up, that she told her Mama she didn't want a birthday party. The most Marianna would agree to was to invite her best friend and fellow chess player, Monique, over to the house for dinner, cake, and a game of chess. After eating Maria's home-cooked meal topped off by a slice of birthday cake, the girls played a game of chess on the set Monique brought over. Marianna went through the motions but her heart wasn't in the game. It was the only time her best friend was able to defeat her at the chessboard. That same evening after it was lights out at the El Paso County Jail, when no one could see or hear him, Jose thought of his daughter turning eight years old and cried himself to sleep.

Over the next three months, Tanner conducted a number of attorney-client conferences with Jose at the El Paso County Jail. He provided Jose with a copy of the "discovery" which included all of the offense reports as well as transcripts of recorded statements taken by law enforcement. He also provided Jose with transcripts of the depositions he took of Judy Doan and of Officer Thomas, the lead investigating officer. Tanner informed Jose that Pablo refused to speak with him and wanted no part of being involved in Jose's case. Jose instructed Tanner not to involve Pablo, to let it be.

As the trial grew closer, only a week away, Tanner and Jose engaged in lengthy attorney-client conferences at the jail. They carefully viewed copies of the Toys R Us security system videos which recorded the masked thief removing the boxed-up chess set from the shelf and exiting through the back door. After viewing the videos, Jose said to Tanner, "The thief's skin color, muscular build, short height, dark hair and mustache appear similar to me. But that's not me! The thief, like me, has a tattoo on his right arm mid-way between his elbow and his wrist. But his tattoo appears round-shaped. My tattoo is heart-shaped."

Tanner and Jose viewed the video one last time. Suddenly, something struck Tanner that he hadn't focused upon previously. He zoomed in and froze the video at the moment the thief was reaching his hands out toward the Renaissance chess set located on the store shelf. With the video still frozen, Tanner asked Jose to hold his hands out toward him with palms open. Tanner's eyes glanced back and forth between the video and Jose's hands. Then he said, "Mr. Rodriguez, I can't make you any guarantees, but I think we've got evidence here that could make a real difference with a jury."

After discussing this matter further, Tanner stated, "The last thing we've got to discuss, Mr. Rodriguez, is that the State has made you a plea offer. As I explained to you previously, an attorney has an ethical obligation to communicate all plea offers to his client. Under the State's offer, you would plead guilty to Burglary. The State would drop the theft charge. You would be sentenced to six months county jail time with credit for the four months you have already served. You would then be placed on 18 months of probation. A fine would be imposed in the amount of $510. An attorney's fee would be imposed in the amount of $150. If you were to be found guilty as charged at trial, the Judge would most likely impose a period of incarceration, perhaps six months to a year in the county jail. There is a strong likelihood that he would impose probation as well, perhaps two or three years of probation. It is also important to note that if the Judge were so inclined, he would have the power to sentence you up to a maximum of five years prison if the jury found you guilty of burglary. He would also have the power to sentence you up to sixty days county jail time in the event the jury found you guilty of theft."

"What do you think of my chances, Mr. Tanner?"

"Your case has specific strengths and weaknesses. The State will argue that you match all of the general characteristics of the masked thief. They'll argue that your tattoo is in the same location and resembles the tattoo of the thief. The State will assert that you had motive to steal the Renaissance chess set in order to give it to your chess playing daughter as a birthday present. They'll argue that when you realized that you couldn't raise the money in time to purchase it before her birthday, you stole it. They'll try to make a "coincidence" argument. That is, the State will argue that only two days after your second visit to the store, at which time you told Ms. Doan that you still lacked the money to purchase the Renaissance chess set, the store was burglarized and a Renaissance chess set was stolen. They will undoubtedly emphasize that Ms. Doan informed you during your first visit to the store, that the Renaissance chess set was a popular item which had been selling at a rapid pace. They will surely argue that when you found out during your second visit to the store that there was only one remaining chess set left for sale- all the others having been sold- you worried that the last remaining chess set would be sold before you could come up with the money to buy it. So you went back and stole it. Of course, we'll counter that you still had over another week to raise the money to purchase the chess set in time for your daughter's birthday. I will argue that your tattoo is heart-shaped while the thief's tattoo as seen in the video appears to be more round- shaped. I believe that our strongest argument is that your hands appear far different than the smooth hands of the thief as seen in the video. The judge will instruct the jury that reasonable doubt may arise from conflicts in the evidence. I will argue that the inconsistencies and conflicts involving tattoos and hands constitute reasonable doubts. There are no fingerprints connecting you to the crime. And, of course, no one is connecting you to the crime by facial identification. I believe in your cause. We can't be sure how the jury will decide. Life has risks. The final decision as to plea or trial is yours to make."

"The bottom line, Mr. Tanner, is that I feel that I must go on to trial. I'm innocent of these charges against me. Setting a good example for Marianna means the world to me. I can't disgrace myself in her eyes by pleading guilty to crimes I didn't commit. Also, my wife needs my income to keep food on the table and pay the bills."

"I understand, Mr. Rodriguez. I respect your decision. If you speak to the jury with the same sincerity you have expressed to me, your testimony will be a strength in your case. So let's prepare for battle! I will be back soon, and we'll go through your testimony, ok?"

"That's fine, Mr. Tanner, I'll see you then."

The day of reckoning soon arrived. The prosecutor, Mr. Winters, wasted no time going after Jose at trial. Judy Doan testified pursuant to a court ordered subpoena. She identified Jose as the man who spoke to her about his desire to purchase a Renaissance chess set for his daughter's birthday. She testified she was certain about her identification because Jose was in her presence at Toys R Us on two occasions. She stated that she'd noticed a heart- shaped tattoo on Jose's right arm midway between his elbow and wrist.

The following is a portion of Tanner's cross-examination of Judy Doan: "Ms. Doan, you've testified that Mr. Rodriguez told you that he wished to purchase a Renaissance chess set as a birthday present for his daughter, correct?"

"Correct."

"He mentioned that his daughter's name was Marianna, is that right?"

"Yes, sir."

"He shared with you that his seven-year-old daughter, Marianna, was the top chess player in her school's chess club, correct?"

"That's correct."

"Without your asking, he told you that she attended Loma Verde Elementary School, right?"

"That's right."

"That registered in your mind because your granddaughter attended Loma Verde Elementary School, correct?"

"Yes, sir."

"Mr. Rodriguez told you that the $40.00 sticker price for the Renaissance chess set was above his price range, is that right?"

"Yes, sir."

"He told you that he believed he could raise the money in about two weeks?"

"That's right."

"You informed him that the Renaissance chess sets had been selling at a rapid pace, correct?"

"Yes, sir."

"He asked if the chess set could be placed on layaway, right?"

"Yes, sir."

"When you told him that it could not be, he responded that he'd be back to purchase it once he had the money?"

"That's right."

"The day he returned to the store, isn't it true that there were many other sales clerks in the store?"

"That's correct."

"He chose to speak with you again?"

"That's right."

"He told you that he hadn't yet raised the money to purchase the chess set, correct?

"That's correct."

"You told him that since his last visit to the store, all the Renaissance chess sets had been sold out, save for one, is that right?"

"That's right."

"So the Renaissance chess set continued to be a very popular item, correct?"

"Yes, sir."

"It proved to be highly coveted, highly desired by the public?"

"Yes, sir."

"Two days after Mr. Rodriguez's second visit to the store, Toys R Us was burglarized, right?"

"Yes, sir."

"Before Mr. Rodriguez left the store during his second visit, he told you that his daughter's birthday was still over a week away, correct?"

"That's correct."

"He told you that he'd be back to purchase the chess set in four or five days, right?"

"Yes, sir."

The security officer testified that the thief wore dark clothing. He stated that it was too dark for him to provide a description of the fleeing thief. He also stated that when he gave chase and began gaining ground upon the thief, he dropped what turned out to be a Renaissance chess set before escaping into the woods.

The security officer also authenticated the store video recordings which were played for the jury. The jury viewed a masked Hispanic looking man whose general characteristics matched those of Mr. Rodriguez, removing the boxed- up chess set from the store- shelf. Mr. Winters went back and froze the video on the thief's extended right arm reaching for the chess set. Doing so allowed the jury to get a good luck at the thief's round- shaped tattoo located midway between his elbow and his wrist.

The video also revealed that the perpetrator was not wearing gloves. It showed that as the thief reached up and removed the chess set, he was careful to touch nothing other than the chess set itself. Law enforcement testimony established that no fingerprints were located on the boxed chess set. In addition, no fingerprints were located on the broken window/point of entry into the store. Winters called a fingerprint expert who explained that the sweat and oil from a person's hand or palm can leave behind latent prints. The expert also testified that sometimes latent prints are left on a surface a person has touched, but sometimes they are not.

Jose took the stand in his own defense. The following exchange occurred between Jose and Tanner during a portion of his direct examination:

"Mr. Rodriguez, where is your tattoo on your right arm located?"

"Halfway between my elbow and my wrist."

"How long has that tattoo been on your right arm?"

"I got the tattoo shortly after my daughter was born, so about eight years ago."

"Would you please describe your tattoo?"

"It is a heart-shaped tattoo, symbolizing my love for my wife and daughter."

"Your Honor, I'd ask the Court's permission for my client to step down in front of the jury in order to display his extended right arm, so as to enable the jurors to get a close look at his tattoo."

"He may step down and do so, Mr. Tanner."

Jose stepped down, extended his right arm, and walked slowly from one end of the jury box to the other so that each juror was able to get a close luck at the tattoo.

"Thank you, Mr. Rodriguez, Tanner stated, please return to the witness stand."

"Mr. Rodriguez, I'd like to show you defense exhibit one for identification only. Do you recognize this photo?"

"Yes sir."

"What is it?"

"That's a photo of my tattoo on my right arm.

"How do you recognize it?"

"It's heart- shaped, and it's midway between my elbow and wrist."

"Do you recall when and where the photo was taken?"

"Your investigator took the photo at the jail on March 27, 2017, a few days after I was arrested."

"Does the photo fairly and accurately depict, represent, and portray your tattoo as it appeared on the day the photo was taken?"

"Yes sir."

"Does the photo fairly, accurately, and substantially portray the way your tattoo appeared a week earlier on March 20, 2017, the date of the crime?"

"Yes, sir."

"Your Honor, I offer defense exhibit one for identification only- into evidence as defense exhibit one."

"Any objections, Mr. Winters?"

"No, Your Honor."

"The photo will be admitted into evidence."

"Your Honor, I'd ask that the photo be published to the jury."

The judge instructed the bailiff to hand the photo to the jury to be passed from one juror to another.

"Mr. Rodriguez, where were you on Monday, 3/20/17, at 10 p.m., the date and time of the burglary and theft?"

"I was fishing on the Rio Grande with my friend, Pablo Torres."

"How can you recall that?"

"For many months, Pablo and I had taken to fishing on Monday and Tuesday nights. It was a way of helping to make sure that our families had enough to eat throughout the week."

"Do you know where Pablo is today?"

"He's a migrant worker as I am. I believe he's working."

"Mr. Rodriguez, in addition to the heart- shaped tattoo on your right arm, are there any identifying features on your hands?

Jose held his hands up in front of him. "Mr. Tanner, are these the hands of a thief?"

"What do you mean by that, Mr. Rodriguez?"

"I've spent most of my life in the fields harvesting crops. It's hard work, and over time it has caused rough, raised, and hardened callouses to form all over my palms and fingers. They didn't form in a day, a week, or a month, but over many years. I earn little pay for my day labor in the heat. But I'm proud of these callouses, Mr. Tanner. I got them supporting my family. Along with my wife, I have taught our eight-year-old daughter, Marianna, to work hard in school and to be honest. I've tried hard to be a good role model for her. I would never risk messing that up by stealing."

"Your Honor, I'd ask permission for my client to once again step down in front of the jury so that the jurors can get a close luck at his palms and fingers."

"He may do so, Mr. Tanner."

"Mr. Rodriguez, starting at the far end of the jury box, please slowly walk a straight line in front of the jurors while holding up your palms and fingers so that the jurors can get a close look at them." Jose did so.

"Thank you, Mr. Rodriguez, Tanner stated. Please return to the witness stand."

At this point, Tanner had Jose identify photos which Tanner's investigator had taken of his palms and fingers on March 27, 2017, at the county jail. The photos clearly displayed the rough, raised, and hardened callouses all over Jose's palms and fingers. The photos were admitted into evidence and published to the jury.

"Mr. Rodriguez, on March 20, 2017, around 10:00 p.m., did you break into Toys R Us as alleged by the State?

"No, sir."

"Did you steal a Renaissance chess set from the store?"

"No, sir."

"Thank you, Mr. Rodriguez, I have no further questions."

The following exchange took place during a portion of State Attorney Winter's cross-examination of Jose:

"Mr. Rodriguez, you've spoken of your deep love for your daughter, correct?"

"Yes, sir."

"You felt that the Renaissance chess set which you spotted in Toys R Us was the perfect birthday gift for her, right?"

"Yes, sir."

"It was perfect given her love of chess, right?"

"Yes, sir."

It was also perfect given the interest she had shown in school in reading about the Renaissance period?"

"Yes, sir, that's right."

When you spotted the Renaissance chess set on display, you asked Ms. Doan what it was priced at, correct?"

"Yes, sir."

"She led you over to five boxed Renaissance chess sets on a shelf available for purchase, correct?"

"Yes, sir."

The chess sets were each priced at $40.00, right?"

"That's right."

"You informed Ms. Doan that the chess set was above your price range, correct?"

"Yes, sir."

"You stated that you believed that you could come up with the money in about two weeks' time, correct?"

"Yes, sir."

"Ms. Doan mentioned to you that the chess sets were a popular item and that Toys R Us had been selling them at a rapid pace, right?"

"That's correct."

"You were quite disappointed that you lacked the money to purchase a Renaissance chess set for your daughter's birthday on the spot, weren't you Mr. Rodriguez?"

"Yes sir, I was."

"In light of the fact that the chess sets were selling at a rapid pace, you asked Ms. Doan if she could place one of the chess sets for you on layaway, correct?"

"That's right."

"She told you that she could not do so?"

"That's correct."

"You were quite disappointed that Toys R Us would not allow the chess set to be placed on layaway, correct?"

"Yes, I was disappointed about that."

"Two weeks later you returned to the store to make sure there were still Renaissance chess sets available, correct?"

"Yes sir, that's right."

"You found out that there was only one remaining Renaissance chess set in the store available for purchase, right?"

"Yes, sir."

"Each of the other Renaissance chess sets had been sold out, correct?"

"Yes, sir."

"You realized how right Ms. Doan had been when she informed you during your first visit to the store, that the Renaissance chess sets were selling at a rapid pace, correct?"

"Yes, sir."

"You still lacked the money to purchase the chess set, correct?"

"That's right."

"At that point, your daughter's birthday was only a little over a week away, isn't that true?"

"Yes, sir."

"You were still very determined, Mr. Rodriguez, to give that chess set to your daughter on her birthday, weren't you?"

"Yes, sir."

"So determined, sir, that when you still lacked the money to purchase it for her, you broke into the store two days later and stole it before anyone else could purchase that last remaining set, right?"

"No sir, that's not true!"

"It's your testimony that at the time of the break-in, 3/20/2017, at 10:00 p.m., you were on the Rio Grande fishing with your friend, Pablo Torres, correct?"

"Yes, sir."

"Your friend's not here at trial, right Mr. Rodriguez?"

"Objection, Your Honor! May we approach the bench?"

"Counsel approach," the Judge responded. Counsel for each side did so.

At this point, a brief sidebar conference was conducted outside the earshot of the jury.

"Make your argument, Mr. Tanner."

"Your Honor, by confronting my client with the fact that Pablo Torres is not here to testify, Mr. Winters improperly shifted the burden of proof. The state has the burden to prove guilt beyond a reasonable doubt. My client has no burden to present witnesses or to prove his innocence. I'd move for a mistrial."

"Your response, Mr. Winters."

"Your honor, once Mr. Rodriguez asserted that at the time of the crime he was on the Rio Grande with Mr. Torres, he opened the door for me to cross-examine him regarding Mr. Torres' absence from the trial."

"My ruling, gentlemen, is that by confronting Mr. Rodriguez as to Mr. Torres' absence from the trial, Mr. Winters did improperly shift the burden of proof. However, I don't believe the error rises to a level requiring me to declare a mistrial. I am ruling that Mr. Winter's cross- examination regarding Mr. Torres' absence from the trial, opened the door to allowing Mr. Rodriguez to explain in full Mr. Torres' reasons for absenting himself from the trial. What would otherwise be forbidden as inadmissible hearsay, will be allowed."

At this point, prior to testimony resuming, the Judge said to Jose in front of the jury, "Mr. Rodriguez, regarding Mr. Torres' absence from the trial, you may explain in full the reasons for his absence."

Jose stated, "Mr. Torres and his wife are undocumented migrant workers. Mr. Torres feared that if he showed up to testify, he and his wife would be arrested and deported by INS. He worried that if they were deported, their two young children who were born in the United States would wind up living in El Paso with their sickly aunt. Jose believed she was incapable of providing proper child care. That's why he avoided coming forward to testify in my trial."

On rebuttal, the following exchange occurred between Tanner and Jose: "Mr. Rodriguez, before you were arrested and charged, what were you planning to do if the last remaining Renaissance chess set at Toys

R Us was sold before you could come up with the money to purchase it for your daughter in time for her birthday?"

"Well sir, my plan if that happened, was for my wife and I to give our daughter a birthday card with an IOU note, promising her a Renaissance chess set. I would have explained to her, 'Listen my darling, birthday girl. Your mama and I wanted to give you a beautiful Renaissance chess set for your birthday; But unfortunately, we couldn't come up with the money to pay for it in time. We are truly sorry. Instead, we are giving you this IOU note. It means that we are promising to give you a Renaissance chess set as a birthday present just as soon as we can.' That's what I would have done."

The following were included among the remarks delivered by Tanner on behalf of Jose during Closing Argument:

"The judge will instruct you that reasonable doubt may arise from conflicts in the evidence. In this case, there is a conflict between the rough, raised, and hardened callouses all over Mr. Rodriguez's fingers and palms, and the smooth hands of the thief as seen in the video! There's a scene from the popular movie, "Jaws," in which Captain Quint questions whether a wealthy oceanographer, Mr. Hooper, has the chops, the right stuff, to go "sharkin"- that is, to go fishing for a Great White Shark. Quint says to Hooper, 'Let me see your hands.' He looks them over and says, 'You've got city hands, Mr. Hooper, you've been counting money all your life!' Ladies and Gentlemen, Mr. Rodriguez doesn't have city hands and he hasn't been counting money all his life. He has earned meager wages as a field worker all his life utilizing his hands to harvest crops. As you saw when Mr. Rodriguez held out his hands during his direct testimony, his fingers and palms are covered with thick and hardened callouses formed over many years out in the field, working his hands to the bone. Projected on the screen before you are the photographs, in evidence, of Mr. Rodriguez's fingers and palms which were taken at the county jail on March 27, 2017, only one week after the break-in at Toys R Us. As you can see, the photographs clearly display the thick and hardened callouses covering Mr. Rodriguez's fingers and palms."

"In contrast, let me zoom in and freeze frame on those portions of the Toys R Us video entered into evidence by the State, which reveal the thief's hands as he reached out to remove the chess set from the shelf. As the video reveals, the thief's palms and fingers appear smooth, completely devoid of rough, raised, and hardened callouses! The reason for the conflict between the hardened callouses on my client's hands and the completely smooth looking hands of the thief as seen in the video, is that they are two different sets of hands! My client is not the thief! This glaring conflict in the evidence demonstrates that the officers jumped to the wrong conclusion and arrested the wrong man!"

"The State noted that my client's tattoo, like the tattoo of the thief as seen in the video, is located half-way between his elbow and his wrist. True enough. However, much more important than the location of the tattoos is what the tattoos look like! As the photograph in evidence of my client's right arm reveals, and as you saw when Mr. Rodriguez held out his right arm before you, his tattoo is clearly heart- shaped, symbolizing his love for his wife and daughter. Upon close review of the video, the perpetrator's tattoo appears more round- shaped than heart- shaped. Once again, reasonable doubt may arise from conflict in the evidence! This conflict, I'd submit, takes on greater weight when it is viewed along-side the glaring conflict between Mr. Rodriguez's deeply calloused fingers and palms, and the smooth hands of the thief as seen in the video."

"The Judge will also instruct you that reasonable doubt may arise from lack of evidence, from things not proven. Mr. Rodriguez's fingerprints were not located on the stolen Renaissance chess set; Nor were they located at the point of entry. The fingerprint expert testified that prints are not always left behind when a person touches a surface. Fair enough. But the point is that there are no fingerprints linking or connecting Mr. Rodriguez to the stolen chess set or to the point of entry. There is no facial identification evidence linking Mr. Rodriguez to this crime. Also, the State has produced no mask. It has presented no evidence tying Mr. Rodriguez to the mask worn by the thief. In addition, the State has presented no evidence of any admissions of guilt made by Mr. Rodriguez to anybody at any time."

"The fact that a Renaissance chess set was stolen from Toys R Us two days after Mr. Rodriguez last spoke with Ms. Doan about his intention to purchase such a set for his daughter's birthday, does not constitute an incriminating, huge coincidence. If that were the case, then anyone who speaks to a clerk about making a purchase, and then fails to follow through for whatever reason, would be in jeopardy if the item was stolen soon thereafter! In addition, Mr. Rodriguez's expression of intent to purchase, does not constitute evidence of intent to steal! Keep in mind also that the Renaissance chess sets were a highly popular, coveted, and desired item among the public. They were selling like hot cakes! The burglary and theft were less of a coincidence and more of an unfortunate event. It was unfortunate for Toys R Us. But mostly, it was highly unfortunate for Mr. Rodriguez. As a result of Mr. Rodriguez expressing an interest in one of those very popular chess sets, combined with the fact that he fit the general description of the masked thief as seen on the video, he was accused of crimes he didn't commit. The fact that both the thief and Mr. Rodriguez were Hispanic males with similar general characteristics, does not constitute an improbable coincidence. Every day experience in the real world reveals that there are lots of folks of Hispanic heritage living in El Paso, and many of them share Mr. Rodriguez's general characteristics."

"You have heard that upon my client's second visit to Toys R Us, he found out that four Renaissance chess sets had been sold, and that there was only one remaining chess set available for purchase. The conclusion drawn by law enforcement as well as the State, is that my client decided to steal that last remaining chess set before anyone else could purchase it. Based upon that conclusion, that assumption, law enforcement shut down their investigation. It was case closed! They looked no further. They dug no deeper. They worked no harder. They failed to analyze the evidence more thoroughly. Do you remember we discussed during jury selection the big difference between accusation and assumption on one hand, and proof beyond a reasonable doubt on the other? If law enforcement had worked a little harder, they would have realized that lo and behold, Mr. Rodriguez's tattoo is clearly heart- shaped, while the thief's tattoo appears to be more round- shaped; And more importantly, they would have realized that Mr. Rodriguez's heavily calloused hands attributable to years of hard work in the field, do not match and are completely inconsistent with the smooth hands of the thief! Remember we discussed during jury selection the importance of thoroughness and attention to detail in conducting a criminal investigation? Law enforcement's failure in this regard resulted in Mr. Rodriguez being accused of crimes he didn't commit. As the Judge will instruct you, ladies and gentlemen, you the jury are the triers of fact. These cases are not decided by law enforcement, or by state attorneys, or by defense attorneys, or by even the Judge. These cases are decided by objective jurors like yourselves who apply the law upon which the judge instructs you to the facts, while holding the State to its burden of proof beyond every reasonable doubt."

"The Judge will instruct you that as jurors, you can utilize your good old common sense. Mr. Rodriguez told Ms. Doan that his daughter attended Loma Verde Elementary School. He told her that his daughter was the top chess player in the school's chess club. He even provided his daughter's name, Marianna. Having provided all of that information, and having twice spoken with Ms. Doan about purchasing a Renaissance chess set for his daughter's birthday, he essentially provided bread crumbs that would lead law enforcement on a path directly to his door! Perhaps pie crumbs would be a more appropriate way to express it, since Mr. Rodriguez would have been making it easy as pie for law enforcement to locate him! The reason none of this makes any sense is because Mr. Rodriguez didn't break into Toys R Us! He didn't steal the chess set! He was accused of crimes committed by another."

"Mr. Rodriguez had an absolute right to remain silent; But he wanted to take the stand and testify under oath. He wanted to tell his story. He willingly opened himself up to cross examination. He's not trained in public speaking; But he knew he was armed with the truth! He was honest and straight forward with you in his testimony. Yes, he wanted to purchase a Renaissance chess set for his daughter, Marianna. Yes, he wanted very much to give it to her for her upcoming birthday. But no, he didn't break into Toys R Us and he didn't steal the chess set!"

"The State argued that my client's desire to give the chess set to his little daughter for her birthday, combined with the fact that he was short on money to purchase the set, constituted his motive for committing burglary and theft. The state emphasized that the judge will instruct you that the case must not be decided because you feel sorry for anyone or are angry at anyone. A few points must be made in response. First of all, Mr. Rodriguez was still working hard in the fields to come up with the money to purchase the chess set. There was still over a week to go before his daughter's birthday. He was honest and straightforward with you. He admitted that he was concerned that the last remaining chess set might be sold before he could come up with the money to purchase it; But he was trying his best. Also, as he explained, he had a Plan B in mind, and it wasn't about stealing! He had decided that if need be, he and his wife would give Marianna a birthday card accompanied by an IOU note, promising her very soon a beautiful Renaissance chess set. That's what he would have done."

"I want to be clear that we are not asking you to decide this case based upon sympathy. As the judge will instruct you, doing so would be improper. Mr. Rodriguez spoke from the heart about his daughter not to invoke sympathy. He did so because he wanted you to understand fully that there was a line that he would never cross. As he explained, there was something even more important to him than giving that chess set to Marianna on her birthday. He and his wife wanted a better life and a better future for their daughter, filled with opportunities that they themselves had never had. They were teaching Marianna the importance of continuing to work hard in school. They were teaching her to be an honest person. It was extremely important to Mr. Rodriguez to serve as a positive role model in his daughter's life. He would never have risked or jeopardized playing that role by stealing."

"Likewise, we didn't present evidence of Mr. Rodriguez's callous covered fingers and palms attributable to endless hours picking crops in the field, in order to appeal to your sympathy. Rather, we wanted you to see that his callous covered fingers and palms were completely inconsistent with the smooth hands of the thief! They were two different sets of hands belonging to two different people!"

"On a related point, the judge will instruct you that one factor in assessing a witness's credibility is whether his testimony is corroborated by other testimony or other evidence in the case. Mr. Rodriguez's testimony that he did not commit burglary or theft was corroborated by the video. It revealed that the thief's round-shaped tattoo as well as his smooth hands matched neither the heart-shaped tattoo nor the calloused over hands of my client! It turns out that Mr. Rodriguez's heart-shaped tattoo on his right arm located midway between his elbow and his wrist, does not constitute an incriminating tell-tale elephant in the room. Rather, it constitutes nothing more than a paper-tiger-lacking teeth, lacking weight, in light of the conflicts in the evidence."

"During his direct testimony, Mr. Rodriguez held up his calloused hands and posed the question, 'Are these the hands of a thief?' As the triers of fact, that is a question for you and you alone to decide, while holding the State to its burden of presenting proof of guilt beyond every reasonable doubt. I'd suggest that the evidence, the lack of evidence, the critical conflicts in the evidence regarding the tattoos and calloused hands, as well as the common-sense considerations I've spoken of, all add up to one thing. The State has failed to prove my client guilty of burglary or theft beyond every reasonable doubt. And the reason they've failed to do so is because Mr. Rodriguez is innocent of both charges which have been filed against him! Therefore, I'm asking you to return the appropriate verdicts of Not Guilty in regard to each count. Thank you."

Because closing arguments concluded at 7:00 p.m., the judge sent the jury home for the night. The next morning at 9:00, the judge read the jury instructions to the jury. He instructed them as to the applicable law they were to apply to the facts during their deliberations. After doing so, he sent the jury out to the jury room to begin its deliberations.

Two hours later, the jurors informed the bailiff that they had reached a verdict. During the entire trial, Maria had waited outside the courtroom. She was too nervous to watch the trial. But now, upon being informed by Tanner that the jury was about to reenter the courtroom to return its verdict, Maria decided to enter the courtroom to hear the verdict read aloud. She sat nervously in the public viewing area of the courtroom. Jose and Tanner sat down together at the defense table. Mr. Winters took his seat at the state attorney's table. Madam Clerk remained seated, while the court reporter prepared to record the reading of the verdict. The bailiff then announced, "All rise," as the Judge reentered the courtroom. The Judge instructed the bailiff to bring in the jury. The attorneys and Jose stood as the jury reentered the courtroom.

"Ladies and gentlemen of the jury, have you reached a verdict?"

The Forewoman, holding the verdict form in hand, responded, "We have, your Honor."

The Verdict Form was delivered by the bailiff to the Judge, who reviewed the form to make sure it was a lawful verdict.

"Madam Clerk, please read the verdict."

"In the Circuit Court of the Criminal Division in and for El Paso County State of Texas v. Jose Rodriguez, Defendant, Case No. CF2007-03276A-XX As to Count 1 (Burglary) – We, the Jury, find the Defendant, Jose Rodriguez, Not Guilty. As to Count 2 (Petit Theft) – We, the Jury, find the Defendant, Jose Rodriguez, Not Guilty. So say we all, dated this third day of December, 2017.

Upon the reading of the verdict, Jose glanced over at his wife who began to silently weep with tears of relief and joy. Jose then sat down and cradled his head in his hands. The judge thanked the jurors for their service and proceeded to dismiss them. As the jury filed out of the courtroom, a couple of jurors glanced over at Jose and smiled.

Soon after the jury was dismissed, Jose was transported from the courthouse to the El Paso County Jail where he'd lived the last four months of his life. From there he was booked-out approximately two hours after his acquittal. He exited the jail into the awaiting arms of Maria. They drove home together where Jose enjoyed lunch with his wife as a free man.

Later that afternoon around 3:00, the two of them drove together to Loma Verde Elementary School. They entered the cafeteria where a big chess tournament involving kids from a number of schools was about to get started. Large numbers of children filled the cafeteria. They were milling about as they excitedly awaited the beginning of the tournament. From the far end of the cafeteria, a high-pitched voice rang out above the buzzing of the crowd: "Papa, Papa!" exclaimed Marianna. She bolted across the cafeteria and leaped into Jose's outstretched arms!

About a week later, a package with an accompanying note arrived at Jose's front door. The note read as follows: "Dear Mr. Rodriguez, I contacted the Circuit Court Clerk's Office following the trial, and learned that you were acquitted of both charges against you. I recall how proudly you spoke about your daughter, and about how well she was doing in school. Please accept the package as a small gesture to set things right for all you have been through. May God Bless you and your family. Judy Doan."

Early one Friday evening, about a month after Jose had returned to work in the fields, he stopped by Marianna's favorite Mexican restaurant, The Tasty Quesadilla, which the family could afford only once in a blue moon. He spoke to the restaurant owner, Carlos Riva. He also spoke to Santiago Diaz who played guitar there on the weekends. Later that evening, Marianna was excited when her parents told her they'd be going out to dinner at the Tasty Quesadilla on Saturday night. She was even happier when they told her that she could invite Monique to join them, and that they would pay for Monique's dinner.

The atmosphere at the Tasty Quesadilla that Saturday evening was loud and festive. Families were enjoying time together, laughing and savoring the aromas and flavors of their favorite dishes. They did so while listening to best-loved Latin standards resonating from Santiago's melodious voice, accompanied by his sweet-sounding guitar. Shortly after Jose, Maria, and the girls finished their dinner, Jose raised his hand signaling both Carlos Riva and Santiago. Santiago finished the song he was playing and then made an announcement.

"Ladies and gentlemen, tonight, a special little girl, Marianna Rodriguez, is here with her family and her best friend, Monique. She doesn't know it yet, so I will tell her. She is here to celebrate, belatedly, her eighth birthday. Her Papa deeply regretted that he could not be with her on her actual birthday. But better late than never! So now, I hope you will please accompany me on my guitar, in celebrating Marianna with a rendition of Happy Birthday!" Marianna smiled and beamed as Santiago serenaded her with the entire restaurant joining in.

The moment the singing began, Carlos Riva appeared from the kitchen while holding high above his head, a birthday cake with eight lit candles. The frosting on the cake was shaped like a queen on a chess board. Written into the frosting were Marianna's initials, "M.R.", next to the words, "Chess Queen!" As Carlos arrived with the cake at Marianna's table, the family's waitress brought over a package.

With two big breaths, Marianna blew out the candles. As Maria prepared to cut the cake, Jose stated excitedly, "Open up the package, Marianna!" As Marianna opened it up, she and Monique suddenly shouted in delight as they feasted their eyes upon the grand and beautiful pieces of a Renaissance chess set!

Marianna excitedly exclaimed, "Papa, Mama, I love it! Thank you! We've got to get home after cake! Monique and I have got some chess playing to do!"

Jose simultaneously laughed and fought back tears, as he savored his daughter's birthday moments which he'd missed and could only dream about during those dark and lonely days he'd spent in the El Paso County Jail, awaiting trial. As the girls marveled over the design of the chess pieces, Jose leaned over to Maria and whispered, "I never thought I'd enter Toys R Us again; But I would like to thank Ms. Doan in person for her kind gesture; And I would like to tell her how overjoyed Marianna was to receive the Renaissance chess set. Will you come with me, dear?"

"Yes, Jose, I will," Maria responded, as she hugged her husband.

As the family stood up to leave, Marianna leaped into her Papa's arms while triumphantly holding up her chess set firmly in her hands. As the family marched out in a birthday procession, the diners looked up and clapped as Happy Birthday once again resonated in the background from the sweet strings of Santiago's guitar.

BRIDGES AND WALLS
(Essay)

Building up bridges and tearing down walls-
Before it's too late to sidestep a fall.
Why don't we do so it's not a tough call-
The ties that bind us are stronger than walls.

Facing up to our feet of clay-
Breaking barriers that lock us away-
Bridging the gap to a peaceful day-
Why don't we do so without delay?

Tearing down walls between the religions-
Building up bridges to other traditions.
Releasing our grip on long held suspicions.
It's up to the people and not politicians.

Envision a world where people unite-
Turning from darkness and seeking the light.
Kindness directed toward every man's plight-
Respect and reverence for human rights.

Picture God painting in colors and shades-
A rainbow of people on canvass is made.
Where racial prejudice melts and fades-
A tolerant world no longer delayed.
Acceptance of others while turning from hate-
The way of salvation before it's too late.

Why don't we cherish our common humanity?
Free ourselves up from conceit and our vanity.
The building of walls a kind of insanity.

Why not forgive all the people we blame-
The things that we cherish are so much the same:
Family and friends as we share the good earth-
A world full of people of equal worth.

Children leave home while spreading their wings-
To seek out their fortune and reach for their dreams.
No matter their setbacks nor how far apart-
Letters from home can lighten their hearts.

When we wall others out, we wall ourselves in-
Cutting off ties and declining within.
Why not opt for a healthier plan-
For friendship with people from far- away lands-
Helping our brothers in need of a hand.

Building up bridges and tearing down walls-
Before it's too late to sidestep a fall.
Should people not do so once and for all?
Rising together and caring for all.

A RAINBOW OF MANY COLORS

(Essay)

What in the world will it finally take-
To quell all the violence and stop all the hate?
Will we choose to do so before it's too late-
Determined to shape the course of our fate?

What is required to stop all the pain-
To throw off the shackles and cast off the chains-
And become what we could be, far more humane?

Will we choose to reject and stop the insanity-
Blinded by vanity, absorbed by inanity-
Embracing instead, our common humanity?

Why all the violence, why all the hatred?
Do religions not teach that love is but sacred?
Ending intolerance based upon race-
Making the world a much better place-
Some would call it, Amazing Grace.

Since we all belong to the human race-
Why all the prejudice based upon race-
Why this enduring age-old disgrace?

Why not repudiate our racial hate-
Celebrate rather our differing traits?
There's no time to lose, no reason to wait.

We're rapidly sinking, trapped in the quicksand-
How much more can we truly withstand?
A critical hour is clearly at hand-
It's up to the people and what they'll demand-
To make the good earth, a better land.

When sunlight passes through rain in a special way-
On a cloudy, dark, and gloomy day-
The beams of sunlight separate into the colors of a
      beautiful rainbow on display.
We savor the moments of its presence-
As we gaze upon the sunlight's essence.

Like beams of sunlight, people come in many colors-
      Like a beautiful rainbow on display.
Can they view each other in this generous way?
Seeing the light at the end of the day-
Sharing in work and sharing in play-
While forging their way to a peaceful day?

Can they look any deeper, deeper within-
Beneath the color of a person's skin-
To his truest colors, the person within?

Not looking down and disparaging others-
Seeing each other as sisters and brothers-
A beautiful rainbow of many colors.

DECENCY, HONOR, AND SIMPLE RESPECT
(Essay)

Whatever happened to decency, honor,
    and simple respect?
Corruptive behavior goes sadly unchecked.
Sexual harassment, attempts to debase-
We fall ever further, further from grace.

Intolerance directed toward other religions-
Disrespect for other traditions-
Hatred preached by politicians-
Demagoguing for their own ambitions.

Betrayal of "Dreamers" and other minorities-
By many of those in the racial majority.
Scapegoating groups for the acts of a few-
Spreading the slander that isn't true-
The thing that despots religiously do.

Profiling suspects on the basis of race-
With excessive force that's "in your face."
Trampling on rights an abuse of authority-
Respecting those rights must be a priority.

If we fail to treat others in a fair and just manner-
The ideals we profess they'll no longer matter.
The question in play at the end of the day-
Will people behave in a civil way?

Or continue to sink and lower the bar?
Is that the essence of who we are?
Consumed by hatred and filled with greed?
Why not opt for a simple creed-
Of respect for others in thought and deed?

Shall we raise the bar like an Olympic star-
Launching herself with all of her might-
Reaching to soar to a much greater height-
That she's never quite reached, try as she might-
But always believing it's still within sight?

Are we losing capacity to care, to empathize?
Our moral compasses woefully compromised?
Mistreatment of others left to agonize?
While the truth is twisted, hidden, or sanitized?

It's a moment of truth, a time of reflection-
About our behavior and needed corrections.
The values we cherish they need our protection.

Decency, honor, and simple respect-
Values our country must never reject.
Justice and fairness must never be lynched-
Preserving these values will not be a cinch.
We can hardly afford to step back or flinch.

If we don't back away-
And we don't go astray-
Then maybe one day we'll be able to say-
We cared for each other and hatred gave way.

WILL PEACE FIND A WAY?
(Essay)

Religious psalms and deadly bombs
      abound in this world;
And I'm left to wonder if
Peace, sweet peace, will find a way?
Or if violence wins the day?
Will it be war on poverty-
Or poverty from war?

New vaccines to heal and new weapons of steel
      abound in this world;
And I'm left to wonder if
Mankind will leave behind the gentler graces of his soul?
Or will safeguarding his children's future be his goal?
Will he choose to soar or plunge into war?
Time will tell us what's in store.

Flights into space and the deadly arms' race
      abound in this world;
And I'm left to wonder if
Peace, sweet peace, will find a way?

A LONG ROAD TO JUSTICE
(Historical Non-Fiction Essay)

"We hold these truths to be self-evident, that all men are created equal,"
    Jefferson wrote in 1776.
But from the beginning, his expression of equality intrinsic to all men, was
    dropped like a ton of bricks.
Those in positions of power decided it meant-
That white men only are created equal, that's how they desecrated the words' intent.

America's slave trade upon which the economy of the South relied, had begun with
    the arrival of slaves upon slave ships in Jamestown, Va., in 1619. Those
    who had survived the brutal and horrendous conditions aboard the ships-
Faced the evil and dehumanizing horrors of slavery, including the lash of the whip.

The slave trade thrived for close to two centuries before slave owner, President Thomas
    Jefferson, finally ended America's involvement in the slave trade in 1808.
    But the enslavement of black people already located in the America South
    continued on, unabated, year after year. Jefferson's expression of equality,
    his self-evident idealistic words-
Were in practice twisted into an evil theater of the absurd.

Slavery was America's original sin-
Tied to the color of a person's skin.
A way of life and an evil ignored-
Which paved the way to the Civil War.

In 1820, Congress passed the Missouri Compromise which was negotiated by the
    "Great Compromiser," Henry Clay. Controversy existed as to whether to extend
    slavery into newly acquired territories. Under Clay's compromise, slavery was
    prohibited north of the 36 30' parallel. Maine was admitted into the Union as a
    free state; But Missouri was admitted as a slave state. Congress thus saw to it that
    slavery would remain alive.
It's sadistic and dehumanizing cruelty would continue to thrive.

Thirty years later, Henry Clay negotiated The Compromise of 1850. As a result
of the Mexican-American War which lasted from 1845-48, America not only
retained possession of Texas, it also acquired an enormous amount of territory
between the Rio Grande and the Pacific. The question, once again, was whether
slavery would be extended into the newly acquired territories? Under Clay's
compromise, California was admitted as a free state. As for all the other
territories between the Rio Grande and the Pacific Ocean, the doctrine of popular
sovereignty would determine the issue. That meant that the people within each of
the newly acquired territories would vote to decide whether slavery would be
permitted- as each of the new territories was admitted.

The Compromise of 1850 also included The Fugitive Slave Act, a moral disaster.
It sanctioned the forced return of all runaway slaves captured anywhere within the
country, to their former masters.
Abolitionists nicknamed it the Bloodhound Law, because bloodhounds were utilized to
track down and capture runaway slaves.
For slaves on the run, the threat was grave.

Under the Kansas-Nebraska Act of 1854, the decision as to whether to extend slavery
into the new territories would once again be determined by the doctrine of popular
sovereignty. This prompted pro and anti-slavery factions to pour into Kansas in an
effort to establish a population advantage regarding the vote for or against slavery.
Violent flashpoints broke out between the pro and anti-slavery armed factions as
they went to war-
Turning the territory into "bleeding Kansas" in 1854.

Just as courageous people a little less than a century later risked their lives
hiding Jews from Nazis, "conductors" of the underground railroad risked
their lives assisting runaway slaves.
They too were highly committed, courageous, and brave.

One such brave and remarkable conductor was Harriet Tubman. Some called her
Moses for taking a stand-
By leading slaves to the Promised Land.
While the journey north to freedom was exhausting, treacherous, and long-
thanks to Harriet Tubman it was well-planned.

Harriet advised runaway slaves to flee north while looking to the North Star
     as their guide.
She instructed them as to places along the way to hide.
The road to freedom contained safe-houses where fleeing slaves could take
     shelter. Runaway slaves learned that safehouses could be identified by a
     candle in the window; And slaves and conductors along the underground railroad
     could identify each other by the greeting, "friend of a friend"-
Signs upon which they came to depend.

At first, the Promised Land was located in the "free" territories and states in the North;
     But following passage of the Fugitive Slave Act of 1850, a slave had
     to travel much further, all the way to Canada to be free.
Otherwise, with slave catchers on his trail, his freedom would never be guaranteed.

In 1857, the U.S. Supreme Court in *Dred Scott*-
Held that a black man's suit for freedom was for naught.
Mr. Scott was held to lack standing to sue in federal court.
The Court ruled that he was neither a complete person nor a
     citizen, nor anything of the sort.

In 1859, abolitionist, John Brown, led an unsuccessful raid on a federal armory at
     Harper's Ferry, Virginia. He seized the armory and seven people were killed. He
     intended to lead an armed rebellion to bring slavery to an end. He was captured,
     tried for treason and murder, found guilty, and hanged. The lyrics, "John Brown's
     body lies a-moldering in the grave but his truth goes marching on," became a
     popular Union marching song.
The raid on Harper's Ferry raised passions which prompted the south's secession
     and the Civil War. It wouldn't be long.

Frederick Douglass rose up from slavery to become one of the most influential leaders
     of the abolitionist movement, and one of the greatest advocates for human rights
     and human decency in history. As a young man he escaped slavery, taught himself
     to read, and developed into a brilliant orator and writer. He wrote three
     autobiographies detailing the cruelty of his enslavement, and castigating with great
     moral clarity the evil hypocrisy of the "peculiar institution" of slavery.

Douglass argued from the beginning that the Civil War should be transformed and elevated from a battle to preserve the Union, into a crusade to abolish slavery. He argued that slaves should be freed and allowed to join the Union army. He insisted that they should receive pay equal to the pay of white soldiers. Lincoln greatly admired Douglass, and he appears to have been influenced by Douglass' voice. In some ways, Douglass was to Lincoln as King was to JFK a century later. Each civil rights leader pushed along and firmed up each President's resolve and commitment to the cause of social justice, and to the need for federal law addressing issues of equal opportunity and racial equality.

Following the Civil War, Douglass became a leading advocate for the rights of freed slaves. In addition, he lent support for the women's suffrage movement in the newspaper he established, The North Star.
When it came to issues of equal justice for all, he passionately strove to raise the bar.

In 1831, William Lloyd Garrison founded an abolitionist newspaper, *The Liberator.*
It was unflinchingly dedicated to the immediate end of slavery, to the detriment of bigots, racists, and haters.
Garrison helped spur a movement as an abolitionist leader.
His paper appealed to the moral conscience of its readers.

In 1852, Harriet Beecher Stowe published her anti-slavery novel, *Uncle Tom's Cabin.* It vividly portrayed the evils of slavery. When Lincoln met Ms. Stowe in 1862, he remarked, "So you're the little lady who wrote the book that started this great war!"
Uncle Tom's Cabin awakened many people to the cruelty and humiliation of slavery, in ways that hadn't been done before.

In 1858, during a speech kicking off his run for a U.S. Senate seat from Illinois, Lincoln asserted, "A house divided against itself cannot stand. I believe this government cannot endure permanently half slave and half free."
During his presidential campaign of 1860, Lincoln expressed his opposition to the extension of slavery into the new territories. Regarding his intentions if elected President, he clearly stated that that was key.

On December 20, 1860, South Carolina responded to Lincoln's recent election as
    President of the United States by seceding from the Union. Many other southern
    slave states followed in short order. On April 12, 1861, the South Carolina
    militia fired upon Ft. Sumter. The Union garrison returned fire. A- day- and a half
    later, the hostilities ended with surrender by the federal garrison; But the Civil War
    had begun!
What followed were four years of unimaginable carnage and bloodshed from the muzzle of
    a gun.

Following the North's victory over the South in 1862 in the bloody Battle of Antietam,
    Lincoln issued the Emancipation Proclamation which went into effect on January 1,
    1863.
The Proclamation Ordered that all those living as slaves within states which were
    in rebellion against the Union, would be forever free.

In his Gettysburg Address delivered in 1863, Lincoln asserted that the nation was
    "…conceived in liberty and dedicated to the proposition that all men are created
    equal." "Now, he continued, we are engaged in a great Civil War, testing whether
    that nation, or any nation so conceived and so dedicated, can long endure."
Lincoln himself could not be sure.
"A new birth of freedom," was Lincoln's vision for the nation he led-
For a Union saved with slavery dead.

Many families were split apart-
Parents were left with broken hearts.
Blood and death were the currency paid-
For the death of slavery and a Union saved.

Lincoln fought for and readily expended political capital
    navigating through Congress the Thirteenth Amendment
    which abolished slavery throughout the United States. But soon thereafter,
    on 4/14/1865, only five days after General Lee surrendered to
    General Grant at the Appomattox Court House ending the Civil War,
    a bullet rang out and Lincoln was dead-
Mortally wounded by a shot to the head.

His post-war vision expressed in his second Inaugural Address, was to "bind up
    the nation's wounds," and to proceed "with malice toward none and charity for all."
Would it live on without him? Not at all.

In the post-war era, the nation's course was forever transformed-
Intolerance and venom were lasting norms.
It was malice toward many and charity for few-
Justice and fairness were driven from view.
Black Codes were passed by southern states-
To hold the freedmen back "in their place"-
As second-class citizens- a moral disgrace.

Lincoln's Freedman's Bureau was intended to assist newly freed slaves in
        locating their spouses and children who had been forcibly sold
        at auction in the marketplace. It was meant to assist them in learning to
        read and write. It was also designed to ensure that that the freedmen were
        no longer treated as slave labor-
To be exploited in the work place and abused by neighbors.

Lincoln's successor, President Andrew Johnson, refused to support the reenactment
        of the Freedman's Bureau. It was vetoed. Although Johnson's veto was
        overridden by Congress, the Bureau was deprived of much of its funding
        by Congress in 1869. The effectiveness of the Bureau was further weakened
        due to intimidation and violence by the KKK.
White supremacist racism and terrorism continued to hold sway-
Keeping justice, tolerance, and equality between the races at bay.

The Fourteenth Amendment was ratified by the states in 1868. Included within its
        language was The Equal Protection Clause.
It stated that no state shall deny any person within its jurisdiction of
        the equal protection of the laws.
This language strictly construed on its face, guaranteed that states could
        no longer pass laws or engage in acts-
Which discriminated on the basis of race against blacks.

But in 1896, in *Plessy v. Ferguson*, the U.S. Supreme Court construed
        the Equal protection Clause as sanctioning state "separate but equal" laws
        known as Jim Crow-
Allowing segregation and discrimination to flourish and grow.

In 1876, Rutherford B. Hayes, an opponent of slavery and supporter of civil rights,
    sold out principle for power in a destructive way.
In order to ensure that the presidential election swung his way-
He promised to remove federal troops from the South which cleared the way-
For continued and unbridled terrorism on the part of the KKK.

As years passed in the "land of the free"-
Apartheid thrived to the nth degree-
Vicious as Stowe's slave master, Simon Legree.

As a result, between 1877 and 1950, between 4000 and 5000 black people
    in the South were lynched.
With federal troops removed from the South, and state law enforcement
    often turning a blind eye, lynchings were committed with
    a sense of impunity; A sense that getting away with it was a cinch.

Ida Wells was a black American educator and journalist. Throughout
    her life, she spoke up against racial prejudice, intolerance, and violence.
    She fought for racial equality and women's rights, including women's
    suffrage. She did so persuasively through the spoken word and through the
    written word. Among her many contributions, she investigated, researched,
    and documented the lynching of black people by racists in the South.
    She was also one of the founders of the NAACP.
When it came to fighting and exposing injustice, she was never one to let it be.

In addition to the thousands of individual lynchings, white supremacists
    attacked and destroyed entire black communities. On top of the
    destruction of black lives, they burned and bombed their homes
    and businesses in places such as Wilmington, N.C., in 1898;
    Tulsa, Oklahoma, in 1921; and Rosewood, Fl., in 1923. The
    destruction of businesses and homes constituted the elimination
    of sources of intergenerational wealth-
Obliterating for future generations of many black people, their economic health.

Black people served their country in WWI and WWII.
Despite being treated as second class citizens, they were
      patriotic Americans through and through.
Upon returning home from war after finishing up their final tour-
Black veterans in the South were barred from "white only"
      public accommodations such as toilets, motels, and
      restaurants, to be sure.

If black people traveled out of town in the segregated South for more than a day-
They needed to consult a "Green Book," listing the lodgings where blacks
      could stay.
They needed to locate eating places and toilet facilities they were permitted
      to use along the way.

Between 1916 and 1970, six million African-Americans left the rural South. They
      moved to the urban Northeast, the Midwest, and the West. They were
      seeking a better life with improved economic opportunities; And they
      sought to be free from the horrors of Jim Crow segregation.
This movement became known as The Great Migration.

Between 1918 and around 1935, a large number of black people who joined the
      Great Migration settled in Harlem. Improved opportunities and a greater sense of
      freedom and self-expression on the part of those who escaped the cruelty and
      stupidity of Jim Crow laws in the southern states, played a part in inspiring what
      became known as the Harlem Renaissance. The Renaissance constituted an
      explosion of intellectual, artistic, musical, and cultural expression. There was a
      "flowering of Negro literature" among writers such as Langston Hughes, W.E.B
      Dubois, and Zora Hurston. Many black jazz musicians played Harlem's Cotton
      Club and the Apollo Theater, including Duke Ellington, Charlie Parker, Miles
      Davis, Dizzy Gillespie, Thelonious Monk, Count Basie, Fats Waller, Louis
      Armstrong, Art Tatum, Bessie Smith, Billie Holliday, and many others. Just as
      the great Jesse Owens won four gold medals in Berlin at the 1936 Olympics,
      exploding Hitler's myth of Aryan supremacy-
The Harlem Renaissance played a role in dispelling the myth of white supremacy.

In 1944, second lieutenant Jackie Robinson was court-martialed after refusing
    to comply with a bus driver's order to move to the back of an army bus.
    Despite blatant racism which the military permitted-
Jackie prevailed, he was acquitted.

In 1947, Jackie set out to tear down walls-
By breaking Major League Baseball's color-line once and
    for all-
He did so with guts and grit while playing ball.

For all of his talent and level of play-
Racist slurs were hurled his way-
Including threats most every day.
He refused to be cowed, intimidated, or discouraged-
His heart was filled with uncommon courage.

One teammate had Jackie's back on and off the field. He did so in an
    effort to stand up for decency and keep the peace.
He was a white man from Kentucky, the Dodger shortstop, Pee Wee Reece.

By holding firm to his principled stand-
Jackie set in motion "ripples of hope" throughout the land.
The man from Ebbets Field did more than tear down walls-
He opened minds while playing ball.

President Harry Truman, by executive order, desegregated the armed
    forces in 1948-
A step toward justice and away from hate-
A measure he felt could no longer wait.
Truman also introduced civil rights legislation which was stopped
    in its tracks-
By those infamous, segregationist legislators known as the Dixiecrats.

In 1955, Rosa Parks was arrested for refusing to give up her seat
    on a Montgomery bus. Her arrest set off the 1956 Montgomery
    Bus Boycott led by Martin Luther King-
A young preacher whose words resonated with inspiration and a freedom ring.

The boycott succeeded when the U.S. Supreme Court affirmed that segregation in
      regard to public transportation was unconstitutional-
Striking down a pillar of racism which Alabama had erected as institutional.

In 1955, a fourteen-year-old black American teen visiting from Chicago,
      allegedly whistled at a white woman inside a Mississippi store.
      His name was Emmett Till.
A few nights later, the woman's husband and half-brother kidnapped
      Emmett from his great-uncle's house. He was brutally tortured, beaten,
      and killed.

The men were tried for the murders they committed.
Tried by an all-white jury, they were each acquitted.
Protected by Double Jeopardy, the two murderers bragged
      to *Look* magazine that they had kidnapped and murdered
      Emmett Till. They had done so with impunity-
As if they were licensed with a kind of immunity-
Safe from punishment within their community.

Beginning in Greensboro, N.C. in 1960, sit-ins took place-
At lunch counters that discriminated on the basis of race.
Black people were refused service and arrested based upon the color
      of their skin.
The "land of the free" was the land of sin.

In 1961, Greyhound Buses carrying Freedom Riders arrived in Anniston, Birmingham,
      and Montgomery, Alabama. The Freedom Riders were testing whether U.S.
      Supreme Court decisions outlawing racial segregation on interstate buses, and
      prohibiting racial segregation in regard to bus depot waiting rooms, lunch counters,
      and toilet facilities, were being complied with and honored. In each city, the
      Freedom Riders were brutally and viciously attacked and assailed-
By members of the KKK wielding bricks, bats, pipes, and chains. The Klan viewed the
      preservation of white supremacy through terror and violence as its holy grail.

The attack on the Freedom Riders in Anniston took place on Sunday, May 14,
      Mother's Day.
Even the day marked to honor mothers wasn't enough to keep the brutality and violence
      of the racists at bay.
They viciously assaulted without delay.

In *Brown v. the Board of Education*, in 1954-
"Separate but equal" was at last struck down by the U.S. Supreme Court, at the
   public schoolhouse door.
While desegregation in public schools was ordered to take place with
   "all deliberate speed"-
State and local officials set up roadblocks- to delay, obstruct, and impede.

As steps toward public school desegregation took place-
Flashpoints followed, a moral disgrace.
In 1957, nine black high school students attempted to desegregate Central
   High School. They were met by violent mobs with threatening signs.
The students courageously placed their physical well-being on the line.
They are honored today as the Little Rock Nine.
President Eisenhower sent in the 101st Airborne Division-
To ensure compliance with the Supreme Court's decision.

In New Orleans, in 1960, six-year-old Ruby Bridges became the first
   black child to desegregate the all-white William Frantz Elementary School.
Racism was fueled and ignited upon Ruby's act of attending school.
What followed was hostility toward Ruby, unimaginably cruel.

Throughout the school year, U.S. Marshals had to escort her to class-
To protect her from mobs which she had to pass.
Many parents of white school children yelled out racial slurs against the child-
As well as threats both callous and vile.
One woman scared little Ruby by holding up and pointing to a
   black baby-doll lying inside a doll-sized coffin-
An act revealing a dark heart that would never soften.

Almost immediately, white parents began pulling their children out of the
   school which Ruby was attending.
The depth and breadth of their intolerance was bottomless

   and never-ending.

In this racist climate, the question arose as to who would teach her?
Only Barbara Henry, a white woman from Boston, was willing to serve as
   Ruby's teacher.
For an entire year, Ruby attended a classroom of one.
Aside from Ms. Henry she was snubbed and shunned.

Discrimination extended beyond Ruby's school.

Many businesses within the community were cowed or cruel.

Ruby's dad was fired from his job as a gas station attendant-

Costing him a paycheck upon which his family was dependent.

The Bridges family had customarily shopped at their favorite grocery store.

Soon they were turned away, no longer permitted to step in the door.

Displaying uncommon courage beyond her years-

Ruby remained in school, regardless of hatred and sneers.

One wonders how many of those racists who discriminated against Ruby Bridges-

Considered themselves righteous, God-fearing, and religious?

In 1962, U.S. Marshals were sent to the University of Mississippi at Oxford,
        by JFK-

To stop the violence which erupted when black military veteran, James Meredith,
        enrolled in school that October day.

With hate and violence on full display-

The rioters displayed their moral decay-

A complete disgrace to this very day.

In Birmingham, Alabama, in April and May of 1963-

Demonstrators marched who wished to be free.

Police Commissioner Bull Conner unleashed upon the marchers
        within his segregated city-

Officers utilizing police dogs, fire hoses, and billy clubs- devoid of
        remorse or pity.

Included among those marching for freedom were children,
        embodying the Children's Crusade.

Adults and children were attacked and sprayed.

Young and old, strong and frail-

Thousands were arrested and thrown in jail.

Police brutality in Birmingham, unleashed upon those peacefully
        marching for equality and justice, was nationally
        televised.

The violent images opened hearts and opened eyes.

The events served as a wake-up call-
As Americans watched the protestors fall.
Television showed the price to be paid-
For marching for freedom and a better day.

On 6/11/63, at the U. of Ala., Governor George Wallace stood in
        the "schoolhouse door." His position was, "Segregation now,
segregation tomorrow, segregation forever."
He wanted the schoolhouse door closed off to minorities forever.

In support of white supremacy, Wallace asserted "state's rights." His
        position was, how dare the big bad dictatorial federal
        government interfere with Alabama's "right" to discriminate-
Against black people living, working, or attending school within
        the state.

The Kennedys pushed back-
Sending in Deputy Attorney General, Nicholas Katzenbach.
Wallace and Katzenbach engaged in a face-to-face stand-off.
After a time, Wallace blinked and backed off.

That evening, JFK took to the airways and addressed the nation.
The President spoke of civil rights as a moral crisis, utilizing moral persuasion.
He called for the country to fulfill its promise.
He announced that he was introducing a civil rights bill desegregating
        all public accommodations, to Congress.

Later that evening in the wee hours of 6/12, civil rights activist
        and military veteran, Medgar Evers, who fought for his
        country at Normandy on D-Day-
Was shot dead by segregationist Byron De La Beckwith while
        standing in his driveway.
At the time of the fatal shot, Medgar Evers was carrying an armful
        of T-shirts containing the logo: "Jim Crow must go."

On 8/28/63, during the March on Washington for Jobs and Freedom,
   MLK delivered his "I Have a Dream" speech in front of the Lincoln
   Memorial on the Washington Mall.
So powerful, inspiring, and persuasive were his words, that in the long
   run, walls of intolerance began to fall.

However, in the short run, less than three weeks later on 9/15/63, at the
   Birmingham 16th Street Baptist Church, white supremacists attacked-
Intent on setting The Movement back.
Four black school girls were tragically murdered, and as many as 22 more people
   were injured when the bomb exploded.
Progress and hope were for a time eroded.

Almost a century earlier, in 1870, the Fifteenth Amendment was ratified granting black
   men the right to vote. Southern states responded by erecting barriers to keep them
   from voting. They were disenfranchised by means of voter suppression provisions
   such as poll taxes and literacy tests.
In addition, racist hate groups employed violence and intimidation in a full court press.
The law, and vigilante law, were together utilized as weapons against blacks-
To suppress their votes and silence their voices- to forever hold them back.

In this context of an endless history of state voter suppression, civil rights and women's
   rights activist, Fanny Lou Hamer, along with civil rights activist Robert Moses
   and others, organized a black voter registration movement in Mississippi. Three
   civil rights workers- James Chaney, Andrew Goodman, and Michael Schwerner,
   who were registering blacks in Mississippi to vote, were murdered during
   "Freedom Summer" in 1964.
Their murders became a national outrage to be sure.
Their bodies were located in an earthen dam.
They were murdered by members of "law enforcement" and the Ku Klux Klan.

On 2/18/65, black American civil rights activist, Jimmy Lee Jackson, while participating in a
   voting rights march in Marion, Alabama, was shot and killed by an Alabama state
   trooper. Jackson's death helped to catalyze the voting rights marches from Selma
   to Montgomery. The initial march setting out from Selma took place on "Bloody Sunday,"
   March 7, 1965.
The marchers, including John Lewis, were brutally beaten by Alabama State Police at the
   Edmund Pettis Bridge. Lewis and many others were lucky to survive.

The march was rescheduled for another day.
This time the marchers were seen safely on their way-
By the federalized Alabama National Guard, sent in by LBJ.

One of those who answered Dr. King's call to action falling the atrocities of "Bloody
　　　　Sunday," was a white woman from Detroit named Viola Liuzzo. She traveled to
　　　　Selma to participate in the voting rights marches from Selma to Montgomery.
　　　　She played an important role in the coordination of the marches. While driving
　　　　after dropping off some fellow activists at the Montgomery Airport, she was
　　　　pursued by members of the Ku Klux Klan-
Who shot and killed her according to plan.

Following successful marches by peaceful demonstrators from Selma to Montgomery, Dr.
　　　　King delivered a speech outside the State Capitol Building. He insisted upon
　　　　federal legislation protecting the rights of minorities to vote. Dr. King spoke of how
　　　　long it would take for progress to be made toward justice:
"How long, not long, because no lie can live forever. How long, not long, because
　　　　truth crushed to earth will rise again. How long, not long, because the arc of the
　　　　moral universe is long but it bends toward justice."

Due to the efforts of all those involved in the Civil Rights Movement, combined with
　　　　President Johnson's persuasive skills-
Landmark civil rights legislation was passed on Capitol Hill.
JFK's Civil Rights Bill of 1963, prohibiting segregation in regard to toilets, water
　　　　fountains, hotels, restaurants, and all public accommodations, was passed as the
　　　　Civil Rights Act of 1964- opening doors as never before.

The Voting Rights Act, passed in 1965-
Was critical to bringing justice alive.
It provided teeth which prohibited poll taxes, literacy tests, the counting of jelly
　　　　beans in a jar, and other state restrictions upon the right to vote-
An advance in justice of historic note.

Racial discrimination in reference to the sale, purchase, rental, and financing
　　　　of housing, was prohibited by The Fair Housing Act of 1968.
It too was a step toward justice and away from hate.

The Greatest, Muhammad Ali, was a man of enormous courage, self-confidence,
        and pride, who often spoke in playful rhyme.
He bolstered the black pride movement of his time.
The Champ personified lyrics by James Brown: "Say it loud-
I'm black and I'm proud!"

At a time that it was not popular to do so, he spoke out against the Vietnam War.
For Ali, many difficulties were in store.
He refused induction into military service based upon his Muslim beliefs.
He was publicly reviled with little relief.

If he had chosen to comply-
He would have remained popular in the public eye-
Putting on exhibitions for the military brass-
As so many athletes had done in the past.
Instead, he chose to risk freedom, fortune, and
        his heavyweight title-
For a principled stand that was far more vital.

In 1967, the U.S. Supreme Court in *Loving v. Virginia*, struck down
        as unconstitutional a Virginia statute prohibiting interracial marriage.
The Court held that marriage was a fundamental right.
The Lovings, who had been convicted and sentenced to prison under the
        racist statute, were victorious in their courageous fight.

1968 was a year of violence, a year of hate.
MLK, RFK, and LBJ had been champions in the struggle for civil rights.
Each had played a critical role in the fight.
But in 1968, they were the subjects of two assassinations and a
        presidential resignation.
Regarding the cause of civil rights and equal justice under law, it was a
        time of setback and devastation.

It was a dark year and a destructive hour-
When Richard Nixon came to power.
Vietnam dragged on for another four years-
Years of death and years of tears.
Nixon's paranoia, disregard for the Constitution, and unbridled hate-
Led directly to his abuses of power known as Watergate.
Due to Watergate and the Vietnam War-
People no longer trusted government as they had before.

When Jefferson wrote, "That all men are created equal," only white
        men were included.
Minorities as well as women were excluded.
Despite the egalitarian words that Jefferson wrote-
It took 144 years for women to obtain the right to vote.

In 1840, two abolitionist women, Elizabeth Cady Stanton and Lucretia Mott,
        attended the World Anti-Slavery Convention in London; Because
        they were women, they were barred from the Convention floor.
They were outraged by this indignity to their core.

In 1848, they organized the first women's rights convention at Seneca Falls. Following
        that convention, Ms. Stanton and Susan B. Anthony formed an alliance. Ms.
        Anthony delivered speeches often written by Ms. Stanton, advocating for women's
        suffrage, equal economic opportunities for women, progressive divorce laws, and
        the right of women to own and inherit property. Despite the progress made through
        their alliance-
Their ideas were met with hostility and defiance.

During her speeches, Anthony was often met with angry mobs who hung her
        in effigy. Often, they hurled food and threats her way.
That was a price she was forced to pay.

In 1864, Lucretia Mott, along with others, founded Swarthmore College, a
Quaker school.
Regarding the cause of women's suffrage, Swarthmore became a source of fuel.
One of its students, Alice Paul, continued the legacy of Seneca Falls.
She fought tirelessly for a woman's right to vote- giving her all.

In 1913, on the eve of President Woodrow Wilson's inauguration, Alice
organized a women's voting rights procession in Washington D.C.
She wouldn't back down or let it be.

She recruited about eight thousand marchers from all over the country to participate
in the parade. The goal was to put pressure on President-Elect Wilson to support
a constitutional amendment guaranteeing women the right to vote. Over 500,000
people viewed the procession. A near riot broke out. The women were blocked
from marching and some were injured. The police did little or nothing to protect
them from the crowd. Eventually, the Massachusetts and Pennsylvania National
Guards were called in to stop the disorder-
Control the crowd and bring about order.

In 1917, Ms. Paul and her close friend and fellow suffragette, Lucy Burns, organized a
campaign of daily picketing in front of the White House for a woman's
right to vote. They refused to call off the picketing even after America entered
WWI. They decided to go right on picketing while allowing their signs to do the
talking. They became known as the Silent Sentinels. Despite spurious attacks upon
the suffragettes' patriotism, Paul and Burns resolved not to back off until the battle
for women's suffrage was won. As they noted, for women, taxation without
representation had never ended.
Nor would it, if the struggle for a woman's right to vote was suspended!

Alice, Lucy, and others were arrested and charged with obstructing sidewalk traffic.
While imprisoned within the Occoquan Workhouse in Va., the suffragettes were
kept in terribly unsanitary living conditions. They faced physical abuse and
brutality during what became known as, "The Night of Terror." After going on a
hunger strike, Alice, Lucy, and others were force fed raw eggs through feeding
tubes placed up the nose or down the throat. At one point, Alice was transferred to
a psychiatric ward. This was the price the suffragettes paid-
For the right to vote and a better day.

Like Dr. King who came after them, Alice Paul and Lucy Burns appeared to view the
    Constitution as well as Jefferson's words, "That all men are created equal," as a
    promissory note.
In 1920, through the dogged nonviolent resistance of Alice, Lucy, and their fellow
    suffragettes, the Nineteenth Amendment was ratified at last, guaranteeing women
    the right to vote!

Despite the ratification of the Nineteenth Amendment over a century ago, equal pay for
    equal work among men and women, is not yet reality throughout the land.
When in the world will the wage gap be eliminated, once and for all through a moral
    stand?

The LGBTQ community has been a target of age-old discrimination and intolerance
    in America and throughout the world. In the early 1950's, gay men and lesbians
    in America formed groups to fight for their human rights. This became known as
    the "homophile movement." Over time, the movement became more outspoken
    and defiant. On June 28, 1969, a police raid upon the Stonewall Inn, a gay and
    lesbian bar in Greenwich Village, set off a series of demonstrations by members of
    the gay community. These demonstrations, which became known as the Stonewall
    Uprising, served as a catalyst in the long struggle for LGBTQ rights. Members of
    The LGBTQ community demanded the right to live openly without fear of
    persecution, arrest, or prosecution because of their sexual orientation. A year later
    on June 28, 1970, to mark the Stonewall Uprising, the first gay pride marches
    took place in many cities across the country.

Despite the Stonewall Uprising, more than thirty years passed before all state laws
    criminalizing same-sex sexual activity were finally invalidated. It was not until
    September 2011, forty-two years after the Stonewall Uprising, that gay and lesbian
    people could, for the first time, serve their country in the military without being
    forced to conceal their sexual orientation twenty-four seven. This became a reality
    as a result of President Obama and Congress ending, once and for all, the military
    policy of, "Don't ask, don't tell."
This was an important step toward justice and away from hell.

It was not until June 26, 2015, almost forty-six years after the Stonewall Uprising, that
    the U.S. Supreme Court in *Obergefell v. Hodges*, upheld the legitimacy of same-
    sex marriage as a fundamental right.
As always, justice was a long time coming through years of darkness before the light.

It was not until 2020, over a half century after the Stonewall Uprising, that the U.S.
Supreme Court *in Bostok v. Clayton County*, held that gay, lesbian, and
transgender employees were protected from discrimination in the work place
by the Civil Rights Act of 1964.
This decision constituted another critical step toward justice which unlocked doors.

The proposed Equality Act would prohibit discrimination on the basis of sexual
orientation or gender identity in areas beyond the workplace- including public
accommodations, housing, education, jury service, and federally funded programs.
Unfortunately, the bill remains tied up in Congress. The long road to justice is a
painstakingly slow, dangerous, and uneven ride.
But history proves that justice is not beyond the reach of freedom fighters filled with
courage, determination, dignity, and pride.

Despite the two century and two score struggle for equality under law-
The outlook today is deeply flawed.
Deep social and economic disparities between the races still exist.
Anti-minority and anti-immigrant hostility persists.

Government officials have sought to deport 690,000 Dreamers who were brought to
America as children through no fault of their own; Dreamers who enrich the
country by working their jobs, attending school, serving in the military, serving
as teachers, and paying their taxes. Will the country choose to be shortsighted
and heartless?
Will it turn its back on the Dreamers and embrace the darkness?

We are and always have been a nation of immigrants. Since its beginnings, right up
through the present day, people have been embarking upon treacherous journeys
from faraway lands to reach America's shores. Often, they are escaping lands
where freedom is stifled, life is cheap, and blood is thoughtlessly spilled.
They come based upon their vision of America as a land of second chances and
opportunity- a "shining city upon a hill."

Is it fair and just to assert that only those whose ancestors came to America first should
have the opportunity to share in the American Dream? Scientists believe that more
than 15,000 years ago during the Ice Age, the "First Americans," the ancestors of
Native Americans, crossed from Eurasia to America by way of a land bridge
known as Beringia. They then spread south over many generations throughout the
Americas. It is Native Americans who have the only true claim to having reached
America first. Historically, they are the only true "native" Americans.

Western European settlers who reached America's shores beginning in the fifteenth
century, systematically exploited Native Americans while occupying their land. In
addition, Native Americans were ravaged by epidemic diseases brought by
European settlers, from which they had no immunity.
The Europeans proceeded to colonize their land and claim the natural resources with a
sense of entitlement and impunity.

As late as 1830, passage of the Indian Removal Act signed into law by President Andrew
Jackson, resulted in the removal of 60,000 Cherokee, Choctaw, Creek, Chickasaw
and Seminole Indians from their fertile lands in the southeastern United States.
They were forcibly relocated onto reservations in relatively infertile areas of the
Oklahoma Territory. Thousands of Native Americans died of disease and starvation
along the Trail of Tears. In light of this long history of land grabs by means of
abuse, exploitation, murder, and forced relocation, is it right to maintain that no one
else has a right to lawfully apply for asylum to come here?
That the American Dream is not to be shared?

Was it just for the U.S. government to establish in 2018, a "zero tolerance" family,
separation policy of deliberately separating immigrants from their children
to discourage them from seeking asylum? From having the chance to establish in a
court of law that if deported they'd face persecution?
Or imprisonment or execution?

In 2013, in *Shelby v. Holder*, the U.S. Supreme Court extracted the teeth from
the Voting Rights Act of 1965-
Paving the way for state voter suppression zombies to return- alive!
Why is it that after so much blood has been shed for so long for the right to vote-
State voter suppression laws targeting minority voting are shoved down the
country's throat?
While Congress stands idly by doing nothing to stop it-
Failing to enact critical, federal Voting Rights legislation to preempt and block it!

Why is it that after more than four centuries of racial injustice and dreams shattered-
The country must still be reminded that "black lives matter?"
Is it so difficult to understand, so terribly elusive-
That support for law enforcement and rejection of racial profiling are not
    mutually exclusive?
And that police use of reasonable force and police use of excessive force
    are two different things?
Does that distinction really have an incomprehensible ring?

Why is it so difficult for so many to "stand in another person's shoes and walk
    around in them?" Or to think about what it's like to "walk in another person's
    skin?"
Why such a history of racial intolerance? Why that Sin?

Why such a long road to justice? Why must it be so slow?
Alas the answers aren't clear, but there's one thing history shows.
For every inch of justice, in every passing year-
A price will be exacted, in blood and sweat and tears.

THE FUTURE OFFERS HOPE SOMEHOW
(Essay)

Some say, "Make America great again"-
Those good old days again, way back when.
But when was it better back then?
Tell me when? What made it better back then?

Was it "separate but equal," instead of co-equals?
Or poisons delivered to our streams and our rivers?
Or tax cuts for the wealthy while neglecting the unhealthy?
Or a failure of reforming to address the global warming in this world?
Favoring the greedy while disparaging the needy?
Or the indigent evicted and their voting rights
     restricted at the polls?

What about equality of treatment and pay between the sexes,
     deferred for so long?
How many years does it take to remedy a wrong?

Some say, "Make America great again"-
Those good old days again, way back when.
But they're wrong.
Those were the days of injustice prolonged.

We must look to the future and learn from the past-
To elevate justice and make it last.
For justice serves as a beacon of hope-
Like discovering cures through a microscope.
When less comes then, and more comes now-
The future offers hope somehow.

TAKE A CHANCE
(Essay)

Why not take a chance, a chance on
    doing better?
Find a way to live together in this world.

The gift of this life-
The gift of our planet-
A world full of so much strife-
That we must come together-

To reject the racist tropes-
Replace distrust with faith and hope.
Set aside our fears-
Of "others" over there-
In foreign lands somewhere.

So much in common that all of us share-
All the people for whom we care.
Those that we cherish, family and friends-
Who remain in our hearts to the very end.

So many needs that all of us share-
A living wage and access to care-
A healthy planet replete with clean air.

Why not resolve to change the equation?
Stand up for justice, rise to the occasion-
Fighting injustice through moral persuasion.
Casting our votes in the face of oppression-
From state-imposed laws of voter suppression.

Acting in concert like birds of a feather-
Taking a chance on reaching for better-
Lifting all boats while working together.

Rejecting the trope of denouncing the "other"-
Coming together as sisters as brothers-
Taking a chance on belief in each other.

CHANGE THE WORLD
(Essay)

It's clear, we must change the world-
Weave a tapestry of justice to unfurl.
When some sink low, we'll reach ever higher-
For the tolerant world that we desire.

Surely, we'll prevail-
The melting pot we cherish must not fail.
We'll resist, giving all and then some-
The power of an idea whose time has come.

We must stem the tide-
Standing tall together side by side.
Step by step, the road is ever long-
Brothers and sisters marching, singing freedom songs.

Answering the call-
Building bridges instead of walls.
Link by link, forging mighty ties-
Forming bonds to cut through all the lies.

We must change the world.